The Thomas M. Cooley Lectures

THE CHOICE-OF-LAW PROCESS

[Based on lectures delivered at The University of Michigan, January 21, 22, 24, 1964, under the title "Policy, Justice, and Principle in the Choice-of-Law Process."]

DAVID F. CAVERS

The Choice-of-Law Process

ANN ARBOR
THE UNIVERSITY OF MICHIGAN PRESS

Published under the auspices of The University of Michigan Law School (which, however, assumes no responsibility for the views expressed) with the aid of funds derived from gifts to The University of Michigan by William W. *Cook.*

Second printing 1966

Library of Congress Catalog Card No. 65-21050
Published in the United States of America by
The University of Michigan Press and simultaneously
in Toronto, Canada, by Ambassador Books Limited
Printed and bound by CPI Group (UK) Ltd, Croydon, CR0 4YY

Paperback ISBN: 978-0-472-75065-8

FOREWORD

A federal system of law, high population mobility, and commonplace interstate transactions combine to provide for the United States a recurring problem in the administration of justice: how to choose between conflicting laws which may be asserted as determinative of a particular controversy. Not that the problem is a new one, for it has been encountered long before this nation was founded. It is only that we encounter the problem with such frequency and in such a variety of contexts that it has at times seemed to defy comprehensive analysis or rational solution.

It is this challenge—to provide a rational analytical framework—to which Professor Cavers has addressed himself in the present work. Whether or not one concedes that the challenge has been fully met, it is certain that a strikingly clear and thoughtful analysis has been produced, and that the bones of contention have been laid bare for ready observation by those whose affairs lead them to this fascinating subject. In a refreshing style, Professor Cavers has summarized the competing views of noted scholars before proceeding with the elaboration of his own ideas on doctrine and method, and there is constant reference to these competing views as he proceeds with analysis of sharply drawn fact situations. Here is a provocative book by a distinguished scholar, designed both to persuade and to stimulate continued dialogue in an area which has engaged the attention of lawyers for centuries.

The lecture series from which the book is derived was named for an eminent jurist—Thomas M. Cooley. He would have reveled in the opportunity to hear the lectures or to read the book.

Allan F. Smith

Ann Arbor
July 1965

PREFACE

In January 1964, I had the privilege of delivering the fifteenth in the series of Cooley Lectures at The University of Michigan Law School under the title "Policy, Justice, and Principle in the Choice-of-Law Process." This volume is based on those lectures.

The reader will find the volume a hybrid: part lecture, part monograph. He will detect evidences of the lecturer's determined efforts to keep his talk of methodologies from being lost in abstractions beyond the reach and interest of his (largely student) audience. The first and second person still appear; imaginary cases are employed; there are traces of autobiography and, here and there, what the lecturer had hoped would seem a light touch. I fear, however, that these residues of the lectures may by now have become largely obscured in the elaboration of analysis and argument and the proliferation of footnotes.

The principal reasons for the dual nature of this work are two. First, I had the benefit of a critique by three distinguished colleagues in the field of conflict of laws, Professors Brainerd Currie of Duke, Willis L. M. Reese of Columbia, and Max Rheinstein of Chicago, who were assembled for a public panel discussion of the lectures at the Law School the week after I had delivered three of the five lectures I submitted. Needless to say, their views, though considerately presented, gave me food for thought and stimulus for self-critical reflection.

I postponed this process for half a year and departed forthwith on a long-deferred sabbatical that led me far from choice-of-law problems. The perspective this interlude provided is the second reason for the lectures' revision. When I reread them upon my return, I was dismayed. I saw many defects and shortcomings.

When I finished responding to all my dissatisfactions and had taken note of intervening events, the five lectures had become eleven chapters, though their central theme remained basically the same. Then, as proofs were being read, a divided New York Court of Appeals decided *Dym v. Gordon*, a case bringing into sharp focus the problems of the new choice-of-law process. Resort to an appendix has made comment on it possible.

I think it fair to say that I have been concerned more with commentators' views and less with court decisions than is customary in American legal scholarship. In this respect our writing in the conflict of laws has tended always to come closer to the scholarship of the civilians. In particular, I have had many occasions to refer to the provocative, yet I believe basically constructive, work of Brainerd Currie. Our points of difference may be more conspicuous in this volume than our area of agreement, yet it seems to me that the latter is, to borrow a phrase, the more significant relationship.

My illustrations, both actual and hypothetical, have been derived with few exceptions from that great manufactory of choice-of-law cases and problems, the fifty United States of America. However, I believe that, if my ideas are valid as applied to the choices of law which our state and federal courts must make, they should also be valid as applied to the choices confronting courts in other countries. A spirit of mutual accommodation leading to agreement on certain principles may spread more quickly through the states of a federal union than among independent nations, yet surely it is not utopian to suppose that the nations of our rapidly shrinking world will come in time to possess a comparable sense of community.

In developing certain portions of this work, notably Chapter X, I have benefitted greatly from the assistance generously afforded me by my colleague, Dr. Kurt H. Nadelmann, who possesses a rich store of learning and wisdom concerning the problems of achieving agreement on conflict-of-laws rules by international conventions and uniform legislation. Moreover, in the formulation and presentation of my ideas, I have profited much from the criticism of my colleague, Professor Henry J. Steiner. Though, of course, our views did not always run parallel, his comment was unfailingly thought-provoking and helpful.

David F. Cavers

Cambridge, Massachusetts
July 1965

CONTENTS

ANALYTICAL CONTENTS

I

CHANGING VIEWS OF THE COURT'S TASK IN CHOICE OF LAW

A. *Six Centuries of Frustration*

Back in the thirteenth century, in the Italian cities which then were rekindling the fires of civilization, two small groups of learned men were working busily at two problems for which solutions were earnestly desired. One problem was scientific: how to make gold out of baser metals. The other was legal: how to choose between conflicting laws. The first group came to be known as alchemists; the second, statutists.

The first group disbanded two or three centuries ago. Their learning relabeled, they settled down to the humdrum business of transforming our material world through the science of chemistry. The task of transmuting elements they let slip into the hands of the physicists. The latter have done pretty well at it, though they no longer bother with gold, preferring instead to turn uranium into plutonium.

The second group came into being after each of the Italian city states had begun to superimpose a distinctive body of law —both customary and legislative—on their common heritage of Roman law. Since their citizens traveled about the peninsula and had dealings in cities other than their own, inevitably controversies arose between citizens of different cities. Controversies between merchants could be decided by the courts merchant by recourse to the common law merchant. However, not all controversies were between merchants, and so, with regard to other citizens, it became necessary to decide whose custom governed whom or whose law governed what transaction. The cities' laws and later even their customs were known as *statuta*; hence the term "statutists."

The statutists tried to find the answers to their problems by classifying the statutes. Some statutes were real, and some were personal. The real statute applied only within the territory of the city whose law it was. The personal statutes followed the city's citizenry wherever they might go. In time, this simple scheme failed to satisfy the intricacies of life and scholarship. As a consequence, a third class of statute was identified—as you can guess, this was known as "mixed."[1]

The scheme was an attractive one, with that illusive simplicity which leads one on in the hope that the final solution to a problem is just around the corner. The doctrine spread over Europe and ultimately came to the United States. Indeed, our first book on the conflict of laws was by an American statutist: Samuel Livermore, Counselor of Law in the City of New Orleans. His little work bore a long title: *Dissertations on the Questions Which Arise from the Contrariety of the Positive Laws of Different States and Nations*. It was published in New Orleans in 1828.

Despite six or seven centuries of labor, the statutists had not eliminated the contrariety of opinion within their own ranks. The trouble was that neither judges nor scholars could agree upon which statute was personal, which was real, and what should be done with those that were mixed. Some statutists emphasized one category; some, the other. The courts of a state that enacted a law could, of course, decide what should be the

[1] For one of the best statements in English of the theory of the statutists, see LIVERMORE, DISSERTATIONS ON THE QUESTIONS WHICH ARISE FROM THE CONTRARIETY OF THE POSITIVE LAWS OF DIFFERENT STATES AND NATIONS (New Orleans 1828). (On this work, see De Nova, "The First American Book on Conflict of Laws," 8 AM. J. LEGAL HIST. 136 (1964).) See also STORY, COMMENTARIES ON THE CONFLICT OF LAWS, FOREIGN AND DOMESTIC, §§ 12 *et seq.* (1st ed. 1834); 3 BEALE, CONFLICT OF LAWS 1886-1912, 1928-30 (1935).

reach of their own statute, but their ideas as to this or as to the reach of the other state's law might differ from the views of the latter state's courts. There was no overall or commonly accepted authority or ideology to which such differences could be referred.

By the nineteenth century, the struggles of the statutists to achieve a neat allocation of competencies among the statutes of the nations of the world appeared hopeless. A commentary on their work that continues to be quoted now and then, for it still seems apt, comes from a famous Louisiana case, *Saul v. His Creditors,* involving creditors' rights in matrimonial property—a topic dear to the statutists. Samuel Livermore was the losing counsel in the case. His learned argument did not persuade the court. Instead, it inspired the bench to the following observation which appears at the start of a lengthy opinion:[2] "[Q]uestions of this kind," wrote Judge Porter, "are the most embarrassing and difficult of decision, that can occupy the attention of those who preside in the courts of justice. The argument of this case has shewn us, that the vast mass of learning which the research of counsel has furnished, leaves the subject as much enveloped in obscurity and doubt, as it would have appeared to our own understandings, had we been called on to decide, without the knowledge of what others had thought, and written upon it."

Apparently it was dissatisfaction with Judge Porter's opinion that led the disappointed Mr. Livermore to write his dissertations, but, despite that work and the succession of scholarly writings that have followed it, the sentiments expressed by Judge Porter might well strike a responsive chord in the minds of judges confronting choice-of-law problems in our courts today.

The eclipse of the statutists in the United States came with the work of Joseph Story. Story's own treatise on the conflict of laws, first published in 1834, drew extensively on the work

[2] 5 MARTIN (n.s.) 569, 571 (La. 1827), reprinted in 4 PHILLIMORE, COMMENTARIES UPON INTERNATIONAL LAW, PRIVATE INTERNATIONAL LAW OR COMITY 734 (1861).

of the statutists,[3] to be sure, but Story used doctrine eclectically and emphasized case law in the manner of the common-law jurist that Story was. Moreover, like many American and English jurists of the day,[4] he was influenced substantially in his thinking by the seventeenth-century Dutch scholars, especially by Ulric Huber. Huber, although viewing laws as territorially limited, found a basis for their recognition in other nations in the *jus gentium,* a doctrine implemented by comity and subject to an exception in the case of laws prejudicial to the forum state.[5]

Abroad, the death-blow to the surviving schools of statutists appears to have been dealt by Carl Georg von Wächter, a German jurist writing in the 1840's.[6] His views as to the choice-of-law process have a singularly contemporary cast.[7] The criticisms of Wächter were followed in mid-century by the work of the great German Romanist, Savigny, who added a final volume on the conflict of laws to an epoch-making treatise on Roman law.[8] As scholars responded to the new conceptions

[3] See Story, *op. cit. supra* note 1, § § 29 *et seq.*

[4] See Nadelmann, "Joseph Story's Contribution to American Conflicts Law: A Comment," 5 Am. J. Legal Hist. 230 (1961).

[5] Huber's famous sketch "*de conflictu legum*" appeared in translation in a note to a Supreme Court case, Emory v. Grenough, 3 Dall. 369 (U.S. 1797). On Huber, see Yntema, "The Historic Bases of Private International Law," 2 Am. J. Comp. L. 297, 306 (1953); Yntema, "The Comity Doctrine," in 2 Vom Deutschen zum Europäischen Recht—Festschrift für Hans Dölle 65 (1963).

[6] On Wächter, see Nadelmann, "Wächter's Essay on the Collision of Private Laws of Different States," 13 Am. J. Comp. L. 414 (1964), including a translation of basic portions of this essay.

[7] A leading German conflicts scholar sees a resemblance to Wächter's own approach in Professor Brainerd Currie's. See Wengler, "The Principle of Equality in the Conflict of Laws," 28 Law & Contemp. Prob. 822, 829 n.31 (1963). But Professor Currie's colleague, Professor Hans Baade, finds a closer resemblance to the views of Professor Ehrenzweig. See Baade, Foreword to "New Trends in the Conflict of Laws," *id.* at 675 n.9. A reading of Wächter, *supra* note 6, leads me to doubt whether either should take satisfaction in these observations.

[8] Vol. VIII of Savigny's System des heutigen Roemischen Rechts (1849) appeared in a translation by a Scottish lawyer, Wm. Guthrie, under the title Conflict of Laws in Edinburgh in 1869 (2d ed. 1880).

found in these works, the day of the statutists seemed ended, and, after six or more centuries of writing and disputation, the statutists seemed destined to go the way of the alchemists.

Savigny did not seek for solutions to choice-of-law problems in the classification of local statutes.[9] Instead, he sought to find a proper seat for each legal relationship in its connection with a given state whose law would thereby be rendered applicable, whatever its terms. He hoped that widespread international agreement might be achieved as to the localization of these relationships.

Later in the century a new emphasis was introduced by an Italian scholar, Mancini. He urged that choice-of-law rules be based on the principle of nationality, thereby reflecting the indigenous cultural elements in national laws.[10] Mancini's principle was enthusiastically espoused in many Continental nations. It has probably left a lasting imprint abroad on choice-of-law rules, especially those relating to personal status.[11] In the Anglo-American common-law jurisdictions, however, the courts have refused to substitute nationality for domicil, influenced no doubt by the needs of federal unions and also by the large migrant elements in their populations.

In Anglo-American jurisdictions, the development of choice-of-law doctrine has been greatly influenced by the works of the English scholar and jurist, A. V. Dicey, and the American law professor, Joseph H. Beale. Dicey adopted the theory that the task of the court in a choice-of-law case was the enforcement of vested rights.[12] Professor Beale coupled this with the terri-

[9] On Savigny, see WOLFF, PRIVATE INTERNATIONAL LAW 34 (2d ed. 1950); Yntema, "The Historic Bases of Private International Law," *supra* note 5, at 309. In England, Savigny influenced Westlake. See WESTLAKE, PRIVATE INTERNATIONAL LAW 24 *et seq.* (2d ed. 1880).

[10] On Mancini's views, see BEALE, *op. cit. supra* note 1, at 1931; De Nova, "New Trends in Italian Private International Law," 28 LAW & CONTEMP. PROB. 808 (1963).

[11] On Mancini's impact outside Italy, see 1 RABEL, CONFLICT OF LAWS: A COMPARATIVE STUDY 10, 200 (2d ed. 1958).

[12] DICEY, CONFLICT OF LAWS, General Principle No. 1, p. 11 (6th ed. 1949) in which the editors explain the modifications in Dicey's original

torial concepts that Story had drawn from Huber and thereby organized a system of choice-of-law rules, simple in structure, which could be applied without regard to the content of the particular laws between which choice had to be made.[13] This theory dominated the American Law Institute's *Restatement of Conflict of Laws* for which Professor Beale served as Reporter.

Professor Beale confronted the welter of conflicting conflicts decisions with bland determination. "Most of the statements in this work will be dogmatic," he wrote at the start of his treatise and then asked—rhetorically: "Does not the Bar desire dogmatic statements?"[14] I need quote only two propositions from the treatise to convey the character of his doctrine and his thought. Thus, at the outset of his discussion of the choice of law as to contracts, he declared: "The question whether a contract is valid . . . can on general principles be determined by no other law than that which applies to the acts [of the parties], that is, by the law of the place of contracting. . . . If . . . the law of the place where the agreement is made annexes no

---

text that they made in an effort (which I believe was only partly successful) to meet the criticisms that had been directed against it. Dicey was influenced by the views of his friend and colleague, T. E. Holland, to be found in HOLLAND, ELEMENTS OF JURISPRUDENCE 288 (1880). See DICEY, CONFLICT OF LAWS vii (1st ed. 1896). *Cf.* Nadelmann, "Some Historical Notes on the Doctrinal Sources of American Conflicts Law," in IUS ET LEX—FESTGABE ZUM 70. GEBURTSTAG VON MAX GUTZWILLER 263-78 (1959). On the relation between Dicey and Beale, see Nadelmann, *id.* at 279.

[13] It is difficult to find a systematic statement of Professor Beale's basic choice-of-law theory. In the first edition of his casebook, he included a 45-page summary of the conflict of laws starting with a definition of the subject; "The topic called 'Conflict of Laws' deals with the recognition and enforcement of foreign created rights." 3 BEALE, CASES ON THE CONFLICT OF LAWS 501 *et seq.* (1902). This definition and certain basic concepts following it were quoted with evident approval in the treatise thirty-three years later. See 3 BEALE, *op. cit. supra* note 1, at 1968. On the territoriality of law, see 3 *id.* at 1962-67.

[14] 1 *id.* at xiii.

legal obligation to it, *there is no other law which has power to do so.*"[15]

And in expounding choice of law as to torts, Professor Beale explained, "It is impossible for a plaintiff to recover in tort unless he has been given by some law a cause of action in tort; and *this cause of action can be given only by the law of the place where the tort was committed.* That is the place where the injurious event occurs, and its law is the law *therefore* which applies to it."[16]

While the *Conflicts Restatement* was still in gestation, Beale's basic conceptions came under attack by what he termed "an ephemeral school" of "self-styled realists."[17] Among these Professor Ernest Lorenzen and Professor Walter Wheeler Cook were the foremost.[18] Professor Charles Wesley Hohfeld, famed for his analysis of jural relations, had also been a dissenter from conflicts orthodoxy of his day, and Professor Lorenzen has credited him with the origin of the "local law"

[15] 2 *id.* § 332.4. (Italics supplied.) Though Professor Beale was wont to cast his propositions in the form of ineluctable deductions from unassailable premises, he always purported merely to be stating common-law doctrine. See, e.g., 1 *id.* § 5.3. For him the test of "power," the Constitution apart, was whether a state's assertion of power would be given extraterritorial effect in a state adhering to common-law doctrine. See 1 *id.* § 50.3.

[16] 2 *id.* § 378.1. (Italics supplied.)

[17] For the allusion to the "ephemeral school," see 1 *id.* at xiii, to the "self-styled realists" (Cook, Lorenzen, and Cavers were named as sources), see 3 *id.* at 1879, where the author explained why he had not dealt with their "new doctrine": "It is a very interesting doctrine, but one with which lawyers in practice have little concern; for it is admitted that the courts do not consciously accede to it."

[18] See Cook, "The Logical and Legal Bases of the Conflict of Laws," 33 YALE L.J. 457 (1924), in THE LOGICAL AND LEGAL BASES OF THE CONFLICT OF LAWS 1 (1942); Lorenzen, "Territoriality, Public Policy, and the Conflict of Laws," 33 YALE L.J. 736 (1924), in SELECTED ARTICLES ON THE CONFLICT OF LAWS 1 (1947). In England, the leading critic of the vested rights theory, Professor Cheshire of Oxford, acknowledged his indebtedness to Professor Cook's views when first he took issue with the theory. See CHESHIRE, PRIVATE INTERNATIONAL LAW iii-iv, 46-55 (3d ed. 1947).

theory[19] that, particularly as championed by Professor Cook,[20] became the principal rival of Professor Beale's "vested rights" theory. These critics challenged the logic of the vested rights theory which they found question-begging, but they also challenged its practicality. They complained of its failure to reflect social and economic needs and policies, though they were seldom specific in identifying these. This, however, was not a cause for concern. In the 1930's the provision of relevant data was viewed as a task for the future: facts were around the corner.

B. *The Lecturer's Indiscretions*

When these attacks were building up just thirty years ago, I published an article, "A Critique of the Choice-of-Law Problem,"[21] in which I not only joined in the attack on the views of my former teacher, Professor Beale, but disagreed with his critics as well.[22] With the brashness of youth, I charged that

19 See Lorenzen, Book Review, "Cook, *The Logical and Legal Bases of the Conflict of Laws*," 52 YALE L.J. 680, 681 (1943). For Professor Hohfeld's chief contribution to the conflict of laws, in which seeds of the local law theory can be discerned, see Hohfeld, "The Individual Liability of Stockholders and the Conflict of Laws," 9 COLUM. L. REV. 492 (1909), 10 *id.* 283, 520 (1910).

20 Professor Cook formulated the theory in 1924 as follows: "[T]he forum, when confronted by a case involving foreign elements, always applies its own law to the case, but in doing so adopts and enforces as its own law a rule of decision identical, or at least highly similar though not identical, in scope with a rule of decision found in the system of law in force in another state or country with which some or all of the foreign elements are connected. . . . The forum thus enforces not a foreign right but a right created by its own law." COOK, *supra* note 18, at 469, in LOGICAL AND LEGAL BASES OF THE CONFLICT OF LAWS, reprinted at 20-21. Professor Cook ascribed the "local law" theory to Judge Learned Hand. See *id.* at 474-75, reprinted at 26-29. That Cook's version differed basically from Hand's is argued in Cavers, "The Two 'Local Law' Theories," 63 HARV. L. REV. 822 (1950). In terms of choice-of-law method, I find little difference between Hand's theory and Beale's.

21 47 HARV. L. REV. 173 (1933).

22 *Id.* at 179-82. My criticism of Professor Beale's position echoed the complaints of Cook and Lorenzen, but his position was more vulnerable

they too had misconceived the task of the court in a choice-of-law case. The new social and economic criteria they were invoking were destined to be frustrated, I argued, because their basic methodology was wrong. Though I joined them in asking, in Professor Lorenzen's words: "What are the demands of justice in the particular situation; what is the controlling policy?"[23] I insisted, nevertheless, that these questions could not be answered as long as the questioners continued to seek what I termed "a jurisdiction-selecting" rule,[24] that is, a rule indicating the source of the law to be applied without regard to the law's content. Without taking the content of the conflicting laws into account, how could one know what would satisfy the demands of justice or the requirements of policy?

In this emphasis on the content of the conflicting laws were the seeds of a misunderstanding: many readers saw implicit in my criticisms the notion that a judge should, when confronted by the laws of two states, simply choose the rule he deemed the better by domestic standards, attaching no significance to the fact that the case was not domestic to either state but had arisen out of events or transactions connected with both of them. I shall seek in a subsequent chapter to dissipate this and other misunderstandings which that youthful article generated, for that

---

than theirs to the criticisms I directed against their views with which I was basically in sympathy.

[23] *Id.* at 179 and 187. The questions I quoted were posed in Lorenzen, *supra* note 18, at 748, reprinted at 15.

[24] Cavers, *supra* note 21, at 194. This concept, launched in the article cited, is gradually becoming current. The jurisdiction-selecting rule makes a *state* the object of choice; in theory it is only after the rule has selected the governing state by reference to the "contact" prescribed in the rule that the court ascertains the content of the state's law. I must concede, however, that a jurisdiction-selecting rule may be the product of two decisions choosing on policy grounds between competing rules in cases in which the law-fact patterns are reversed. If the court concludes that the same contact should be controlling in each case, economy in stating the results would yield a choice-of-law rule stated in terms of the jurisdiction where that contact is located. However, in the use of a rule thus synthesized, its origin should always be kept in mind.

article is the proximate cause of the subject I have chosen for these lectures. I hasten to add that my hosts did not call for the presentation of this sequel to it, but a sequel is long overdue. Perhaps I may be forgiven if I indulge in an autobiographical note in explanation of that fact.

When I wrote in 1933, I viewed my article as the first of a series, each dealing with the troubles that the search for jurisdiction-selecting rules had created in a particular field of choice of law. However, these well-laid plans soon went agley. I had proposed the creation of, and had been given the task of editing, a quarterly at the newly reincarnated Duke University School of Law. This quarterly, *Law and Contemporary Problems,* was to be devoted to symposia by legal scholars, practicing lawyers, officials, and social scientists on contemporary problems in which law played a significant part. In the 30's the nation did not lack contemporary problems. Bold new legal measure followed bold new legal measure, with major repercussions on the organization of our economy and society. As I explored these problems, the choice-of-law problems I had dealt with in my 1933 article began to shrink. Did it really matter whether one view or another prevailed in a field where law review articles and comments greatly outnumbered important judicial decisions? True, the rebels against the *Restatement* were gaining new adherents and my own article was widely read—perhaps I should say, widely misread—and widely cited, the citation ordinarily being prefaced by the words, "But compare . . . ." However, even the chance that my views might ultimately win recognition did not then seem to me very important.

This attitude was accentuated by World War II's challenges to legal creativity. As far as conflict of laws was concerned, I became a "tired progressive"; more aptly, perhaps, a "tired realist." In this mood I wrote a review of Walter Wheeler Cook's collected essays in which, though paying tribute to a great teacher, I dealt with the competing schools of choice of law in the spirit of Mercutio's "A pox on both your houses!"[25]

As I look back on that review, I find in it a lesson. For that particular utterance, Mercutio's timing is the only appropriate one: it should be a dying declaration. It alienates your own house; it earns you an unwanted welcome in the house of your adversaries. My sentiments were treated as apostasy and hailed with undisguised satisfaction by the beleaguered advocates of the *Restatement* who found in my "give-it-up" spirit a vote of support for their system.

In the post-war period, I began to observe here and there signs of judicial use of the approach to conflict-of-laws problems developed by the rebels against the *Restatement*. Moreover, within the law schools and among law review writers, the ranks of the rebels were swelling. Though, when the American Law Institute undertook the second *Restatement*, I remained skeptical of the feasibility of reducing the choice-of-law problem to the *Restatement* format, I was nevertheless pleased to observe that the new *Restatement* no longer adhered strictly to the old orthodoxy. While the Institute was not fully converted to the heresies of the 30's, there was, to mix metaphors, a considerable injection of new wine into the old bottles, and, here and there, even the bottles were new. A prophecy I had uttered near the close of my 1933 article seemed near fulfillment.

I had there anticipated the charge that my proposals would be dismissed as "academic." I was obliged to concede this as true, but in response I declared, "Fortunately, however, we have academies, and the nurture of ideas which are quite clearly academic is still a responsibility of theirs. . . . In the law schools alone can ideas of this sort take root; once having rooted there, the process of transplanting them to less sheltered fields may be gradual but it is sure."[26]

If this prediction is broadened to embrace the ideas of Cook,

[25] Cavers, Book Review, "Cook, *The Logical and Legal Bases of the Conflict of Laws*," 56 HARV. L. REV. 1170 (1943).

[26] Cavers, *supra* note 21, at 204.

Lorenzen, and the other dissenters from the first *Restatement* as well as my own, I believe the developments of the intervening years have borne it out. These ideas have been transplanted in the world of affairs by writings that emanate from the law schools and even more from their graduates at the bar and on the bench.

C. *The Transitional Period*

We have been witnessing the accelerating erosion of a choice-of-law doctrine—a doctrine never deeply fixed in our case law—and its piecemeal replacement by a small but increasing number of cases and a swelling body of scholarly writing, a theoretical literature in which disagreement with the original *Restatement* is the principal common characteristic. The process has not greatly altered my earlier judgment as to the relative social importance of the problems with which the choice of law deals. These are, to be sure, increasing in consequence because of the increasingly complex interrelationships among our states and between our nation and the rest of the world. They reflect the greater ease and speed of communication, trade, and travel. However, with respect to the whole body of our law, we are in a period that resembles the 1920's more closely than the 1930's. I suspect a new set of major problems is building up. Some of them—in civil rights, for example—are already coming to the fore. Nonetheless, we are still in a period of consolidation. Law and legal thought have been absorbed in assimilating and perfecting the changes of the 30's and 40's, rather than in breaking new ground and creating new doctrines and institutions. Since in this period changes have gone further and cut deeper in the conflict of laws than in most fields, especially in that dwindling preserve, "private law," we can pause to consider some implications of the developments that have been taking place in conflicts doctrine.

The conception of the courts' function in the choice of law has been the most significant target of these changes. For the courts and their critics in the reviews, this trend is creating problems of decision-making that are unfamiliar, that are both intellectually exciting and philosophically disturbing. Though it has long been apparent to the critical scholar that some courts were taking advantage of the diversity of choice-of-law rules to utilize them selectively, yet the familiar protective façade of conventional doctrine and precedent was well preserved until recently. Now, as the courts themselves begin to break through this screen, they are confronting the need in choice of law for new premises and a new methodology.

This does not often happen in contemporary law, though if we were to search our law's history, we would find judicial creativity as the source of now-settled doctrines. However, we are more accustomed to observe courts choosing between competing premises already established in law and extending or contracting them. I can think of few areas of law in this century where the courts have had to lay a foundation of new premises before our very eyes.

One of these is that body of law and method that the Supreme Court constructed to guide the process of judicial review of railroad and utility rate decisions, starting from *Smyth v. Ames*[27] and virtually abandoning the attempt in the *Hope Natural Gas*[28] case half a century later. In the interpretation of the broad charter of the Sherman Antitrust Act, the federal courts have been developing a body of doctrine which has progressed far beyond its antecedents in the historic learning on restraints of trade.[29] Perhaps the civil rights cases of the past decade may be set aside as simple, if emotion-charged, exercises in the application of *Brown v. Board of Education*,[30] but clearly

[27] 169 U.S. 466 (1898).

[28] Federal Power Comm'n v. Hope Natural Gas Co., 320 U.S. 59 (1944).

[29] For a report of the doctrine thus developed, which may be all the more illuminating because of its English source, see NEALE, THE ANTITRUST LAWS OF THE UNITED STATES (1960). For their implications for foreign trade and investment, see, BREWSTER, ANTITRUST AND AMERICAN BUSINESS ABROAD (1958).

[30] Brown v. Board of Educ. of Topeka, 347 U.S. 483 (1954).

in 1962 the Supreme Court in *Baker v. Carr*[31] embarked upon uncharted seas when it dared to consider the problem of legislative redistricting as justiciable, a venture for which "one-man, one-vote" is not likely to prove an adequate rule of navigation.[32]

The Court's decisions in these fields represent a series of difficult exercises in the art of statecraft, in which issues as to the allocation of power in our polity are grave and momentous. In choice of law, on the other hand, we can examine a jurisprudentially similar process without these disturbing involvements. How choice-of-law cases are decided is not going to upset basic values on any pervasive scale: the cases are few and their impact is limited. In many respects, the field is unique.

Nonetheless, even here one encounters concern lest we are witnessing a flight from reason and certainty to the *ad hoc*, unprincipled decision. Will discontent with rigid conceptualism and mechanical decision-making induce the impractical pursuit of the elusive will-o'-the-wisp of justice in the particular case? Some are troubled lest emphasis on specific laws and policies result in excessive localization in grounds of decision and preclude the development of an international or even an interstate consensus. The champions of the new theories disagree as to the respective roles of the courts and legislatures in building a new methodology of decision. And, to report a dismaying view, one of our most distinguished colleagues, Professor Max Rheinstein, has sorrowfully stated that the new American methods in choice of law represent a return to the errors of the statutists.[33] After six centuries the cycle is complete.

31 369 U.S. 186 (1962).

32 Reynolds v. Sims, 84 Sup. Ct. 1362 (1964), requiring apportionment to be on a population basis, has already led to a division in the court. Fortson v. Dorsey, 85 Sup. Ct. 498 (1965).

33 See Rheinstein, Book Review, "How to Review a Festschrift," 11 Am. J. Comp. L. 632, 633 (1962): ". . . present-day American scholars have remained within the framework of statutist thought. . . . American conflicts law has thus been led into a dead-end alley. . . ."

D. Back to the Case Method

To identify these fears more specifically, to evaluate them, and to examine a possible, principled approach to the choice-of-law process that will help to allay at least some of them is the chief task of these chapters. But in this attempt I am confronted by half a dozen or more methods of choice of law in the writings on the subject, if not in the cases. As expositor, my task becomes formidable.

In this predicament, I have had recourse to the familiar tactic of the law teacher: the case method. However, as I have remarked, the actual cases reflecting new approaches to choice of law are still relatively few. Moreover, they have cropped up in a variety of unrelated fields of law, and seldom are the courts' opinions of much help—for reasons with which I sympathize. Hence, I would be in serious straits if I had to rely on actual cases.

A law teacher, however, is never at loss for a case. If a case in point does not exist, he makes up a hypothetical case. Never, however, does he provide a hypothetical opinion, my colleague, Professor Lon Fuller, excepted. He is the author of a notable series of imaginary judicial opinions for the teaching of jurisprudence.[34]

My own purpose is far less ambitious. I shall start with a case representing a fairly close approximation of an actual case decided a few years ago. I shall follow this with three more cases presenting variations on the same set of facts but posing new questions. I shall then add a fifth case which is identical to the first one except for the fact that the relation of the state laws to the facts—what I call the law-fact pattern—has been reversed. The cases are not in series; each decision is to be viewed as independent of the others, even though, to

[34] See for the best known of these Fuller, "The Case of the Speluncean Explorers," 62 HARV. L. REV. 616 (1949). This "case" has been translated into Spanish for use in instruction in Latin America, FULLER, EL CASO DE LOS EXPLORADORES DE CAVERNAS (Abeledo-Perrot, 1961), and Professor Fuller tells me that a Japanese translation is in process.

avoid repetition, I shall not restate a judge's views which have already been reported in an opinion of his on the same point.

Of course, it is necessary that you know the reasoning of the judges, but no living bench can provide the diversity of approaches that I desire. Therefore, I have had to invent one, and the only place I could find the judges reflecting the needed variety of viewpoints is in the law schools. Accordingly I have envisaged a court of law-teacher-judges. I could, of course, have converted this lecture into a roman à clef and left you guessing as to the identity of the bench. However, I have decided to be more candid. I have named as judges the following: Dean Erwin N. Griswold of Harvard; Professor Max Rheinstein of the University of Chicago, formerly of the famous Kaiser Wilhelm Institute of Comparative and International Private Law in Berlin; Professor Willis Reese of Columbia University, Reporter of the *Restatement of Conflict of Laws Second*; Professor Brainerd Currie of the Duke University School of Law, whose *Selected Essays on the Conflict of Laws* has only recently been published; and, finally, your author.

You will note that my bench numbers only five—a little small for the New York Court of Appeals whose role it must play, but this limitation on numbers was compelled by the fact that these distinguished jurists could never agree upon a single opinion for the court. As a consequence, I have been driven to assume that the judges will render their individual opinions *seriatim* in the English manner.

The opinions I presented orally in the lectures were all written by me; their ingredients reflected the views of the professors as I interpreted them. I took this liberty without giving to any of the professors I placed on the bench a chance to approve or disapprove, or to edit, the opinions bearing their names. Accordingly, I besought the audience to hold me solely responsible for what I put in my characters' mouths and never to attribute to the professors any of the sentiments the judges expressed.

The opinions, I should add, were not models of the opinion-writing art; the need for brevity and for illustrating different methods of resolving choice-of-law problems had required the sacrifice of thorough inquiry into the (imaginary) facts and careful evaluation of the precedents and the views of commentators.

The University of Michigan Law School had arranged for a panel discussion of the lectures in the week following their oral presentation, the panelists being Professors Currie, Reese, and Rheinstein. In advance of that occasion, I provided the panelists with copies of the lectures in the version from which the oral lectures were drawn. This gave to each of them an opportunity to criticize the views of his judicial counterpart. This was done informally, except that Professor Currie provided draft opinions which he thought were more representative of Judge Currie's views than those I had ascribed to him in Cases 3, 4, and 5. I have used those three opinions in somewhat condensed form in this published version of the lectures.

Though Professor Reese vigorously disavowed all of Judge Reese's conclusions except the one involving the Massachusetts plaintiff in Case 4, I have nonetheless preserved Judge Reese's original opinion in Case 1 and by annotation have recorded Professor Reese's dissent from Judge Reese's views. However, in Cases 3 and 4 I wrote new, short opinions for Judge Reese which hopefully brought his views in these cases into accord with Professor Reese's. Professor Rheinstein suggested changes in the opinions of Judge Rheinstein, giving greater stress to the expectations of the parties and, in consequence, changing the position I had ascribed to that jurist in Case 3 and the claim of the New York plaintiff in Case 4.

Recently I have availed myself of the fact that Judge Griswold's counterpart is my colleague, Dean Erwin N. Griswold, to obtain his reaction to Judge Griswold's opinions. Without changing the basic position taken by Judge Griswold, Dean Griswold expanded and invigorated the original statement of that jurist's views, adding in the process a somewhat greater element of flexibility. I have revised or supplemented Judge Cavers' opinions in certain cases to reflect the changes I have made in the opinions of other members of the bench.

Despite this greater participation of the real professors in the judicial processes involving their imaginary counterparts, I believe fairness still requires that the reader dissociate the professors from the opinions bearing their names, Cavers, J., perhaps excepted.

Now for the cases.

II

FIVE IMAGINARY CASES

Case 1

Adams v. Knickerbocker Nature Study Society, Inc. Adams is a dues-paying member of the Society (hereafter called "Knickerbocker"). Knickerbocker is a nonprofit corporation organized under the laws of the State of New York to promote nature study. Its principal office is in New York City, but it maintains a summer camp for adult nature lovers in New York's Adirondacks. In 1961 Andrew Adams, a New York domiciliary and botanist, enrolled for a two-week session. He was taken in a camp truck with fellow-campers to visit Mount Greylock, tallest peak in the Berkshires in Massachusetts. After lunch, at the foot of the mountain, the truck driver carelessly started up in reverse and in so doing ran over Adams who had stooped to observe an unusual species of toadstool.

Adams sustained serious injuries and was hospitalized for two months in Pittsfield, Massachusetts. In June 1962, the New York trial court in which Adams was suing for damages granted Knickerbocker summary judgment. Knickerbocker had shown that, under Massachusetts law, a charitable corporation is not liable for its servants' torts. Under New York law (as a consequence of a series of judicial decisions[1]), Knickerbocker would have no immunity; so if Adams had

[1] The gradual erosion of the limited immunity granted by New York law to charitable institutions seems to have been completed by Bing v. Thunig, 2 N.Y.2d 656, 143 N.E.2d 3 (1957).

been allowed to show the driver's negligence, the corporation's charitable character would have been no defense to it. The Appellate Division affirmed the order below in a memorandum opinion, one judge dissenting without opinion. The case now comes to the Court of Appeals which, after hearing extensive argument developing a number of the current methodologies, renders its decision in a series of opinions from which I am quoting the following excerpts.

GRISWOLD, J. ". . . The object of our legal system, I suppose, is to provide 'equal justice under law.' This is something different from 'justice,' which is a very elusive concept, and surely as much of an unruly horse as 'public policy.' If we are to have 'equal justice under law,' there must be law, which means that there must be rules of law. Cases must be put into groups or categories, and cases which rightly fall within the same category should receive the same decision. This need not be a mechanical process. Indeed, it cannot be such a process, for the problems which arise in human relations have infinite variation. Nevertheless, we should not be deluded by the variation. We should recognize that our function is to develop rules of law so that, in so far as possible, similar cases will be similarly decided.

"This problem, which runs through the law, becomes especially acute in the field of conflict of laws. The conflict of laws is, I take it, 'the subject which determines the effect to be given to extra-state elements in any situation.' (Griswold, 'Renvoi Revisited,' 51 Harv. L. Rev. 1165, 1198 (1938).)

"Though a case has extra-state elements, it is still incumbent upon us to find or develop rules of law for its decision, if we are to meet our responsibility to establish, so far as possible, 'equal justice under law.' Through long experience, American courts have developed the basic rule that many problems in the law of torts are to be decided by the law of the state where the tort occurred. For the time being, we can put aside difficult problems presented when the tort occurs in more than one state—when, for example, the force originates in one state and takes effect in another. Nothing like that happened here. All of the events directly connected with the injury in this case occurred in Massachusetts.

"The rule which has been developed in such cases was stated succinctly in Section 378 of the original *Restatement of the Conflict of Laws.* This Section reflects the great weight of authority in this country, both before and since its promulgation. Since, in this case, the place of the tort was clearly in the Commonwealth of Massachusetts, its law renders the charitable character of a defendant corporation a defense to all actions for personal injuries caused by its servants, whether these actions are brought by the beneficiaries of its activities or by strangers. Section 388 of the *Restatement* specifically provides, 'If there is a defense on the merits to the plaintiff's claim by the law of the place of wrong, no recovery can be had on the claim in another state.'

"In reaching this conclusion, I am not unaware of criticisms of the 'place of tort' rule; nor have I overlooked recent ferment, both academic and judicial, in the field of conflict of laws. I do not think that the place of tort rule should be applied woodenly. For example, it may well be unwise to apply it to the question of survival of causes of action, either on the plaintiff's side or on the defendant's. This means that each problem must be considered carefully and thoughtfully. Nevertheless, in such considerations, we should never forget that what we are seeking is a rule of law. The rule that basic aspects of a tort are covered by the place of the tort is such a rule of law. I know of no other rule which shows any capacity of replacing it. The decision of each case on an *ad hoc* basis should be plainly recognized as the antithesis of a rule of law.

"Earlier in this opinion a definition of conflict of laws has been given. But what is the purpose or objective of the conflict of laws? It is not simply to provide a means of deciding cases, for that could be done by flipping a coin, or by always applying the domestic law of the forum. Is it not true that the conflict of laws 'can have as its only purpose the effort to make the result reached in a particular case independent of the forum in which it is brought'? (Griswold, 'In Reply to Mr. Cowan's Views of Renvoi,' 86 U. of Pa. L. Rev. 257, 261 (1939).)

"This is especially true and important within the confines of a Federal system. If we were setting up the United States today, we would almost surely think it foolish to have different rules of law applicable every few hundred miles within its territory. But we have a Federal system, with more than fifty separate legal units. Quite apart from the function of conflict of laws in the international scene, its function within the United States is to bring order out of this chaos, and to provide some rules of law which will make it possible for states to decide cases having some external elements on a rational and reasonably consistent basis.

"Within the United States, there can very rarely be any legitimate basis for one state to apply its 'public policy' against the laws of another state. Nor should any state, in seeking 'justice,' fail to apprehend that there will be no justice unless cases are decided in accordance with law, that is, in the conflict-of-laws area, on a basis which will be accepted by other states, and will lead, in so far as humanly possible, to the same decision of a controversy no matter where the suit is brought.

"Thus, as it seems to me, to say that each state must seek the result which it regards as just under all the circumstances, including the extra-state elements and laws, is simply to deny the existence and purpose of the conflict of laws. It is as much a denial of the purpose of the conflict of laws as is the decision of each case by law of the forum, regardless of its extra-state elements. This should be apparent on its face. It is made apparent when the question of forum-shopping is considered. If each court simply decides what it regards as 'just,' or, on the other hand, if it applies only its own law, then diverse precedents will surely develop, and counsel for plaintiffs will be remiss in their duty if they do not study all the cases in all the states, and file their suit (as they often can) in a state which will give them a favorable result.

"Not only is this a denial of true justice, a denial of the purpose of the conflict of laws, but also it is a denial of law itself. It provides no opportunity for certainty in the law. It makes it difficult to plan transactions having interstate elements. Even after an injury of some sort has occurred, there is, under such a rule, no basis for advising a client as to his rights, or for settling or adjusting the dispute without litigation. All that the lawyer can say is, 'Well, it depends upon the state in which the suit is brought. We will have to see where we can serve the defendant, and then try to find the state where the prospects are best. Perhaps we should sue in three or four states, and then nurse the several cases along until we see how the precedents develop.'

"All of this is fun for lawyers, and provides much for the law professors to write about. But it is not law. It is not conflict of laws, if that term has any real and constructive meaning and objective. We will not have law in this area, we will not fulfill the objectives of the conflict of laws, unless we can provide rules for cases under which the same cases will be decided the same way no matter where the suit is brought, to the extent that this is possible within the limits of human frailty. We will not always be successful in achieving uniformity, but we will surely have more success if we constantly hold up uniformity of result as a major objective, and recognize that there can be no true justice without it.

"To this end, the rule that the law applicable in such a case as the one now before us is the law of the place of the tort seems to me to be well calculated to provide a rule of decision which is understandable by lawyers both before and after an injury has occurred. In order to achieve this rule of law, this measure of certainty and uniformity, we will no doubt have to give up a measure of flexibility. But if flexibility is carried to the point where each case must be decided on all its facts, we no longer have any rule of law. Between the two, I prefer some law to chaos which seems to the particular court dealing with it to be resolved in terms of justice.

"In the long run, therefore, it seems to me more in the interest of justice under law to persist in the position taken by the court below, unless and until a significantly better rule can be offered in place of the one we have. No alternative rule has been advanced having comparable virtues of simplicity and certainty, and therefore I would affirm.

"I should add, however, that the case before us illustrates the possibilities for flexibility, and the opportunity for refinement, which exist under the rule that such cases should be decided in accordance with the law of the place of tort. We still have to decide what that law is, and it may, in some cases, be different when there is an external element in the situation than it would be in a case where all of the facts are internal. Thus, if it had been shown that Massachusetts would, in a case exactly like the instant case, hold that its immunity laws did not apply to corporations mainly active in, and organized under the laws of, other states denying immunity, then adherence to the *Restatement* rules in this case would not advance the goal of uniformity. In such a situation New York should not be more royalist than the king. It should follow the Massachusetts law by applying its own law. (See Griswold, 'Renvoi Revisited,' 51 Harv. L. Rev. 1165 (1938).) However, we have no showing here that a Massachusetts court would not apply its own rule to this case."

RHEINSTEIN, J. ". . . My brother Griswold has invoked the authority of the *Restatement* and adjures us not to depart from it. However, as experience throughout the world shows, efforts to secure adherence to mechanical rules for choice of law will not procure uniformity in the long run. The rule that the law of the place of wrong should apply involves circular reasoning to begin with, as Savigny noted long ago. Moreover, it is not firmly supported by authority where the place of injury is not the same as the place where the defendant acted. (See Rheinstein, 'The Place of Wrong: A Study in the Method of Case Law,' 19 Tulane L. Rev. 4, 165 (1944).) Finally, though I recognize a place for the doctrine of renvoi in choice of law, Judge Griswold's own willingness to depart from the *Restatement* by recourse to renvoi, permitting reference to the Massachusetts conflict-of-laws rules, reinforces the validity of my observation. Use of sound choice-of-law method in the instant case would make renvoi here unnecessary.

"We should take advantage of this case to adopt the methodology developed on the Continent over the past half century, under the leadership of German scholars—particularly the late Dr. Ernst Rabel, whose monumental study of the conflict of laws on a comparative basis has been published under the auspices of the University of Michigan Law School. The approach there developed calls for avoidance of broad sweeping rules, such as the one Judge Griswold invoked, which purports to cover all civil wrongs. Instead, one would recognize that the court in choice-of-law cases must deal with much narrower, more specific problems. If our rules for choice of law are no broader than the problems, then we can find a specific jurisdiction-selecting choice-of-law rule for each problem, and these rules can embody specific policy judgments that make good sense. Courts will find it possible to adhere to them, and, in time, the uniformity of result that Judge Griswold rightly prizes can be attained.

"Applying this approach to the principal case, I find the specific problem confronting this court is what law should govern the question whether a charitable corporation is immune from liability for its servant's torts. Now this problem has arisen because states have sought to conserve the assets of such corporations for their charitable uses and not to allow persons injured by them, especially their beneficiaries, to jeopardize a charity's continuance by claiming what might be a large share of the corporate assets for such damages. Other states, taking account of insurance, have changed this rule and think it better to protect injured persons by subjecting their charitable corporations to all claims for liability—in practice imposing on them only the need to carry adequate liability insurance.

"The foregoing makes it clear that this problem is one which should be resolved by the law of the state of incorporation, at least where the corporate defendant's office and the bulk of its activities are in that state and where the plaintiff, a beneficiary of those activities, was domiciled there and also had entered into his relationship with the defendant there.

"By applying the law of New York in these circumstances, the court will be giving effect to the reasonable expectations of both parties and will subject neither to a surprise. The plaintiff would have every reason to suppose that disputes arising out of his relationship with the defendant would be resolved by reference to New York law. Certainly he could not be expected to have taken out accident insurance for risks due to his participation in Knickerbocker's activities outside New York State. And, needless to say, the defendant has not sought to allege that the insurance protection it required for its New York activities did not extend to out-of-state risks.

"The protection of reasonable expectations is one of the most important objectives of the conflict of laws. As the foregoing analysis makes plain, it can be attained here by holding the New York law denying immunity to charitable corporations applicable to this defendant. I would therefore order the judgment below reversed."[2]

Reese, J. "My brothers Griswold and Rheinstein have

[2] This opinion has been revised along lines suggested by Professor Rheinstein to give greater emphasis in Judge Rheinstein's opinion to the prior relationship of the parties and their consequent expectations. This emphasis required some revision in my report of Judge Rheinstein's reasoning in Case 2.

divided on the question whether this case should be rested on the authority of the *Restatement of the Conflict of Laws.* But that 1934 work is being extensively revised, and, in the spring of 1963, the American Law Institute brought out Tentative Draft No. 8 of the *Restatement of Conflict of Laws Second* dealing with "Wrongs." To be sure, Draft No. 8 has not yet been passed upon by the Institute's annual meeting, but the Tentative Draft has the approval not only of the advisers to the Reporter, but also the Institute's sixty-member Council.

"Section 379 of *Restatement Second,* which states 'The General Principle' for the 'Torts' topic of the 'Wrongs' chapter, has adopted a different approach to choice of law in the field of torts from that reported in its predecessor. Taking account of the diversity of questions that may arise in torts cases, the draftsmen have used a far more flexible concept than the place of wrong to identify the proper source of law. Instead of the place of wrong, the new provision would require the application of the law of the state which has 'the most significant relationship with the occurrence and with the parties.' The succeeding section adds, however, that where a personal injury and the defendant's conduct occur in the same state, its law will 'almost invariably' be applied (*Id.* § 379a (1).)

"In my opinion this court should lend its support to this reformulation of the principles of American case law. The language, to be sure, is unfamiliar, but it reflects the spirit of flexibility to be found in our case law dealing with choice of law.

"If we adopt this formulation, we must ask ourselves what state has the most significant relationship to this tort. The question cannot be answered easily. Here tortious conduct by the defendant's agent occurred in Massachusetts and the harm also occurred there. Yet the local law of Massachusetts to which we are referred would deny liability. Section 379 of the *Restatement Second,* presenting the rationale of the new criterion, recognizes that the significance of the relationship may vary with the issue raised, but this does not appear to be helpful here. We note that the comment on this point does not include charitable immunities among the several examples in which the separate treatment of issues leads to differentiated appraisals of significance. In dealing with the analogous question of intra-family immunity, *Restatement Second* in § 390 adopts a special rule referring that matter to the local law of the family domicil. Yet, in § 390a, *Restatement Second* deals specifically with the problem of charitable immunity and relegates it to its general formula. I can scarcely believe this would have been done if the draftsmen had intended the issue to be resolved by a reference to the place of incorporation. In that event, they would have done as they did in the case of the intra-family immunity and referred to that source of law specifically.

"The comment to § 390a recognizes that, if the immunity rule of the place having the most significant relationship is designed to protect only local charities from tort liability, it should not be applied to an out-of-state charity. But, as Judge Griswold observed, we have not been shown that such is the intent of the Massachusetts law.

"Somewhat reluctantly, in view of the cogent argument of my brother Rheinstein, with whose approach the new *Restatement* is in closer agreement than may have been recognized, I conclude that the state having the most significant relationship with the occurrence giving rise to this claim is the Commonwealth of Massachusetts, and so I agree with my brother Griswold that the judgment below should be affirmed."[3]

[3] Professor Reese disapproves of Judge Reese's opinion. He views the state of the charity's incorporation and principal activities as having the "most significant relationship with the occurrence and with the parties," at least in this action by a New York plaintiff against a New York defendant. His opposition may foreshadow a change in the current Tentative Draft of *Restatement Second*. However, as recently as his comment on *Babcock v. Jackson*, Professor Reese wrote: "But what of issues that in-

Currie, J. "The authority on which Judge Griswold would have us rely is bankrupt and discredited. *Restatement Second,* in its efforts to conceal the fact with new verbalisms, only leads us deeper into the morass wherein our efforts to develop a body of international 'rules' for choice of law have left us floundering. Moreover, the appeal of Judge Rheinstein's proposal disappears when one realizes that, like the rules of the first *Restatement,* the specific problems to be identified by this method would have to be approached without regard to the particular policy underlying each of the conflicting laws. We should have to choose laws without knowing the interests of the respective states involved in the litigation. Our decision might, therefore, frustrate the policy of one state without advancing the policy of the other.

"In this case, as in every choice-of-law case involving a controversy in which this state may have an interest, it is our duty sitting as a court of New York State to ascertain the State's policies that may be engaged in the litigation. When, as to any issue, such a policy is identified, we should determine whether there is any reasonable basis for asserting a New York interest in applying that policy to the instant case. If New York has such an interest, then, as a New York court, we should advance that interest by applying New York law. To be sure, we may often have occasion to ask whether the other state has a con-

---

volve neither standards of conduct nor a special relationship? The measure of damages, charitable immunity, survival of actions, and the effect of a release given to one joint tortfeasor upon the liability of other tortfeasors are examples. The state of conduct and injury does not have as great an interest in the resolution of these issues as in issues involving standards of conduct. Yet conduct and injury are the most important elements of a tort. When these two elements are grouped in a single state, it is believed that for purposes of guidance and predictability the law of this state should control unless there is some countervailing reason for applying another law. It may be that, generally at least, a state where both parties are domiciled will have a demonstrably greater interest in these issues than the state of conduct and injury." Reese, "Comment on *Babcock v. Jackson,*" 63 Colum. L. Rev. 1251, 1255 (1963).

flicting policy which we should take into account in formulating New York policy or in the identifying of its interest. Plainly there is no need to exercise that precaution here.

"The case we have before us is a clear example of a false conflict. The policy of New York in seeking to assure compensation to New Yorkers injured by charitable corporations' negligent activities is to deprive such New York corporations of their common-law immunity. Obviously this New York policy is concerned with New York corporations, not with Massachusetts corporations. We should therefore apply the New York law and so give effect to New York's interest. In so doing, we shall not in any way frustrate or impair the Massachusetts policy to conserve the assets of its charitable corporations. That policy reflects the traditional, albeit dubious, trust-fund theory. No Massachusetts corporation will lose assets by our granting judgment to this plaintiff against this defendant. I would reverse the decision below."

Cavers, J. "I agree in substance with the criticisms which Judges Rheinstein and Currie have directed to the first *Restatement* and which Judge Currie directs to the alternative approach that Judge Rheinstein would have us adopt. Both would compel us to employ jurisdiction-selecting rules, and, in so doing, to use what I have elsewhere termed 'a blindfold test' which would oblige us to choose between two states without regard to the content of their respective laws. (See Cavers, 'A Critique of the Choice of Law Problem,' 47 Harv. L. Rev. 173 (1933).)

"I regret that my brother Reese finds no support for reversal in the language of *Restatement Second*. Advantage might be taken of § 379(3) to give weight to the issue before the court in determining the 'most significant relationship.' Here we are dealing with the claim of a New York citizen who had been taken to Massachusetts and negligently injured there by the servant of a New York charitable corporation. Given these facts the relationship of the New York rule denying immunity with the 'occurrence' and 'the parties' is far more significant on the immunity issues than the relationship of the Massachusetts rule granting immunity. That state's only connection is the circumstance that the injury happened to occur there. Judge Reese's lawyerly argument based on § § 390a and 390g, which deal with charitable and family immunities respectively, would be more impressive if *Restatement Second* were not in tentative draft. If we reverse this decision, the American Law Institute may bring its charitable immunity section into line with our position.

"I agree with Judge Currie's conclusion that what we have here is a false conflict. Properly viewed there is no real conflict between the laws of New York and Massachusetts. If we consider fairness to the parties as well as the purposes of the two states' laws, the case for reversal is reinforced. Knickerbocker's liability is one with which it must live in all its day-to-day activities in New York State. No doubt it has long since insured itself against the resulting risk, and its insurer could scarcely have reduced its premiums on the chance that Knickerbocker would do damage in a state with a law like Massachusetts'. The impact of variations in state tort laws on insurance premiums is easily exaggerated. Professor Peck could not even detect differences in premiums caused by the adoption of a comparative negligence rule in a neighboring state. (Peck, 'Comparative Negligence and Automobile Liability Insurance,' 58 Mich. L. Rev. 689, 718-25 (1960).) As for the plaintiff, he is one of those whom this state in doing away with immunity was seeking to protect.

"Judge Griswold fears uncertainty in the law if we depart from the *Restatement's* broad formula. But our decision in this case would provide a clear guide for any like case. If, in a like case, the plaintiff should seek a Massachusetts forum rather than our own, I should hope that Massachusetts would also apply the New York rule. However, our decision now should not depend on evidence that Massachusetts is prepared to take that step. Once we are satisfied that considerations of policy and fairness require New York law to be applied, we should not hestitate to invoke it simply because we cannot be sure that a Massachusetts court at some future time will do as we have done. I vote for reversal."

Voting to reverse the judgment for the defendant: RHEINSTEIN, CURRIE, and CAVERS, JJ.

Voting to affirm: GRISWOLD and REESE, JJ.

Case 2

In Case 2, the laws of the two states are the same and the facts differ from Case 1 only in that there is a new plaintiff, John Ball, a Massachusetts citizen residing in the neighborhood who had been struck and seriously injured when the truck backed up. He, too, had lost below on the immunity ground.

In this case, Judges Griswold and Reese[4] find no difficulty in reaching the same results as they had reached in the previous case and on essentially the same grounds. Accordingly, they voted to affirm. Judge Rheinstein, who in Case 1 had placed some emphasis on the relationship of the New York plaintiff to the New York defendant, could not find in Case 2 any basis for an expectation on the part of the Massachusetts plaintiff that New York law would be applied to his claim. However, since Judge Rheinstein considered the central choice-of-law problem posed by a case involving a charitable corporation's claim of immunity to involve the financial position of such corporations, he concluded that the New York law imposing liability should be applied. As a New York corporation, Knickerbocker's expectations would

[4] Professor Reese, having disapproved of Judge Reese's opinion in Case 1, see note 3 *supra*, was not prepared to accept it in this case, though the Massachusetts domicil of the plaintiff would strengthen the grounds for applying that state's law if one were to follow the analysis the former uses in the passage quoted in note 3, *supra*.

be shaped by the New York law, and presumably it would have protected itself by insurance. Accordingly, he voted to reverse. Judge Currie also found Case 2 a bit troublesome. To quote from his opinion:

"In abolishing common-law immunity for a charitable corporation, New York was legislating for the protection of New York citizens. If its law is to be extended to protect John Ball, a citizen of Massachusetts, it must be that New York recognizes another and different interest here, an altruistic interest to protect whoever may be injured by the negligence of a New York corporation, in whatever state he may be. Yet this seems a reasonable assumption; it avoids the possibility of inter-state retaliation and the resulting need to resort to reciprocity.

"I detect nothing in the adoption of the New York rule that would restrict its benefits to New York citizens. Moreover, if such a restriction were imposed here while New York citizens injured in Massachusetts were permitted to recover, the discrimination might be viewed as a violation of the Privileges and Immunities Clause of the Constitution. Such would not be the case, of course, if this extension of New York's financial protection to cover a Massachusetts citizen injured in that state were in any sense an intrusion into Massachusetts affairs. (See Currie & Schreter, 'Unconstitutional Discrimination in the Conflict of Laws: Privileges and Immunities,' 69 Yale L.J. 1323, 1361, 1377-78 (1960).) The contrary is true; the compensation paid by way of damages to an injured Massachusetts citizen can only be a benefit to the Commonwealth. I would vote to reverse."

Judge Cavers agreed with Judge Currie's conclusion in the following passage: "When a few years ago this court finally did away with the last vestiges of its former policy to grant charitable immunity, it seems plain that it simply wished to put nonprofit corporations on the same footing as other corporations with respect to civil responsibility. I see no reason why Knickerbocker should have an immunity thrust upon it simply because its victim is a Massachusetts citizen. It has been argued that to allow Ball to recover is to grant him a windfall that he would not have recovered if he had been hit by the truck of a Massachusetts educational institution. I doubt the aptness of the term 'windfall' to describe the recovery of damages by anyone who had been in contact with the rear end of a reversing truck. The plaintiff obtained no more than compensation for the injury sustained. It would be fair to deny him that compensation only if this were the necessary consequence of furthering the purpose of a Massachusetts law. Such is not the case."

Since Judge Rheinstein had cast his vote for the plaintiff, this case also goes to the plaintiff by 3-2 vote.

Voting to reverse the judgment for the defendant: RHEINSTEIN, CURRIE, and CAVERS, JJ.

Voting to affirm: GRISWOLD and REESE, JJ.

Case 3

Case 3 is more complex. It differs from Case 1 in the way the accident comes about and in its date, 1958. On the trip to Mount Greylock, the Knickerbocker truck broke down in Massachusetts ten miles from the destination, and an accommodating farmer offered to rent the Knickerbocker representative an old truck of his for use while the Knickerbocker truck was being repaired. When the farmer explained that he had not registered his truck that year, the Knickerbocker representative said, "Oh, we'll chance it." As in the first case, the truck-driver backed into the plaintiff, Adams, the New York camper, on a highway, but this time under circumstances where neither party could be shown to have been negligent. Yet in 1958, under Massachusetts law, the driver of an unregistered motor vehicle was an "outlaw on the highways," liable for whatever injuries he caused.[5] New York had no such rule. The plaintiff, of course, relied on the violation of the Massachusetts statute to establish liability. The defendant moved for a summary judgment, relying on the Massachusetts law granting charitable immunity, and the plaintiff's failure to allege negligence. The motion was granted on both grounds and the order sustained in the Appellate Division.

Judge Griswold, of course, voted to uphold the decision below on immunity ground but also expressed the opinion that, but for the defendant's immunity, the Massachusetts law governing unregistered vehicles would have been applicable. His belief that the same state's law should govern both issues led him to remark, "I cannot refrain from observing the paradox which would have been produced had a majority been ready to follow Judge Cavers in denying defendant the immunity which Massachusetts law would confer while giving plaintiff the benefit of the Massachusetts strict liability rule. If all the facts of this case had been in New York, plaintiff would have lost for failure to prove negligence. If all the facts of this case had been in Massachusetts, plaintiff would have lost because of the Massachusetts charitable immunity rule. Now, by reason of the division of the facts of the case between the two states, Judge Cavers would perform the miracle of creating a cause of action where none existed in either state. If this represents justice, then so does the principle: 'Heads I win: tails you lose.' "

[5] The Massachusetts statute, which had been interpreted to render an unregistered motor vehicle on the highway a "nuisance" and the owner or operator liable for damage caused by it without proof of negligence, Koonovsky v. Quellette, 226 Mass. 474, 116 N.E. 243 (1917); *cf.* Strogoff v. Motor Sales Co. Inc., 302 Mass. 345, 18 N.E.2d 1016 (1939) (out-of-state owner not liable for driver's unauthorized, unanticipated entry into Massachusetts), was amended in 1959 to remove such vehicles from the nuisance category and to render violation merely evidence of negligence. MASS. ANN. LAWS ch. 90, § 9 (Supp. 1963).

Judge Rheinstein, having dealt with the charitable immunity issue in the manner indicated by his opinion in Case 1, calling for the application of the law of New York, then turned to the question whether the defendant should be subjected to absolute liability by an application of the Massachusetts law.

"For the reasons noted," Judge Rheinstein continued, "the relationship of plaintiff and defendant was centered in New York and their expectations framed with reference to New York law. New York law should therefore determine the extent to which its own immunity rule can be said to have been abandoned. It is one thing to expose our charities to vicarious liability when the harm done by their servants is the consequence of those servants' careless or intentionally wrongful conduct in another state and to invoke the law of the place of injury for the standards to govern that conduct. It is quite another thing, however, to expose our charities to a drastic sanction of strict civil liability for failure to register a motor vehicle pursuant to the law of another state, an omission unconnected with the actual infliction of plaintiff's injury. I would therefore reject the application of the Massachusetts 'outlaw-on-the-highways' rule to this defendant, at least in a case in which the defendant is sued by its New York beneficiary.

"The Massachusetts statute should be disregarded for the following additional reasons: The statute is meant to deter Massachusetts people from driving on Massachusetts highways automobiles for which no license fee has been paid to the state of Massachusetts. The statute is essentially a fiscal law, reinforced by the penal provision. The fact that the penalty goes, as a windfall, to a private individual rather than to the public treasury is irrelevant. Whether we like it or not, at present, states still adhere to the tradition that they will not mutually assist each other in the enforcement of their fiscal and penal laws."[6]

Judge Reese, though prepared to hold that Massachusetts' relationship to the occurrence was the most significant and that therefore its law should govern the issue of charitable immunity, noted that he appeared to be in a minority position on this point. Observing that, on the issue as to the standard of liability to govern the defendant's conduct, the relationship of Massachusetts to the occurrence was even more clearly the most significant, Judge Reese nevertheless voted to reverse the order granting the defendant's motion for a summary judgment but to dismiss the plaintiff's case without prejudice. Judge Reese's explanation of his decision is contained in the following passage from his opinion.

"I do not rest my position on the ground that the Massachusetts 'outlaw-on-the-highways' rule is a 'penal law in the international sense' (see *Huntington v. Attrill*, 146 U.S. 657, 673 (1892); *Loucks v. Standard Oil Co. of New York*, 224 N.Y. 99, 103, 120 N.E. 198, 199 (1918)) though a strong argument could be made for such a characterization. Rather, I rest my vote for dismissal on the ground that the imposition of civil liability for personal injuries on this defendant in the circumstances of this case would be so outrageous an injustice that, as a matter of sound public policy, we should refuse to give effect to the Massachusetts rule. Although the implementation of such a decision calls for dismissal without prejudice rather than a summary judgment for the defendant on the merits, I take comfort in the realization that a Massachusetts forum can—and doubtless would—protect this defendant by applying its own rule of charitable immunity. I also note with satisfaction that, since the occurrence leading to this

[6] I prepared this opinion after Professor Rheinstein had intimated that the special relationship of the parties would have led Judge Rheinstein to apply New York law rather than Massachusetts law as I had originally supposed.

action took place, Massachusetts has abandoned its draconic rule. (See, in this connection, the observations of Holmes, J., in *Union Trust Co. v. Grosman,* 245 U.S. 412, 417 (1918).)"[7]

Judge Currie, after having been led again by his governmental interest analysis to apply New York law to the immunity issue, addressed himself to the question whether it would be proper to give effect to what would appear to be the clear interest of Massachusetts in imposing a civil sanction on this violation of the control which it exercises over vehicles on its highways through its vehicle registration law. He decided that it would not be proper. His opinion on the point follows:

CURRIE, J. ". . . Agreeing as I must with Judge Griswold that the result reached by Judge Cavers in applying both the New York law denying charitable immunity and the Massachusetts law of strict liability for unregistered vehicles is paradoxical, I would affirm the judgment for the defendant.

"True it is that choice of law must proceed on an issue-by-issue basis; but modern conflict-of-laws analysis can make no more serious mistake than to indulge in an unprincipled eclecticism, picking and choosing from among the available laws in order to reach a result that cannot be squared with the interests of any of the related states. Issue-by-issue analysis should not result in the cumulation of negative policies to produce a result not contemplated by the law of either state.

"The problem has its counterpart in other choice-of-law situations. For example, I find unprincipled eclecticism in the case of *Lillegraven v. Tengs,* 375 P.2d 139 (Alaska 1962), in which the Alaska court allowed an Alaskan injured in British Columbia to recover from the Alaskan owner of the automobile causing the injury under the British Columbia owner-liability law, despite the facts that the built-in one-year limitation period in that statute had expired before the suit was brought

[7] This opinion, which I prepared after ascertaining the view of Professor Reese, was substituted for the original opinion by Judge Reese, which applied Massachusetts law to both issues.

in Alaska and that Alaska had no owner-liability law. This strikes me as a perversion of the government-interest analysis, not to be avoided by the classification of limitations as procedural, and I am glad to endorse the convincing criticism of the decision which appears in 1963 Duke Law Journal at 762.

"Unlike Judge Cavers, I do not find distressingly paradoxical the results even of such cases as *Marie v. Garrison* and *Scheer v. Rockne Motors*, cited by him, where the courts reach results at variance with the identical laws of the states concerned. Their results might be reached, if with some difficulty, by a fair approximation of the governmental-interest analysis. A plaintiff's claim may fall between two stools and be governed by the common law rather than by the statute of either state.

"In our case, however, the problem is different. While Massachusetts has a policy of deterring the operation of unlicensed vehicles, it does not extend that policy to charities (here I follow Judge Cavers in his apparent assumption that Massachusetts would impose vicarious liability on the driver's employer, but not in the case of a charity). While New York has a policy of requiring compensation for its injured residents, it has no policy of imposing liability in the absence of negligence. To impose liability on this New York corporation, which has been free from fault, simply in order to carry out a nonexistent Massachusetts policy of deterrence, seems to me entirely unjustified. (I hope my brethren will note that I have not found it necessary to refer to the doctrine that no state enforces the penal laws of another.)

"It is one thing to fall between two stools; it is quite another to put together half a donkey and half a camel, and then ride to victory on the synthetic hybrid."[8]

[8] This opinion represents a condensation of a draft opinion prepared by Professor Currie and substituted for Judge Currie's original opinion which applied Massachusetts law to the liability issue while applying New York law to the immunity issue.

Judge Cavers noted that there was no conflict between the Massachusetts outlaw-on-the-highways rule and the New York law which attaches no civil consequences to nonregistration since New York had no reason to assert the applicability of its law to conduct on the Massachusetts highways. Moreover, while admitting that the Massachusetts law was a "drastic" method of assuring more responsible ownership and use of automobiles on the state's highways, he rejected the view that the civil sanction was merely a fiscal measure and observed that a strict liability rule providing for compensation to injured persons could no longer be viewed as penal in the international sense. "Surely," he added, "the day has passed when we should resort to public policy to provide a haven in our state for a defendant who is being called upon to reimburse the plaintiff for damage that the defendant has caused in the state whose law he has violated. Nor do I find myself ready to join Judge Rheinstein in what appears to me to be a piecemeal restoration of New York's former charitable immunity doctrine. Are we prepared now to hold that New York would deny recovery to a beneficiary of a New York charity in a case of injury outside New York in which New York's domestic rule imposed strict liability?"

Judge Cavers next addressed himself to the characterization by Judges Griswold and Currie of the result he would reach as "paradoxical" in permitting the plaintiff to recover in a two-state case when he would fail if the accident had been localized in either state.

"I find nothing paradoxical in the differing results to which Judge Griswold points. That a paradox may seem to exist is due to our habituation to choice-of-law thinking that requires us to choose between legal systems rather than between specific conflicting rules. Otherwise, we should think it natural enough that a two-state case involving two distinct policy problems should not always have the same result as a one-state case involving the same problems. (*Cf.* Harper, 'Policy Bases in the Conflict of Laws: Some Reflections on the Reading of Professor Lorenzen's Essays,' 56 Yale L.J. 1155, 1163 (1947).) Where both states have the same policies on the problem at issue then I agree it would be paradoxical, to put it mildly, for a two-state case to produce a different result than the same case in either state. Yet traditional conflicts thinking has permitted such results. (*Marie v. Garrison,* 13 Abb. N.C. 210 (N.Y. 1883); *cf. Scheer v. Rockne Motors Corp.,* 68 F.2d 942 (2d Cir. 1934), discussed in Cavers, 'The Two "Local Law" Theories,' 63 Harv. L. Rev. 822 (1950).)

"Judge Currie's joinder in the charge of paradox cannot be laid to addiction to jurisdiction-selecting rules, and I agree with him that, when laws are chosen on an issue-by-issue basis, care must be taken not to combine rules in such fashion as to work injustice. I am prepared to accept his quarrel with the Alaska court's action in using its longer statute of limitations to permit an action to be brought against a party who could be held liable only by invoking a rule of liability in a jurisdiction whose 'built-in' period of limitation had expired. The case is rather suggestive of the case that *Kilberg* would have presented if New York had neither a survival nor a wrongful death statute. On the other hand, Judge Currie's acceptance of the results of *Marie* and *Scheer* leads me to distrust the process of interest analysis that can produce them. If pushed too far, it can yield unrealistic delimitations of state interests.

"What characterizes the case where it is improper to join rules drawn from two states to produce a cause of action that would be recognized as a domestic cause in neither state is the fact that the rules thus combined are closely related in purpose—the 'built-in' statute of limitations being an example. Another example is suggested by the law-fact pattern of *Brewster v. Boston Herald-Traveler Corp.,* 188 F. Supp. 565 (D.C. Mass. 1960), though the actual case did not pose the issue. Massachusetts denies truth as a defense to a malicious libel and also denies the recovery of punitive damages, whereas Maine allows truth as an absolute defense and also allows the recovery of punitive damages for malicious libel. I submit —and I am sure Judge Currie would agree—that a Maine court should not grant punitive damages for a true but defamatory statement maliciously published in Massachusetts concerning a Maine plaintiff. It is reasonable in that situation to assume that the Massachusetts rules are related, that in requiring publishers to compensate persons maliciously harmed by true statements, the Commonwealth's lawmakers did so with an awareness that the recovery would be limited to the actual harm sustained. For a Maine court to impose liability for malicious truth, which it could do only by reason of the Massachusetts law, without at the same time adopting the Massachusetts measure of damages, is for it to exploit the interstate situation unfairly. (Perhaps I should add that this hypothetical case would resemble *Kilberg* and that bulwark of the vested rights theory, *Slater v. Mexican National R.R.* 194 U.S. 120 (1904), only if Maine also allowed recovery for the malicious publication of truth.)

"What Judge Currie has done in the principal case is to insist that two rules, unrelated in policy, be drawn from a single source. Massachusetts' policy of granting immunity to charitable corporations has no relation to its policy of imposing strict liability on drivers of unregistered vehicles. Massachusetts excepts its charities from that rule just as it excepts them from all its rules imposing liability for tort. The fact that the liability is strict introduces no distinguishing element. Must a New York court refuse to impose liability for tortious conduct in Massachusetts on a New York charitable corporation unless it can be shown that the defendant would have been liable under the New York law of torts? If so, then we are letting the Massachusetts immunity rule in by the back door. Yet I had supposed that most of us were agreed that the state of injury had no reasonable basis for injecting its immunity rule into a case in which the charity's state of incorporation and principal activities had done away with the immunity doctrine.

"As I see it, New York has given to its charities just the same status with respect to vicarious liability for their servants' conduct as it has given to any other legal entity of its creation. The policy embodied in that action is not delimited by New York views as to the basis of tort liability or by the views of other states as to the status of their charities. The New York charitable corporation in Massachusetts should be held answerable to Massachusetts law governing conduct there.

"I would reverse."[9]

Voting to affirm the summary judgment for defendant: GRISWOLD, RHEINSTEIN, CURRIE, JJ.

Voting to reverse the summary judgment for defendant but to dismiss the plaintiff's action: REESE, J.

Voting to reverse the summary judgment for defendant: CAVERS, J.

Case 4

Case 4 will be recognized by conflicts cognoscenti as the product of plagiarism rather than imagination. In it both the New York nature lover and a Massachusetts citizen are the victims of the truck-driver's negligence—a New York truck this time—but the accident is fatal to both. The relicts of the victims sue as personal representatives for the wrongful deaths of their spouses in the New York courts for $100,000 each. The defendant, in addition to pleading the Massachusetts law on charitable immunity, pleads the Massachusetts wrongful death act, which at that time restricted damages for wrongful death from a minimum of $2,000 to a maximum of $20,000, the amount between those limits being determined by the degree of the defendant's culpability. Again the defendant pre-

[9] All of this section of his opinion following the first paragraph was added by Judge Cavers after the revision of Judge Currie's opinion, reported in note 8 *supra*.

vailed below on the immunity issue. Since on appeal the majority voted to apply New York law on the immunity issue on grounds we have already reported, the excerpts from the opinions presented below relate only to the damage issue.

On that issue Judge Griswold voted that Massachusetts law should be applied, quoting from Mr. Justice Holmes's opinion in the *Slater* case,[10] in which Holmes said, "It seems to us unjust to allow a plaintiff to come here absolutely depending on the foreign law for the foundation of his case, and yet to deny the defendant the benefit of whatever limitations on his liability that law would impose." Judge Griswold also invoked *Loucks v. Standard Oil Co. of N.Y.*,[11] an action by the widow of a New Yorker killed in Massachusetts, in which the New York Court of Appeals, *per* Cardozo, J., enforced the Massachusetts rule limiting damages for wrongful death against a New York corporate defendant.

In taking this position, Judge Griswold had to dispose of *Kilberg v. Northeast Airlines, Inc.*,[12] the case that inspired Case 4. In *Kilberg*, the New York Court of Appeals in an elaborated dictum—virtually a letter of advice to plaintiff's counsel—declared that New York's strong public policy, manifested by a constitutional provision forbidding limitations on recovery for wrongful death, justified a refusal to apply the Massachusetts limitation to a case arising out of the death of an airplane passenger, a New York domiciliary, in a Massachusetts crash which ended a flight that had begun in New York, even though the liability for wrongful death had to depend on Massachusetts law, the New York wrongful death act having long been held not to apply to out-of-state deaths. This rule was later sustained against constitutional attack when the full bench of the Second Circuit in *Pearson v. Northeast Airlines,*

[10] Slater v. Mexican National R.R., 194 U.S. 120, 126 (1904).

[11] 224 N.Y. 99, 120 N.E. 198 (1918). The plaintiff did not contend in *Loucks* that the New York rule be applied.

[12] 9 N.Y.2d 34, 172 N.E.2d 526 (1961).

Inc., reversed a 2-1 decision by a three-judge panel.[13] The Supreme Court denied *certiorari.*

To narrow *Kilberg*, Judge Griswold relied on the emphasis given in the *Kilberg* opinion to the fact that the place of injury in an airplane accident is highly fortuitous. In view of the considerations special to air travel, he insisted that the dictum should be confined to the type of situation that gave rise to the *Kilberg* case.

Judge Rheinstein saw the damage claims of the two plaintiffs as giving rise to separate problems. He voted to apply the Massachusetts limitation to the claim of the Massachusetts plaintiff, Mrs. Ball, but not to that of the New York plaintiff, Mrs. Adams. He explained his position as follows:

"The Massachusetts plaintiff has never entered into any special relationship with the defendant corporation. Neither he nor his survivors had any reason ever to expect that, in the case of his being injured or killed in Massachusetts, any law other than that of Massachusetts would determine the amount of recovery. If he regarded the Massachusetts law as insufficient for his needs or those of his family, he had the opportunity of supplementing a potential recovery by taking out accident insurance.

"In contrast, the New York decedent has a close relationship with the New York corporation of which he had become a member. He could reasonably expect that his relationship to that body would be determined by New York law in all respects, including the corporation's out-of-state activities. For him, no reason existed why he should take out accident insurance to supplement claims he or members of his family might have against Knickerbocker."[14]

[13] 309 F.2d 553 (2d Cir. 1962), *reversing* 307 F.2d 131 (2d Cir. 1962). The court divided 6 to 3.

[14] This opinion represents a slightly condensed version of an opinion provided by Professor Rheinstein and substituted for the original opinion by Judge Rheinstein, which applied Massachusetts law to both plaintiffs' claims.

Judge Reese, though voting with Judge Griswold to apply Massachusetts law on the issue of immunity, was obliged by reason of their minority position to consider whether the Massachusetts ceiling on damages should apply to the claims of either or both plaintiffs. He called attention to the fact that, while Tentative Draft No. 8 of *Restatement Second* applied the general test of "most significant relationship" to find the source of the measure of damages for torts generally (see § 390b), nevertheless, the Draft promised in a Reporter's Note (at 129) that there "will be a separate section dealing with damages for wrongful death." Judge Reese's opinion continues:

"Though it would be premature to assert what the American Law Institute's position will eventually be, I suspect it not unlikely that it will reflect the position taken in *Kilberg* which, as I read that opinion, certainly calls for the application of the higher measure of damages in the law of the state from which both parties come if that state has a strong public policy calling for its use.

"As *Kilberg* made plain, New York's public policy against a ceiling limitation on the damages recoverable for wrongful death is strong. I believe the plaintiff, Mrs. Adams, the widow of a New York citizen, should have the benefit of this policy. On the other hand, I see no basis for projecting this policy to the claim of the plaintiff, Mrs. Ball, as the widow of a Massachusetts citizen, for the wrongful death in Massachusetts of her husband. I concur with Judge Rheinstein in holding that, if the defense of immunity is to be denied, the New York measure of damages is to be applied in the case of Mrs. Adams and the Massachusetts measure in the case of Mrs. Ball."[15]

Judge Currie saw a false problem in the claims of the New Yorker's representative and therefore had no difficulty in applying New York law. Unlike *Kilberg* where the defendant

[15] This opinion, which I prepared after ascertaining the view of Professor Reese, was substituted for the original opinion by Judge Reese, which applied Massachusetts law to both plaintiffs' claims.

was a Massachusetts corporation, here there was no conflicting Massachusetts interest. Moreover, Judge Currie voted to apply the New York measure of damages in the case of the Massachusetts decedent's representative, expressing his views in an opinion from which the following excerpt is taken.

Currie, J. ". . . It would be possible, of course, for New York's courts to hold that the policy of compensation without arbitrary limitation is designed primarily for New York people, and to classify nonresidents on the basis of the laws of their home states in order to deny them the protection of New York law when it is withheld from them by their own law. I would not make such classifications arbitrarily, however. In some situations—for example in the case in which domestic law protects married women from liability for the debts of their husbands—I would be quick to classify and to deny the nonresident married woman a protection, or a disability, not bestowed or imposed by her home state. In other cases—concerning, for example, debtors' exemptions—I should much prefer the principle of equal treatment for all. (See Currie, 'Selected Essays on the Conflict of Laws,' 545-57 (1963).)

"Here, since New York will apply its law to give full compensation to the survivors of the New York citizen killed in Massachusetts, I would apply the principle of equality and do the same for the survivors of the deceased citizen of Massachusetts. I find comfort in the fact that the New York defendant's liability insurance will cover it in both cases; in the arrangement of such insurance there is no way to predict whether the victim will be a citizen of New York or of Massachusetts.

"Of course I am here venturing to define the scope of New York's policy, which is essentially a task for the legislature. If I am wrong I invite the legislature to correct our decision should I lead my brethren into error as well. But if New York's policy is to be narrowly and selfishly defined in this situation, out of consideration for those local interests that would benefit from such a definition, the decision should be made by the legislature, which is the proper institution to respond to pressures from local private interests—not by this court, in which sensitivity to such pressures would be, to say the least, unbecoming."[16]

As to the New York plaintiff, Judge Cavers joined with Judges Rheinstein, Reese, and Currie in their conclusion, but his opinion manifested some misgivings. Why, he asked, in the New Yorker's case, should a New York court be free to disregard the ceiling that the Massachusetts legislature had persisted in imposing on recoveries for wrongful death if, as he assumed, it would be ready to recognize a Massachusetts rule to determine whether strict liability or negligence was the basis of the plaintiff's case? On this point Judge Cavers said: "Here we find both states in agreement that wrongful death is actionable and differing only as to the measurement of compensation. On that latter issue, is not the New York law the preferable source of the measure not only because New York has expressed a strong policy against limitations on wrongful death recoveries but because the representative of a New Yorker is claiming compensation from the New York defendant corporation which had taken the plaintiff's decedent from New York into Massachusetts in carrying out a transaction imposing a duty of care on the defendant to the decedent? That relationship provides a ready basis for the application of New York law, and there are no countervailing considerations calling for the Massachusetts ceiling.

"In contrast, in the case of the Massachusetts decedent, there seems little reason in the fatal chance encounter with an out-of-state stranger to afford his survivors a far higher

[16] This opinion represents a slightly condensed version of a draft opinion prepared by Professor Currie in substitution for Judge Currie's original opinion, which I had prepared and which applied the New York no-ceiling rule to the New York plaintiff's claim and the Massachusetts ceiling to the Massachusetts plaintiff's claim.

standard of recovery than is available to them under the laws of their home state. The cases of a Massachusetts patron of Knickerbocker and of a New Yorker, who without prior relationship to a New York defendant was killed in Massachusetts, would be more difficult. Fortunately, we need not decide them now.

"Though I sympathize with Judge Currie's desire to assure equality of treatment in our courts to the two widows whose bereavement occurred in the same accident, I believe the implications of his position should be carefully weighed before this court should accept it. I view the advantage which I would have us accord the New York plaintiff, Mrs. Adams, as exceptional, one that springs not merely from the fact that her husband was a New Yorker and the defendant, a New York corporation, but from the further fact that, as I pointed out above, they were in Massachusetts as a consequence of a prior special relationship which they had formed in New York. Suppose we were to hold now that Mrs. Ball can recover unlimited damages for the death of her husband, a stranger to that relationship. How then could we justly deny the claim to full recovery under New York law of the next Massachusetts plaintiff widowed by a New York corporation's Massachusetts operations, even though no New Yorker were hurt in the same accident? Surely the mere coincidence that a single negligent act claimed two victims is not a firm basis for distinguishing between those two cases.

"Yet ought we to take the position that a New York citizen or corporation always carries the New York rule against ceilings on wrongful death recoveries wherever that citizen or the corporation may go? Moreover, if we insist on our no-ceiling law as a rule always to be observed in the New York courts, regardless of the out-of-state decedents and the state laws involved, I see no reason why the courts of other states should not also apply it when their citizens sue New York defendants in their own forums. (Though I write of out-of-state decedents and New York defendants, I scarcely need remark how simplistic those labels are and how many and diverse the connections between the respective parties and states can be.)

"I submit that we are not required by considerations of policy or justice to impose as heavy a burden as Judge Currie's chivalrous response to Mrs. Ball's distressing plight would cast on New York defendants. I am not resigned to that prospect by the realization that their liability insurance carriers would absorb all or a considerable part of the cost and that this in turn would probably not bulk large when spread over the premiums paid by all New Yorkers. We are dealing with damages for wrongful death. In these days when six-figure verdicts in wrongful death actions are becoming a commonplace, the comfort Judge Currie takes in the defendant's liability insurance coverage in the instant case (if it in fact suffices) may easily be unjustified in cases involving individual defendants or accidents less commonly insured against.

"The remedy to prevent such hardships as the anachronistic damage ceiling of Massachusetts may impose on Mrs. Ball in this case lies, I submit, in the hands of the Massachusetts legislature.

"I would reverse as to Mrs. Adams and affirm as to Mrs. Ball."[17]

Voting to affirm as to Mrs. Adams: GRISWOLD, J.

Voting to reverse as to Mrs. Adams: RHEINSTEIN, REESE, CURRIE, and CAVERS, JJ.

Voting to affirm as to Mrs. Ball: GRISWOLD, RHEINSTEIN, REESE, and CAVERS, JJ.

Voting to reverse as to Mrs. Ball: CURRIE, J.

Case 5

Ball v. Berkshire Natural History Society, Inc. We have examined four cases, each of which has been patterned on

[17] This opinion was substituted by Judge Cavers for his original opinion, after reading the new opinion by Judge Currie. The original opinion reached the same result as the substitute.

the first: the charitable corporation of New York injuring the plaintiff or causing wrongful death in Massachusetts. Case 5 reverses the law-fact pattern by switching the facts, not the laws. The charitable corporation is now the Berkshire Natural History Society, Inc., a Massachusetts educational corporation (which I shall call "Berkshire") with activities centered in the Commonwealth, including a camp for nature lovers near Mount Greylock in the Berkshire Mountains of Massachusetts. The campers, who include John Ball of Boston, go on a trip in a camp truck to the Adirondack Mountains in New York State. There the negligence of the truck driver results in the serious injury of Ball. He is rushed to an Albany hospital where he spends two months before returning to his home in Boston for convalescence.

When sued in New York under the New York Non-Resident Motorist Statute,[18] Berkshire moves for summary judgment, setting forth the Massachusetts law on charitable immunity. The trial court grants defendant's motion, and the Appellate Division affirms 3 to 2. Once more we shall poll our judges sitting as the New York Court of Appeals.

Judge Griswold adheres to the place-of-injury rule and votes to reverse. However, he cannot refrain from observing wryly that, despite the critical attitude displayed by his brothers Currie and Cavers toward the *Restatement*'s rules, they show no hesitancy to apply the law of the place of injury in this case. This leads him to speculate whether they find the place-of-injury rule acceptable in this case because it favors plaintiff. Judge Rheinstein would, as before, classify the problem of charitable immunity as one of special concern to the state of incorporation, which not only was the seat of the corporation's activities but also the home of the plaintiff. In the light of these facts and the parties' expectations resulting therefrom, he would apply Massachusetts law. He would therefore affirm. Judge Reese, having found the "most significant

[18] N.Y. VEHICLE & TRAFFIC LAW § 253.

relationship" to have been with Massachusetts in Case 1, now is led by the coincidence of the place of the defendant's servant's conduct with the place of injury to conclude that that relationship is now with New York. Accordingly, he votes to reverse.[19]

Judge Currie is prepared to deny immunity in this case. Excerpts from his opinion follow:

CURRIE, J. ". . . It is plain that Massachusetts has an interest in the application of its immunity rule to protect the defendant Massachusetts charitable corporation. But does New York have a conflicting interest to assure the compensation of the plaintiff, a Massachusetts citizen temporarily in New York at the time of injury?

"Certainly this court could declare an interest on the part of New York in applying its policy of compensation to all persons injured in the state in order to compensate medical creditors, and to avoid a burden on our public institutions, merely on the ground that a real tendency to create such a burden exists. That such a construction of New York law would not unconstitutionally encroach on the interests of Massachusetts is the teaching of *Carroll v. Lanza,* 349 U.S. 408 (1955). I would not rush to the conclusion, however, that so broad a construction should be given to New York's law. Our esteemed colleague in California, Justice Traynor, recently refrained deliberately from giving California policy a construction as broad as could constitutionally be sustained, preferring a moderate construction that would avoid conflict. (*Bernkrant v. Fowler,* 55 Cal. 2d 588, 360 P.2d 906 (1961).) A construction of the Jones Act that refrained from asserting

[19] Professor Reese disapproves of Judge Reese's opinion and would apply the law of Massachusetts in this case. He views the state of the charity's incorporation and principal activities as having the "most significant relationship with the occurrence and with the parties," at least in this action by a Massachusetts plaintiff. *Cf.* note 3, *supra.*

an American interest in protecting local medical creditors when foreign seamen are injured aboard foreign vessels in our ports has met with approval. (See Currie, Selected Essays on the Conflict of Laws ch. 7 (1963).)

"In one aspect at least, the question is whether the domestic gain achieved by the broader construction, judged in relation to the impairment of foreign interests, is such that the purpose to achieve it can reasonably be attributed to the legislature. In another aspect, the question is perhaps how particularistic the courts can afford to be. Would it be practical for us to assert New York's interest in foreigners injured here only when the apprehended burden on local people and institutions actually materializes? Doubt has been expressed as to the willingness of courts to particularize very much in matters of this kind. (See Currie, 'Mutuality of Collateral Estoppel: Limits of the *Bernhard* Doctrine,' 9 Stan L. Rev. 281 (1957).) Happily this appears to have been too pessimistic. (See *Teitelbaum Furs, Inc. v. Dominion Ins. Co.*, 25 Cal. Rptr. 559, 375 P.2d 439 (1962); *United States v. United Air Lines, Inc.*, 216 F. Supp. 709 (D. Nev. 1962).)

"I need not decide in this case whether to give New York's policy in that respect a broad or a narrow construction, however, for I construe New York's policy of full compensation as designed to discourage the negligent operation of motor vehicles within this state, irrespective of who the victim may be. I am satisfied that such laws as this are designed to have a deterrent effect, though we may all be skeptical as to how effectively they accomplish that purpose. (See Currie, Selected Essays on the Conflict of Laws 210, 294, 323, 371, 488, 540, 701 (1963); Currie, 'Comment on *Babcock v. Jackson*,' 63 Colum. L. Rev. 1212, 1237 (1963).)

"We need not speculate what a court in a disinterested third state would do if such a case were to come before it under circumstances that prevented dismissal on the ground of an inconvenient forum. (See Currie, 'The Disinterested Third State,' 28 Law & Contemp. Prob. 754 (1963).)[20]

"I would apply New York law and therefore vote for reversal."

Judge Cavers reached the same conclusion as Judge Currie, but in doing so may have projected the position noted in the next-to-the-last paragraph of the latter's opinion beyond the point which Judge Currie would find acceptable. "I am not content," Judge Cavers said, "to rest my decision simply on the ground that it advances the domestic policy of this state to do so, if it is possible to justify our preference of the New York law on a principle that would seem persuasive to a court of a disinterested third state, or even to a Massachusetts court. I believe grounds for such a principle of preference exist.

"A basic function of this and, indeed, of any modern state is to provide a highway system and regulate its use, including the prescription of standards of safe motoring. Another mode of regulation is the imposition of civil liability for damages on the motorist who negligently injures another. Still another mode of regulation is to require the provision of financial protection to persons injured on its highways and so to the institutions that minister to them. This state has now determined that these needs are paramount to the protection of charitable institutions from liability, and, therefore, as a part of its scheme of highway regulation, subjects them to its civil liability laws.

"A principle preferring this policy determination by the state of the highway accident to the contrary policy of a state from which the plaintiff and defendant highway users have come preserves the integrity of the state system of regulation

[20] This opinion represents a slightly condensed version of a draft opinion prepared by Professor Currie in substitution for Judge Currie's original opinion which I had prepared and which had rested the New York interest in the application of New York law on New York's concern for the burden of medical care.

without intruding unfairly upon the responsibilities of the other state. To exclude from the New York policy either out-of-state residents who are injured here or out-of-state institutions whose agents have caused injuries here could be justified only if their inclusion were unreasonable or otherwise unfair. Certainly to impose New York law need cause no hardship to institutions operating under the laws of other states which afford them more protection. They have the option to conduct their activities elsewhere. If they enter New York State, they, like New York institutions, can seek such protection as insurance can provide against the financial risk they are assuming.

"I should hope that the reasonableness of this principle would be recognized by courts of other states, whatever their laws as to charitable immunities. I would include in this hope the Commonwealth of Massachusetts, if it continues to adhere to its ancient rule for injuries inflicted there by the servants of its charities.

"It does not follow from the foregoing that a New York charitable corporation whose servants negligently inflicted injury on a New York plaintiff on the Massachusetts highways should enjoy the protection of the Massachusetts immunity. There is no inconsistency in allowing the Massachusetts plaintiff to recover for his New York injury against a Massachusetts corporation while allowing a New York plaintiff to recover for his Massachusetts injury against a New York corporation. A principle is reasonable which would give preference to the law denying immunity when that law exists in the state of injury since that state in denying immunity is by the same token expressing concern that injured persons be compensated. The injury that takes place within the state plainly falls within reach of that concern. On the other hand, a principle is also reasonable which, in a case against a charitable corporation from a nonimmunity state, would deny preference to the law granting immunity when that law exists in the state of injury. The latter state in granting immunity is by the same token subordinating any concern that injured persons be compensated to its concern for the financial health of its charities. It is not the fact that an injury has taken place within that state which arouses the latter concern; it is whether the defendant is connected with the immunity-granting state.

"The imposition of liability in both cases would also be defensible against a charge of inconsistency if one were to apply the 'significant relationship' test of § 379 of *Restatement Second* with a view to the respective purposes of the competing rules, as § 379(3) permits. The fact that an injury takes place within a state which denies immunity for injuries is significant; the same fact in a state that grants immunity for injuries is not in itself significant. To find a significant relationship with the latter state's law, one should ask why it grants immunity. If it is due to the desire to protect the funds of charitable corporations, then the location of the charity, not the fact of injury, becomes significant, although not necessarily controlling.

"I vote to reverse."

Voting to affirm judgment for defendant: RHEINSTEIN, J.

Voting to reverse judgment for defendant: GRISWOLD, REESE, CURRIE, and CAVERS, JJ.[21]

The Five Cases in a Massachusetts Forum

I shall not attempt to report the cases that would parallel Cases 2 through 4 with the new law-fact pattern. I shall follow instead the law teacher's practice of leaving some cases for the class to worry about. Suppose, however, that the five cases had been litigated in Massachusetts. A Massachusetts court devoted to the first *Restatement*'s analysis and ready to accept the *Restatement Second* variant would find no difficulty

21 But it should be recalled that Professor Reese would have Judge Reese join Judge Rheinstein. See note 19 *supra*.

in applying its own law in the first four cases; if it were prepared to follow the *Restatement Second* variant, its decisions would depend on whether it adopted Judge Reese's reading of the black letter or Professor Reese's. However, in Case 5, a Massachusetts forum being asked to hold its charity liable to compensate the Massachusetts plaintiff for his New York injury by application of "the law of the place of the wrong" might take shelter in that ready refuge of a parochially-minded court, public policy, and refuse to allow the New York claim to be enforced. This position could, of course, be circumvented by means of a New York judgment against the charity which the Full Faith and Credit Clause would compel Massachusetts to enforce.[22]

A Massachusetts court, if converted to the approach in Case 1 of Rheinstein, Currie, or Cavers, JJ., should not find it hard to adopt that approach in holding the New York corporation liable, though in Case 3 it might be glad of a chance to restrict the application of its obsolete "outlaw on the highways" rule and though in Case 4 it would probably refuse to allow damages for a wrongful death in Massachusetts to exceed the limit set by the Massachusetts law, even in the case of the New York widow. However, in Case 5, all the New York judges save Judge Rheinstein had held the Massachusetts charity liable in New York by applying the New York law.[23] As Massachusetts judges, presumably, Judges Griswold and Reese would hold fast to the same position. However, Judge Currie would regard Massachusetts, a state having a clear interest in protecting its charities from liability, as being well nigh bound to stand by that policy rather than hold its charity liable. Judge Cavers can

[22] Massachusetts could not constitutionally refuse to enforce the New York judgment on the ground that the claim on which it was based was contrary to the public policy of Massachusetts. Fauntleroy v. Lum, 210 U.S. 230 (1908).

[23] As to Judge Reese, see note 21 *supra*.

do no more than express the hope that Massachusetts would apply the New York rule.

How do these results square with the actualities? What decision would have been reached had any one of these cases really been carried to the New York Court of Appeals? I shall not attempt to answer these questions for all the cases. However, as I indicated earlier, Case 1 was based on an actual decision in that court, a 1961 decision, the authority of which has been shaken by a still more recent decision of the same court. I shall begin the next chapter with a brief report of those two cases.

III

CHOICE-OF-LAW METHODOLOGIES: HEREIN OF "JUSTICE IN THE INDIVIDUAL CASE"

A. *The Kaufman and Babcock Cases*

The actual case from which *Adams v. Knickerbocker Nature Study Society, Inc.* was drawn is *Kaufman v. American Youth Hostels. Inc.*,[1] a decision by the New York Court of Appeals. The case involved a New York charitable corporation which conducted tours in New York and other states. During a mountain-climbing tour in Oregon under its auspices, the plaintiff's daughter, a fifteen-year-old girl, was killed, allegedly because of the defendant's negligence. In the New York Appellate Division,[2] the court applied the Oregon law, which, unlike the New York law,[3] holds charities immune. The court first examined the Oregon decisions to see whether they applied any different rule to charities incorporated elsewhere but found no indication of this. The Appellate Division also held that an alleged release given in New York by the father to the Youth Hostels before the journey was also a valid defense to the action, at least against a motion to strike. The Court of Appeals struck the defense based on the release but

[1] 5 N.Y.2d 1016, 158 N.E.2d 128 (1959).

[2] 6 App. Div. 2d 223, 177 N.Y.S.2d 587 (1958).

[3] The always limited recognition given by New York to the charitable immunity doctrine was gradually eroded by restrictive decisions until it was finally done away with in Bing v. Thunig, 2 N.Y.2d 656, 143 N.E.2d 3 (1957).

allowed the immunity defense to stand. Its memorandum opinion did not discuss the choice-of-law issue.

The case that has undermined the authority of *Kaufman* is *Babcock v. Jackson,*[4] decided in May 1963. In *Babcock,* the New York Court of Appeals by a 5-2 vote reversed a 4-1 decision below.[5] It applied the New York common law permitting an injured automobile guest from New York to recover for the New York driver's negligence in an Ontario accident, despite an Ontario statute denying a guest any cause of action against a driver. The court analyzed the policies underlying the two rules and found the Ontario law designed to prevent collusion between passenger and driver against the driver's insurer. This policy would not be advanced by application to a New York driver. On the other hand, New York's policy could readily be held applicable to a passenger-driver relationship created in New York, as was the relationship in *Babcock.*

The court quoted *Restatement Second*'s "significant relationship" test with approval, but, at one point in its opinion, citing Professor Albert Ehrenzweig's article on the guest statute problem, used language suggestive of the approach I have associated with Professor Rheinstein.[6] No doubt, this approach would identify the liability of automobile drivers to

[4] 12 N.Y.2d 473, 191 N.E.2d 279 (1963).

[5] 17 App. Div. 2d 694, 230 N.Y.S.2d 114 (1962). The majority were content to file a memorandum opinion; Justice Halpern wrote a long, brilliant dissent.

[6] See Babcock v. Jackson, *supra* note 4, at 483-84, 191 N.E.2d at 285 (1963), where the court stated: ". . . the rights and liabilities of the parties which stem from their guest-host relationship should remain constant and not vary and shift as the automobile proceeds from place to place," a proposition that would reject an application of a liability-imposing law in the place of injury. I have discussed this in Cavers, "Comment on *Babcock v. Jackson,*" 63 COLUM. L. REV. 1219, 1222-26 (1963). The court noted the beneficial implications of its view for insurance, quoting from Ehrenzweig, "Guest Statutes in the Conflict of Laws," 69 YALE L.J. 595, 603 (1960).

their passengers as a special problem to which a jurisdiction-selecting rule would be applied, perhaps, as in *Babcock*, the law of the state where the guest relationship was created, the driver resided, and his car was garaged.[7]

I have joined in the general applause that has greeted *Babcock*,[8] in my opinion the most important judicial departure from the first *Restatement*'s orthodoxy to date. However, I hope the court will not prove to have adopted a jurisdiction-selecting rule in *Babcock*. In commenting on *Babcock*, I have raised the question: What would the New York court now hold if an Ontario passenger were injured by his Ontario driver's negligence in New York?[9] That case would pose a difficult choice, introducing considerations not presented by the law-fact pattern in *Babcock*. I cannot believe *Babcock* makes it clear that New York would deny the Ontario plaintiff compensation.

Be that as it may, the undermining of *Kaufman* by *Babcock*

[7] The court did not attempt to distinguish between those factors. More recently a Supreme Court justice, in a sophisticated opinion, applied the New York law to a driver-guest passenger relationship created between two New Yorkers who had met in Colorado where they were summer school students. Dym v. Gordon, 41 Misc. 2d 657, 245 N.Y.S.2d 656 (Sup. Ct. 1963). The decision was reversed by the Appellate Division, which in a memorandum opinion noted, *inter alia*, the parties' temporary residence in Colorado and the fact that their relationship was confined to Colorado, concluding that Colorado had "the dominant contacts and the superior claims to the application of its law." 22 App. Div. 2d 702, 253 N.Y.S.2d 802 (2d Dep't 1964) (mem.). The *Dym* case is discussed in an appendix, *infra* at p. 293, in the light of its affirmance by the New York Court of Appeals, July 8, 1965.

[8] Six law professors, all teachers of conflict of laws, myself included, contributed comments on the case to the *Columbia Law Review*. See "Comments on *Babcock v. Jackson*, A Recent Development in Conflict of Laws," 63 COLUM. L. REV. 1212 (1963). They tended to see in its result, and, in some instances, in its reasoning, support for their respective views. Since, as reported in the appendix, the Court of Appeals, while following *Babcock*, has divided as to its application to *Dym*, *supra* note 7, continued unanimity among the scholars is doubtful.

[9] See Cavers, *supra* note 6, at 1224.

was recognized by the dissenting judge in *Babcock* who cited the *Kaufman* case at the start of his dissent.[10] Although I should predict a New York decision for the plaintiff today in Case 1 (the action against the New York charity for the Massachusetts injury), perhaps resort to a jurisdiction-selecting rule would lead to a decision for the defendant in Case 5 (the action by the Massachusetts plaintiff against the Massachusetts charity for the New York injury). The recognition the New York court gave *Restatement Second* in *Babcock* would not, I hope, lead to the restrictive reading of its provisions that we saw in the opinion of Judge Reese.[11]

The *Babcock* case is but one of a number of recent decisions that require the professors' methodological discussions to be taken seriously. Though New York and California are the leaders, decisions deviating from the first *Restatement*'s orthodoxy are cropping up in all parts of the country.[12] The Supreme Court has given the trend its blessing in a recent decision construing the Federal Tort Claims Act in such a way as to encourage state experimentation.[13] Underlying this experimentation is, as I suggested earlier, a change in the courts' conception of their task in choice-of-law cases.

[10] Babcock v. Jackson, *supra* note 4, at 485, 191 N.E.2d at 285. Judge Van Voorhis' prediction has already been translated into a decision. In a case arising out of the same accident that led to *Kaufman*, a lower New York court has applied New York rather than Oregon law. Blum v. American Youth Hostels, 40 Misc. 2d 1056, 244 N.Y.S.2d 35 (Sup. Ct. 1963).

[11] A reading from which, it will be recalled, Professor Reese dissented. See Chapter II, *supra* p. 28. One may hope that *Babcock* will lead to a revision of the provisions of the *Restatement* relevant to the charitable immunity issue.

[12] I have surveyed the leading choice-of-law decisions reflecting change in the fields of contract, tort, and property law in Cavers, "Change in Choice of Law Thinking and Its Bearing on the *Klaxon* Problem," ALI, Study of the Division of Jurisdiction Between Federal and State Courts 154, 159-82 (Tent. Draft. No. 1, 1963).

[13] Richards v. United States, 369 U.S. 1, 12-13 (1962).

B. *Four Methodologies for Choice of Law*

Now that our cases have shown judges approaching their task in diverse ways, perhaps we can formulate their views in more general terms. There are more than the four conceptions I am summarizing below, but plainly we can cope with no more than four. Moreover, I shall state only the bare bones of each method and not the considerations of policy or logic that seem typically employed in each.

(1) The court is first to identify the legal category into which the case before it falls—torts, contracts, property, etc. —and then to apply the proper connecting factor for that category of case in order to choose the state whose legal system will determine the parties' respective rights, duties, and other legal relations.

(2) The court is first to identify the specific problem or problems in the case before it which pose choice-of-law questions and then, for each problem, to apply the proper connecting factor in order to choose the state whose legal system will provide a solution for that problem. In making this choice, the court should recognize that ordinarily the most important choice-of-law concern is the protection of the expectations of the parties.

(3) For each issue in a case as to which the laws of the states involved are potentially in conflict, the court is to apply the ordinary processes of construction and interpretation to those laws in order to decide whether, in the light of the respective policies expressed in the laws and of the circumstances of the case, the states involved would have an interest in the application of their respective laws to that issue. If only one state has such an interest, its law should be applied to the issue; if both have, the forum's law should be applied. However, in determining whether the interests of two states are actually in conflict, the forum should be prepared, when the circumstances warrant, to give a moderate and restrained

interpretation to the policy or interest of one state or the other and thus avoid the conflict.

(4) If application of the processes of construction and interpretation to the laws in apparent conflict, as proposed in the third methodology, does not reveal a false or readily avoidable conflict, the court is to seek a rule for choice of law or a principle of preference which would either reflect relevant multistate policies or provide the basis for a reasonable accommodation of the laws' conflicting purposes. A principle of preference would be applicable to all cases having the same general pattern of law and fact and would identify a preferred result on choice-of-law grounds. If the case could not thus be generalized, the court should state the reasons leading it to prefer one result to the other on choice-of-law grounds. In either case it should apply the law leading to the preferred result.

If I were to ask you to associate each of our five judges in the *Knickerbocker* cases with one of these methods, I suspect most of you would associate Judge Griswold with the first one; Judge Rheinstein with the second; Judge Currie with the third; and Judge Cavers with the fourth, though you might wonder why he was not more explicit on the score of principle. (He had not read these lectures.) You might fit Judge Reese under more than one method. I should agree with this classification, including your difficulty in placing Judge Reese. Now, however, that I have laid bare Judge Cavers' preference—for, as the psychiatrists would say, I identify with Judge Cavers—I should explain the difficulties I have with each of the other methods and then attempt to distinguish the views I am supposed to hold from those that I do hold and, in later chapters, to present and defend my affirmative views from their critics, present and prospective. In so doing, I shall introduce the conception of principles of preference that I have incorporated in the fourth methodology, a conception to which I have been gradually led by the implications of my discontent with other doctrinal solutions.

C. *The Methodologies Criticized*

(1) *The First Restatement Method.* The first methodology is essentially the first *Restatement*'s. It strives for simplicity by seeking choice-of-law rules that ordinarily will allocate each case to the legal system of a single state.[14] But rules prescribing connecting factors to cover a diversity of issues in a broad category of cases (torts, for example) must be very general and therefore the policy considerations supporting these rules must also be very general, as, for example, certainty, ease of application, facilitation of transactions. Furthermore, once the connecting factor for a category of cases has been fixed, all that remains to be done in a later case is to make sure the case falls within the category and to ascertain the state in which the connecting factor is located. These jurisdiction-selecting rules render irrelevant the specific content of the laws in conflict and hence the specific purposes which the respective states adopting them had in view.

Simples rules working in this way are supposed to be conducive to uniformity and certainty in choice of law and to give assurance that, in whatever forum a case is brought, it will always be decided by the application of the same law. But choice-of-law rules do not work well when the connecting factors they prescribe are based on broad criteria which ignore the special facts of the cases, the purposes of the conflicting laws, and the results produced by the laws they choose. They may dictate the choice of laws having little reasonable basis for application to the question at issue. Moreover, they block inquiry whether a real conflict of policies exists and, if so, how it can best be accommodated.

[14] The division in the *Conflicts Restatement* between the law of the place of contracting to govern the validity and obligation of a contract (§ 332) and the law of the place of performance to govern the sufficiency of performance (§ 358), excuse for nonperformance (§ 358), and damages for breach (§ 372) is perhaps the most conspicuous example of allocation of one transaction to the laws of two states, an allocation calling for a line of demarcation which a *Restatement* comment (§ 358, comment *b*) confesses cannot be logically drawn.

This price, I submit, is too high for the benefits of uniformity and certainty. I suspect these benefits are often hypothetical for I see little evidence that forum-shoppers are exploiting the existing lack of uniformity and certainty.[15] Moreover, experience indicates that diversity and uncertainty in choice of law are likely to persist because courts are unwilling to adhere to broad and necessarily mechanical choice-of-law rules when the results these rules dictate arouse their "sense of injustice," to echo the late Edmund Cahn's insightful phrase.

For the reasons stated by Judge Cavers in the first *Knickerbocker* case, I do not think the inherent defect of the method is cured by Judge Griswold's readiness to resort to renvoi and so to permit New York to apply its own law imposing liability on the New York charity if it were shown that the courts of the place of injury, Massachusetts, would do so. This would preserve uniformity of results between Massachusetts and New York despite their different choice-of-law rules. This can mitigate the effects of a bad choice-of-law rule in the forum; it does not justify the method that produces bad results.[16] Moreover, if the place-of-injury rule were really defensible on grounds of fairness and policy, why should it be

15 This is an opinion based on watching for choice-of-law cases in the *Federal Reporter* and *Federal Supplement* for many years. See Cavers, "The Changing Choice-of-Law Process and the Federal Courts," 28 LAW & CONTEMP. PROB. 732, 740 (1963). I have no statistics to support it. Of course, uncertainty can create difficulties for counsel engaged in planning transactions.

16 The view that *renvoi* has exerted an attraction for those who are discontented with the conventional rules yet are not ready to reject them is persuasively developed in von Mehren, "The Renvoi and its Relation to Various Approaches to the Choice-of-Law Problem," in XXTH CENTURY COMPARATIVE AND CONFLICTS LAW 380 (von Mehren, Nadelmann & Hazard, eds. 1961). (*Renvoi,* I should perhaps explain, is the name accorded a much-disputed doctrine that a court, in referring to the law of another state, may include that state's choice-of-law rules in its reference and, if these differ from its own, obtain a reference back (*renvoi*) to its own law, thereby setting up a logical circle from which it may break by "accepting" the *renvoi* and applying its own internal law.)

abandoned by New York because Massachusetts had ruled otherwise? And if, in a case like *Knickerbocker*, a choice of the New York law were defensible on grounds of fairness and policy, why should its application have to depend on whether the place of injury, Massachusetts, has registered its agreement?

(2) *The Rheinstein Method.* I am not persuaded of the desirability of the second methodology embodying Judge Rheinstein's views despite his proposal to narrow the problems for which he seeks choice-of-law rules. I remain troubled by the fact that he seeks his solution—as does Judge Griswold—in jurisdiction-selecting rules. That is, to resort to our series of cases, the place of the charity's incorporation might be held the source of the law to govern the problem of its tort liability, regardless of whether that law would hold the corporation liable or grant it immunity. But, as I think our cases show, the considerations introduced when the charity's law exposes it to liability are quite different from those introduced when that law grants it immunity. There is no need for judicial concern for the protection of charitable funds in the former case; that concern is the essence of the problem in the latter case. With some difficulty, I can concede that courts may reasonably decide to apply the law of the place of incorporation in both cases, but I submit that a rule requiring this result can be reasonably formulated only after both sets of considerations are taken separately into account. This is not done by a choice-of-law rule that simply identifies narrower problems for solution than those selected by the first *Restatement*.[17]

[17] For example, the 1951 Hague Convention on the Law Applicable to International Sales of Goods, translated in 1 Am. J. Comp. L. 275 (1952) (which has only recently come into force, see Chapter X, p. 256, *infra*) has chosen to govern international sales (in the absence of a choice of law by the parties) by the law of seller's "habitual residence" at the time he receives an order unless the seller receives the order in the country of the buyer's habitual residence, in which case that country's law is to be applied. This solution was opposed by those who would deny effect to

I suspect, moreover, that the task of breaking down the *Restatement's* broad categories into narrower categories for which satisfactory choice-of-law rules might be constructed would often prove hard to do. For example, two competing rules may be similar but not mirror images, as when, say, the State X rule has policy goals *a* and *b* whereas State Y's rule has policy goals non-*b* and *cc*. Moreover, by multiplying the number of problems on which a consensus would have to be sought, the method makes the odds against attaining a consensus very high indeed.[18] Accordingly, in terms of simplicity and acceptability, I believe that Judge Rheinstein's problem approach would prove disappointing.

As I noted in connection with Judge Rheinstein's opinions in Chapter II, several of his opinions had been elaborated at the instance of Professor Rheinstein in order to lay more stress on the expectations of the parties as to the law to be applied. Indeed, I now believe that Professor Rheinstein sees, as a

---

the habitual residence of the buyer, and their countries may never ratify the Convention. But, whichever contact is preferred, in one case the buyer's law may favor the seller and the seller's law the buyer. In the next case, the pattern may be reversed. It is hard to find a rational basis for preference, as between the habitual residences of either party, and this difficulty would persist if like choice-of-law rules as to sales contracts were formulated along commodity lines.

18 Professor Rheinstein has described the "method of problem classification" which he advocates as reflecting the views of modern German conflicts scholars. See Rheinstein, Book Review, "How to Review a Festschrift," 11 Am. J. Comp. L. 632, 633 (1962). But in his as yet unpublished lectures at the Hague Academy in the summer of 1964 on "The Crisis in Conflict of Laws," Professor Gerhard Kegel of the University of Cologne said, "The conflicts rules embrace *large groups* of the private law rules of *all states* such as those that apply to the form of legal transactions, agency, statutes of limitation, contracts, torts. . . ." and so on to the end of a long list. (Italics in original.) Any belief that the broad terms in the list are used merely for convenient reference is rebutted by the sentence that follows it: "The purpose of an individual substantive rule need therefore only be discussed where a classification problem appears."

cardinal virtue of narrowing the problems to which choice-of-law rules are to be directed, the likelihood that this will aid the courts in identifying the parties' expectations. That focusing on a specific problem may be on occasion helpful to this end can be conceded without accepting the role of the parties' expectations as more than an auxiliary consideration in justifying choice of law. Reliance on this factor seems especially dubious with respect to tort questions, but, even in the field of contracts, it is difficult often to escape the suspicion that a finding of the parties' expectations is simply a vehicle to express the court's conclusion that the choice of law it approves is a fair one.[19]

(3) *The Second Restatement Method.* The method advanced by Judge Reese and *Restatement Second* is hard to classify. When one seeks the "local law of the state which has the most significant relationship with the occurrence and with the

[19] For a discussion of the way in which the parties' expectations have been employed in choice-of-law cases, see Cavers, "Oral Contracts to Provide by Will and the Choice-of-Law Process: Some Notes on *Bernkrant*," in PERSPECTIVES IN LAW: ESSAYS FOR AUSTIN WAKEMAN SCOTT 38, 48 (Pound, Griswold & Sutherland, eds. 1964).

The importance which Professor Rheinstein attaches to the protection of expectations as a means of establishing "a minimum measure of predictability in a society of credit, investment and individual planning" has been made evident in a statement of his philosophy of choice of law appearing in a review of Professor Ehrenzweig's treatise too late for integration into my statement of "The Rheinstein Method." Rheinstein, Book Review, "Ehrenzweig, *Conflict of Laws*," 32 U. CHI. L. REV. 369, 375 (1965). He recognizes that the "policies pursued in the shaping of conflicts rules may . . . be manifold" (e.g., to "determine behavior," to avoid aiding in law evasion, to "facilitate a harmonious co-existence of states pursuing potentially different policies of behavior"), but he warns "every framer of rules of conflicts law, be he a legislator, a judge, or scholar" never to lose sight of the policy of "mitigating for individuals the inconveniences and problems" arising from differing state norms of decision and to recognize that "an attempt by the states to build a system of conflicts law on the demarcation of state spheres of legislative jurisdiction is doomed to failure" since "no state is bound to abide by the efforts of any other state." *Ibid.*

parties,"[20] one must ask with what are the "occurrence and the parties" involved in a dispute to be related. I see at least three possibilities. *First*—and the one that is in accord with a literal reading of the black letter—the relationship might run to the states involved, that is, to their entire legal systems (excluding, where "local law" is used, as in the provision quoted, their choice-of-law rules). *Second*, the relationship might run to laws of those states that bear on the specific legal issues in dispute, without regard to the content of those laws in the respective states. A comment to the black letter notes this possibility. *Third*, the relationship might run to the laws of the same states on the same issues, due account being taken of their respective provisions in gauging their relative significance. The difficulty of reaching a rational judgment as to degrees of significance except in this third way is the main basis for giving this reading to the black letter. Note in this connection that the black letter of § 379(3) explicitly authorizes the court to "consider" not only the issues and "the character of the tort" but also "the relevant purposes of the tort rules involved."

If one gives the first reading to the relationship, then *Restatement Second* becomes simply a fuzzier version of the first *Restatement*, and so could be fitted under the first methodology. The second reading would adopt, in effect, the Rheinstein approach and so would come under the second methodology. Finally, the third reading might permit *Restatement Second's* conversion to the fourth methodology.

I have argued elsewhere that my third reading is the proper one, at least for the "Contracts" chapter, and at certain points the black letter and the comment there supports my conten-

[20] RESTATEMENT SECOND, CONFLICT OF LAWS § 379 (Tent. Draft No. 8, 1963). The formula quoted is from the general section in the topic on "Torts" in the chapter on "Wrongs." The "Contracts" chapter has a similar formula posing the same three possible interpretations: "the local law of the state with which the contract has its most significant relationship." *Id.* § 332 (Tent. Draft No. 6, 1960).

tion.[21] However, I can also find support for the first reading and even more for the second. I note also that Professor Rheinstein seems to have found typical portions of *Restatement Second* acceptable.[22] Those who have been most sharply critical of the "most significant relationship" test have tended to assume that either the first or second reading is correct and that the application of the test is to be achieved by a process of "counting contacts." Suppose, however, they conclude that they have been mistaken in thus excluding an examination of the purposes of the laws in conflict in the light of their "contacts," a process that my third reading would permit. Suppose, accordingly, they widen their inquiry to include a consideration of the laws' purposes. Sooner or later this will bring them to the question how to resolve a case in which the purposes of each of the laws in conflict would be advanced by its application to that case. Which law's connection is then

[21] See Cavers, "Re-Restating the Conflict of Laws: The Chapter on Contracts," in XXth Century Comparative and Conflicts Law 349, 356-58 (1961). Either of the other alternatives is easier to reach as a matter of literal interpretation.

[22] See Rheinstein, *supra* note 19, at 656-58. In the "Contracts" chapter, *Restatement Second* prescribes specific contacts which are to govern, respectively, each of eleven different types of contracts in the absence of an effective choice of law by the parties. See Restatement (Second), Conflict of Laws §§ 346e-346n (Tent. Draft, No. 6, 1960). However, with few exceptions, each of these must yield to a contact having a more significant relationship to another state. See, e.g., *id.* § 346e(2). In a recent book review, Professor Otto Kahn-Freund of the University of London also indicates a preference for determining the applicable law (in the field of contracts) "in terms of the type of contract" rather than of "the issue under discussion." Nevertheless, he views the importance of considering the purpose of a legal rule as "almost a commonplace." Kahn-Freund, Book Review, "*XXth Century Comparative and Conflicts Law*," 76 Harv. L. Rev. 223, 229 (1962). He does not explain how he would achieve the *tour de force* of considering the purpose of a legal rule without considering the issue which the rule is designed to resolve. Incidentally, he finds that "invoking the magic of policy at the expense of principles" has become "a fetish" in the United States. As will appear, one of the purposes of these lectures is to find principles of choice of law that can implement policy.

the more significant? Must there not be some basis for preferring one law as against the other?

Restatement Second provides in its black letter a good many jurisdiction-selecting rules which provide specific answers to such questions, but those answers are often simply the heritage of decisions left behind by mechanical rules of the sort from which *Restatement Second* is seeking to escape. Moreover, it usually accompanies these black-letter rules with a warning that the law the rule prescribes must yield if another law reflecting "a more significant relationship" is found to be in conflict with it. It seems clear that the questions that must be answered, though couched in terms of significant relationship, are which law is to be preferred and on what grounds. For such questions, principles of preference of the sort suggested in the fourth methodology would be designed to provide answers.

(4) *The Currie Method.* When I come to evaluate Judge Currie's method, summarized as the third methodology, I must proceed with caution. My past and current writings, not to mention the third and fourth methodologies, reveal considerable areas of agreement in our views, thereby creating a problem of differentiation that Professors Currie and Ehrenzweig seem to have experienced.[23]

Professor Currie and I both see the choice-of-law problem as posed by the need to choose between two specific rules of law, not between the legal systems of two jurisdictions. I predict that, for years to come, he will be held by many to insist that the law of the forum must always be applied in a case in which the court can find any reasonable basis to apply the forum's law. This notion, based on Professor Currie's earlier

[23] The authors have endeavored to differentiate their views, a process in which comparison has tended to the invidious. See Currie, Book Review, "Ehrenzweig, *Conflict of Laws*," 1964 DUKE L.J. 424; EHRENZWEIG, CONFLICT OF LAWS § 122. Each has given a succinct statement of his method in CHEATHAM, GRISWOLD, REESE & ROSENBERG, CONFLICT OF LAWS, CASES AND MATERIALS 477-79 (5th ed. 1964).

writings, especially on summarized statements of his position,[24] has been dispelled by his latest articles. Now it is plain that he would permit an interested forum to take account of the other interested state's law and the latter law's claim to application in deciding the proper reach of the forum's own law. Presumably, in this process he would permit the court to take into account the particular facts of the case in construing both its own and the other state's law. My reference in stating the third methodology to a "moderate and restrained interpretation" is drawn directly from a relatively recent article by Professor Currie.[25] Its result is to add the category of what I shall term "avoidable conflicts" to the category of false conflicts, leaving only an intractable residue of true conflicts where he would always have the interested forum employ its own law. The opportunity to avoid conflicts in this fashion is also open to a disinterested forum, a forum Professor Currie claims to have rarely encountered. Hence it is only when such a forum encounters a true and unavoidable conflict that it may have to resort to its own law in order to discharge its duty to adjudicate the case before it—and, even in this situation, he now concedes for the American state court the possibility of ruling as it opines the Congress would legislate if it were to do so under the Full Faith and Credit Clause.[26]

The difference between Professor Currie's views and my

[24] Especially the much-quoted five-point summary in Currie, "Notes on Methods and Objectives in the Conflict of Laws," in CURRIE, SELECTED ESSAYS ON THE CONFLICT OF LAWS (hereinafter cited as SELECTED ESSAYS) 177, 183-84 (1963), reprinted from 1959 DUKE L.J. 171, 178.

[25] Professor Currie's descriptions of his method in his *Selected Essays* should be read in the light of two more recent writings: Currie, "Comment on *Babcock v. Jackson*, A Recent Development in Conflict of Laws," 63 COLUM. L. REV. 1233, 1242 (1963); Currie, "The Disinterested Third State," 28 LAW & CONTEMP. PROB. 754, 763-64 (1963).

[26] Professor Currie has recently suggested that, in this predicament, the disinterested forum, if one of the United States, might undertake to reach the decision that it thinks "Congress would reach if it were to consider the matter." *Id.* at 778.

own seems to me to go chiefly to the degree to which each of us expects those "ordinary processes of construction and interpretation" to resolve choice-of-law problems, a difference which reflects my own skepticism that those processes can be expected regularly to yield a relevant policy for each law subjected to them, a policy that will point reliably the direction in which the state's interest lies. Moreover, as I shall explain in the next chapter, I feel that his terminology may create difficulties in the application of those processes by tending to exaggerate the interest of a state in the application of its own law and to undervalue the importance of factors that are not reflected in the domestic policies of the respective laws between which a choice is to be made. It should also be noted that Professor Currie does not consider the decisions holding conflicts to be false or avoidable which result from "the ordinary processes of construction and interpretation" to constitute the source of choice-of-law rules; on the contrary, he would reject all choice-of-law rules which are not statutory. This austere position would, I believe, tend to inhibit a forum that was faithful to it from recognizing another state's interest.

Professor Currie's readiness to do without judge-made choice-of-law rules may reflect more a strategy of escape from the rules we now have than a rejection of these rules for all time. If, however, he were to reject all such rules for the future, I would have to disagree with him, and for three reasons. First, I believe the "ordinary processes of construction and interpretation" are inadequate to discharge the inescapable choice-of-law function for, in difficult cases, the considerations that should control choice will not be found immanent in the terms or objectives of the conflicting laws but must be drawn from other policy sources. That is why the cases are difficult. Second, however earnestly a court sought to follow Professor Currie's counsel, it would inevitably be led to produce choice-of-law rules. Third, a system in which choice-of-law rules were strictly taboo would provide little guidance to courts and counsel.

This is peculiarly the case when, an apparent conflict having been found in the policies or interests of the states involved in a private litigation, the court is advised to consider the wisdom of a "restrained and moderate interpretation" of its own or the other state's law. Virtually every case other than the false conflict cases (which are excluded *ex hypothesi*) presents this opportunity for conflict avoidance. But when should the court take advantage of this freedom to deny recourse to its own law and why? When should it remain resolute and insist upon the (unrestrained and immoderate?) application of the *lex fori?* Though the court may cast its decision in terms of interpretation, the questions it must nonetheless answer are which law is to be preferred and on what grounds? In other words, the questions appear to be basically the same as the questions with which the significant relationship test of *Restatement Second* would confront the court. And Professor Currie's method would provide no more clues to the answers to those questions than does *Restatement Second.*

In the next and succeeding chapters I shall develop further the reasons for the points of difference in our views. In noting them, I am displaying the mark of the true conflict-of-laws scholar: a keen sensitivity to the deficiencies in the theories of his fellows. But, of course, some methodological ideas of my own have been exposed to the scrutiny of a generation of scholars, all possessing a similarly heightened sensitivity. What are the deficiencies that these scholars have seen in them?

D. "*Justice in the Individual Case*": *The Cavers Method?*

These are many and varied, but, as to one characteristic, my critics are well-nigh unanimous: I am identified—and often deplored—as the man who wants the court to do justice in the individual case. This has become almost a trade-mark for my position, a slogan like "Mild, but They Satisfy." Law review editors who cite my 1933 article[27] frequently make its message

[27] Cavers, "A Critique of the Choice-of-Law Problem," 47 HARV. L. REV. 173 (1933).

plain to their readers by adding parentheses after the citation with some variant of that revealing phrase: "justice in the individual case." Commentators listing objectives of the choice-of-law process will enter "justice in the individual case," citing Cavers. Professors Cheatham and Reese in a survey of nine such objectives listed it as No. 9, grudging it a brief paragraph and a citation to you know whom.[28] Its vitality is remarkable; for me it has given real meaning to the term "stereotype."

When I find myself beginning to wince each time I encounter the phrase, something comes along to cheer me up. For example, in that casebook favorite, *Siegelman v. Cunard White Star, Ltd.*,[29] Judge Jerome Frank, dissenting, confessed near the end of his opinion: ". . . I grant that, in this context, I am stressing the need to do justice in particular instances. I do so unashamedly. For it is generally agreed that the decisions of conflict-of-law cases by mechanized rules, without regard to particularized justice, cannot be defended on the ground that they have promoted certainty and uniformity, since such results have not been thus achieved. Several wise commentators have urged that the element of justice should have a dominating influence."[30]

My article was among those cited to this last sentence. Needless to say, a listing as one of "several wise commentators" was exhilarating. However, I could not take full satisfaction in this compliment for, in truth, I am not the champion of justice in the individual case that I have been made to seem. I never have been.

This widespread misapprehension merits discussion for such light as it may throw on the role of justice in the choice-of-law process. I believe a fair rendition of the meaning which

[28] Cheatham & Reese, "Choice of the Applicable Law," 52 COLUM. L. REV. 959, 980 (1952).

[29] 221 F.2d 189 (2d Cir. 1955).

[30] *Id.* at 206.

"justice in the individual case" has for the users of the stereotype of my views is about as follows:

Cavers, they think, believes that:

(1) The choice-of-law rules of the first *Restatement* and their ilk are mechanical and whether they produce justice in any given case is a matter of chance (unless the court juggles the rules to assure it).

(2) The prospect of getting better rules by heeding the critics of existing doctrine is hopeless.

(3) Every case should, therefore, be decided on its individual facts, fully particularized, the decision being based on (a) the judge's intuitive sense of the just result; or (b) the judge's preference for the domestic rule of one or the other of the states involved.

The phrase denotes the process, so-called, of "free law" decision, a fighting cause at the turn of the century, now so faded that it can scarcely serve as a bugaboo.

Of the three propositions I have just stated, the first I think valid as a general proposition for which undoubtedly some exceptions can be found. The second I think was true as long as the critics continued to build doctrine only out of jurisdiction-selecting rules. This is no longer the case. The third seems counsel of despair but not too inaccurate as a description of what goes on behind the façade of conventional choice-of-law rules.

E. *The Relation of Justice to Rules*

When I argued for justice in the individual case, it was in protest against rules which made that result accidental. I was echoing Professor Lorenzen, no champion of "free law." As I noted in my first lecture, he put the problem of choice of law in the two questions which I quoted in the previous lecture and twice in my article: "What are the demands of justice in the particular situation; what is the controlling policy?"[31] I fol-

[31] See p. 9, *supra*.

lowed my abstract, intricate, and obscurely phrased summary of the process I would have the courts adopt in choosing a law with this sentence: "The choice of that law would not be the result of the automatic operation of a rule or principle of selection but of a search for a just decision in the principal case."[32]

It is at that point that quotations stop. Almost no one has quoted the next sentence: "But lawyers are a rule-making sect." That sentence prefaced a discussion, several pages in length, in which I tried to identify—again abstractly—the nature of the rules and principles I hoped would emerge from the process I had outlined. I insisted that they not trammel inquiry into factors otherwise pertinent by imposing "artificial limitations on relevancy," that they should "guide, not stifle, inquiry." I pointed hopefully to the working of stare decisis "with its pragmatic limitations on the scope of precedent in lieu of the present recourse to broad rules."[33] Finally, I argued that "the creation and fruitful employment of rules" of the sort I urged "must be attended by the development of standards for the evaluation of the facts which they render significant." I was alluding to the need I had stated for determining the significance of connecting factors "from the standpoint," as I put it in my ill-fated summary, "of justice between the litigating individuals or of those broader considerations of social policy which conflicting laws may evoke."[34]

This forecast of a body of rules, principles and standards of a new sort, developing through the workings of stare decisis and the combined efforts of courts and scholars, scarcely represents a call for a "free law" jurisprudence. Indeed, why should the application of a just rule seem incompatible with justice in the individual case? Perhaps the response to my

32 Cavers, *supra* note 27, at 193.

33 *Id.* at 196, citing the presidential address to the Association of American Law Schools of Professor Herman Oliphant of Columbia, one of the leaders of the newly fledged realist movement, "A Return to Stare Decisis," 14 A.B.A.J. 71, 107, 159 (1928).

34 Cavers, *supra* note 27, at 192.

critique is due to the fact that we take it for granted that our rules of law will do justice, and so the doing of justice, like the speaking of prose, is seldom mentioned. Now and then, however, one of our rules appears to be miscarrying in an atypical situation. We become disturbed, alarmed. It is then that we cry out for "justice." Justice, as a consequence, has come to look like a drastic, emergency remedy, a goal to be pursued outside the rules, not to be embodied in them. Therefore, anyone who suggests that we should always ask, "What are the demands of justice in the particular situation?" must be viewed with suspicion as one who, if permitted, would probably subvert all rules.

My contention, of course, was that the choice-of-law rules which the first *Restatement* was proposing to propound were not designed to achieve justice in the individual case. Rules that could not be counted on to work justice in the individual cases to which they applied would not in my opinion, then and now, be just rules.

This criticism of choice-of-law rules takes on special consequence from the distinctive nature of the problem of justice in a choice-of-law case. The court will be choosing between two rules of law. In most cases, it will have no occasion to challenge the justice of either rule as applied to a wholly domestic situation. Yet to apply one of these rules in a case with which it has no reasonable connection or where its application furthers no rational purpose is to deny the defeated party the benefit of a rule of law which does have such a connection or purpose and which would have favored him. This, I submit, is unjust. It does little to palliate such a result to show, as sometimes can be done, that the jurisdiction-selecting rule that produced the injustice did so at random, that it was used without concern for the results it was working.

The injustice which I was decrying in 1933 was the injustice worked by a process that seemed essentially irrational and therefore unfair. Since my 1933 article was a critique of an existing methodology and a call for a new one, it did not provide an occasion for the formulation of affirmative criteria by which the users of the new methodology, when perfected, would be able to test the justice of the results it produced, save perhaps in those easy cases wherein the justice of one result becomes virtually self-evident when that result is compared with the various alternatives to it.

I believe nonetheless that affirmative propositions can be developed which, when applied to specific cases, can yield just solutions to choice-of-law questions, solutions which are just not only because they provide a fair accommodation of conflicting state policies but also because they afford fair treatment to the individuals who are caught in the conflict between state policies. Later in these lectures, I shall hazard the formulation of certain broad principles of preference which I believe could guide courts to just solutions of the individual cases falling within their reach.

Of course, not every choice-of-law case presents an issue in which one result must be just and the other unjust. Take our Case 5, for example.[35] I can argue that to apply New York law to support the Massachusetts plaintiff's claim is the better solution to a hard problem of choice; I could not contend that the contrary result would be unjust. Such a case poses a difficult issue of judgment, which, when resolved by judicial decision, can be given stability through the operation of stare decisis and, in time, the formulation of a principle of preference. Yet, even when the application of neither law in such a case would itself be unjust, the process whereby the choice is made can be unjust.[36] This complaint can be sustained if the rule of choice

[35] P. 50, *supra*. In that case, a Massachusetts charitable corporation asserts immunity under Massachusetts law for an injury its agent has carelessly inflicted on a Massachusetts beneficiary in New York State. The plaintiff relies on the New York rule which rejects charitable immunity.

[36] The applicability of constitutional requirements of procedural due process is seldom dependent on whether the results actually reached in proceedings ignoring those requirements could be stigmatized as unjust.

has placed "arbitrary limitations on relevancy" and stifled inquiry into policy considerations that might otherwise be controlling.

F. *The Atomization of Precedents*

Perhaps some critics might concede that my purpose had not been to advocate the intuitive disposition of every case on its individual facts and yet contend that my illustrations of the method made it plain that, as a practical matter, the judgments it would compel would be no more useful than if they had been the products of judicial hunch. They would insist that I was bent on atomizing each case so that no choice-of-law decision could serve as a controlling precedent for any later case, the facts of each being viewed as materially different.

I can see wherein I fired such fears. In my 1933 article, I used variations on only one illustrative hypothetical case[37]—a problem relating to the capacity of a minor married woman making a purchase on credit in State A where she lived, the goods being sold to her by a seller in State B. Having first posed the problem by supposing that State A denied capacity while State B conferred it, I then reversed the law-fact pattern so that it was State B, the seller's state, that denied capacity. The disposition of this second case was simple. To my rhetorical question whether sellers in State B should be "penalized in their extra-state business, because of the anachronistic legislation of that commonwealth,"[38] I answered "No" on the ground that to apply State A's law produced "an eminently sensible result." From that obvious example of a false conflict, I then turned back to the first case where the law of the domicil, State A, was the stringent one and observed that the "fact that now the application of State A's law will defeat the contract confers a radically different aspect upon the problem."[39]

This tactic of reversing the law-fact pattern is now familiar

[37] Cavers, *supra* note 27, at 180. [38] *Id.* at 190. [39] *Ibid.*

to those joining in my assault upon jurisdiction-selecting rules or in Professor Currie's search for false conflicts. However, in trying to resolve the true conflict when State A denied its domiciliary's capacity and the seller's State B did not do so, I opened the door to a wide-ranging factual inquiry.

It seemed plain to me that the spot where technically the contract was entered into (if one were entered into) had no relevance to solving the conflict, but whether the seller's agent had gone to the defendant's home and, if so, whether this was an isolated transaction, perhaps intitiated by a coupon clipped from a magazine, or instead was part of a sales campaign waged in State A might well be significant. So, too, might be the fact that the bargain had been negotiated in the seller's state. I intimated that a sale of a set of books might present a different problem from a sale of securities or even of household wares.[40] Whether the married minor was technically domiciled in State A seemed less important than whether she was a settled resident there.[41] In noting the need for these discriminations, I pointed to "the new significance with which the suggested approach would invest the 'contact.' "[42] I declared that "if a law is to be chosen with some consideration of the result it effects in a given litigation, then the contact should itself be significant in relation to that result."[43]

This effort to give the contact greater significance in the process of choice went largely unheeded. To scholars whom conventional choice-of-law rules had accustomed to inserting into the appropriate slots such standardized contacts as "place of contracting," "place of performance," and "domicil," this kind of speculation doubtless verged on the irresponsible, if not the anarchic. They saw every case resting on its own facts: the difference between a children's encyclopedia and a washing machine might be crucial. Whither were we tending?

Today, with everyone enured (if not always happily) to the

[40] *Id.* at 189. [41] *Id.* at 191. [42] *Ibid.* [43] *Id.* at 192.

"grouping of contacts"[44] this type of speculation would seem less aberrant. Doubtless I was tactically unwise to propose introducing such new elements into choice-of-law process without at least demonstrating more specifically how they could be used. This I think could have been done, but, in the terminology of trials, I failed to lay a proper foundation.

We all know of many areas in the law where the court is called on to apply a rule or principle one of the ingredients of which is a legal standard—"due care," "good faith," "probable cause," "foreseeability," to mention only a few—in which the court's judgment is based on a constellation of facts that is rarely if ever duplicated. Not only are these decisions reached by the triers of fact, but, converted into issues of law, they can be reviewed on appeal. Moreover, reported opinions deciding such issues are consulted carefully by counsel. They are taken into account in negotiating case settlements or planning against legal hazards though everyone knows that no new case will ever be the same as the old ones.

"Ah," you will object, "in those cases there was not only a standard, but also a rule or principle of which the standard was a part and against which the facts could be judged. The significance of the difference in facts posed by the new case could be appraised not only against prior cases applying the standard but also against that rule or principle and in the light of its purpose. Where is the counterpart of such a criterion in your argument? Having neither rule nor principle to guide him, aren't we obliged to assume that the judge will have to

[44] This phrase is beginning to appear with some frequency in choice-of-law opinions involving contracts. See, e.g., Auten v. Auten, 308 N.Y. 155, 160, 161, 124 N.E.2d 99, 101, 102 (1954). The fact that the concept is not accompanied by criteria for evaluating the contacts after grouping has led to its criticism. See, e.g., Cavers, "Re-Restating the Conflict of Laws: The Chapter on Contracts," *supra* note 21, at 355; Currie, "Conflict, Crisis and Confusion in New York," 1963 DUKE L.J. 1, 39 *et seq.*, in SELECTED ESSAYS, 690, 727 *et seq.*; EHRENZWEIG, CONFLICT OF LAWS § 142 at 400 (1962).

consult either his own intuition or his preference for one of the competing rules?"

Here I think is a telling point. The process I was advocating did look to the future development of criteria of judgment, rules, principles, and standards to provide the judge a basis of adjudication other than his personal, subjective preferences. I could, of course, have said to the critic, "read on, and you will see that I have called for such criteria and have charged legal scholarship with direct responsibility for their development." Alas, this might have evoked the retort, "I'll believe in the possibility of such objective criteria when I see them. In the meanwhile, how about that paragraph of yours at the bottom of page 190?"

G. *The Result-Selective Forum*

I can't wave a wand and have it disappear, so let us read that paragraph. After having posed on page 190 the conflict between State A's law denying capacity and State B's law conferring it, I then suggested that the court's decision choosing between them might be based broadly either on the policy of protecting the incapable or on that of fostering interstate business or, instead of being rested on a broad policy ground, might be individualized in the light of the relative claims of the respective parties to judicial solicitude. I then went on to say the following:[45]

"Be that as it may, in the course of this evaluation, the court's, opinion as to the desirability of limitations upon the contractual capacity of infants and married women will inevitably enter. Any effort to exclude it would operate only to distort the intellectual processes of adjudication. This factor in the decision may, of course, render of consequence the choice of forum. Judges in state *B* or in state C, having laws similar to *B*'s, may not attach the same importance to the

[45] Cavers, *supra* note 27, at 190.

limitations on wifely capacity that would be encountered in state A. Such differences are inevitable; it is important only that they be frankly encountered. Today, as in the past, their influence may not appear on the surface of opinions, but, if the uncertain course of decision characteristic of most conflicts problems is evidential, such influence had not been wanting. Moreover, a recognition of the necessity for a thorough understanding and appraisal of foreign law should tend to diminish the parochial 'affectation of superiority' which now leads the forum so frequently to reject foreign law."

This resigned acceptance of a fact of life, coupled with the belief that a more suitable conception of the choice-of-law process would diminish its significance, seems to me to fall well short of an adoption of what Professor Moffat Hancock has termed "a result-selective approach." As he explains, this calls for "choosing the law which best accords with present-day ideas of justice and convenience."[46] Although the

[46] Hancock, "Three Approaches to the Choice-of-Law Problem: The Classificatory, the Functional and the Result-Selective," in XXTH CENTURY COMPARATIVE AND CONFLICTS LAW 365, 374 (1961). Professor Currie found me result-selective in this sense but subconsciously so. In his article on "Married Woman's Contracts," he called attention to a "pleasantry" of mine: an effort to characterize the competing laws in my hypothetical case in terms I thought mildly humorous. I noted the immateriality for the conventional choice-of-law rule that one law may be "reminiscent of those days when husband and wife were one" and that the other "mirrors the latest views of the National Woman's Party on sex equality before the law." Cavers, *supra* note 27, at 180. Professor Currie sees in this a "subliminal statement of a proposition that cannot with comfort be stated baldly," namely, that a judge may take advantage of the "looseness in the joints of [the choice-of-law] apparatus" to "frustrate . . . all that is archaic and foolish in the law." Currie, "Married Woman's Contracts: A Study in Conflict-of-Laws Method," 25 U. CHI. L. REV. 227, 250 (1958), in SELECTED ESSAYS 77, 105. Since my striving for a light touch was surely not needed to reveal my widely-shared preference for the emancipation of married women and since I had dealt explicitly with the problem of the judge's preference in the paragraph quoted above, this recourse to my subconscious, though interesting, has always struck me as a little superfluous.

result-selective approach thus defined has an ancient lineage, having been espoused, Professor Hessel E. Yntema points out, by a glossator named Aldricus *circa* A.D. 1200,[47] I deny that I am the intellectual heir of Aldricus. If I am suspect, I suppose it is due to my insistence that the process of making a just choice between two laws requires that one take into account the respective results worked by the laws between which one chooses. However, in a choice-of-law case, the court is not engaged in an exercise in comparative jurisprudence, appraising the respective merits of two rules of law. Rather the court is passing upon the conflicting claims of two parties, each of whom insists that the facts of the case justly require that one of the rules, and not the other, be applied in its decision. It is therefore to the circumstances of the case that one must look for the problem. To neutralize these by asking the judge simply to express a preference between the two rules on the score of "justice and convenience" is to abolish our centuries-old subject.

In giving my grudging recognition to the inevitable operations of judicial preference and even parochialism, I did not try to make a virtue of the application of the forum's law, as it sometimes seems to me Professors Currie and Ehrenzweig come close to doing—so close, I fear, that it will take only a little oversimplification of their respective views for them to be cast as advocates of applying forum law simply because it is forum law. That this should come at a time when, if we are to believe Justice Traynor, our state courts are prepared to free themselves from parochialism,[48] seems to me unfortunate. Yet both these scholars could protest this conclusion. Professor Ehrenzweig would have a court "whose jurisdiction is properly invoked" apply its "own law except where legislative or

47 Yntema, "The Comity Doctrine," in 2 VOM DEUTSCHEN ZUM EUROPÄISCHEN RECHT: FESTSCHRIFT FÜR HANS DÖLLE 65, 68 (1963).

48 Traynor, "Is This Conflict Really Necessary?" 37 TEXAS L. REV. 657, 675 (1959).

settled judicial rules of choice of law or the policy of the forum's municipal rule have required a different answer."[49] He insists that his approach should result in more applications of the other state's law than the *Restatement* rules have been producing.[50] And now that Professor Currie would permit a court to examine the forum's law and the foreign law together and give the court freedom to place a "moderate and restrained" interpretation on its own law, in the light of the foreign law,[51] occasions would not be uncommon where this would lead to the foreign law's use.

[49] Ehrenzweig, "The 'Most Significant Relationship' in the Conflicts Law of Torts," 28 LAW & CONTEMP. PROB. 700, 703 (1963).

[50] EHRENZWEIG, CONFLICT OF LAWS 350 (1962).

[51] Currie, "The Disinterested Third State," *supra* note 25, at 763.

IV

THE USES AND LIMITATIONS OF THE "ORDINARY PROCESSES OF CONSTRUCTION AND INTERPRETATION"

Near the start of the preceding chapter, I listed in capsule form four choice-of-law methodologies. It was evident from that listing that the third and fourth methodologies (with which I associated Judge Currie and Judge Cavers respectively) were rather closely linked. There is a considerable overlap in the two methodologies, an overlap that I think derives from the fact that both start with the belief that the court must view its task in terms of a choice between competing rules of law. Accordingly, it must begin with inquiries into the terms and purposes of those rules of law as well as into their connections with the event or transaction giving rise to the controversy.

At least the initial processes in which a court engages when it pursues these inquiries can be termed "the ordinary processes of construction and interpretation," as Professor Currie would have us call them, though that characterization is not without its difficulties and the process itself encounters problems of terminology and application that are far from ordinary. These matters will be discussed shortly. Before I turn to them, I wish to suggest the nature and dimensions of the area common to both the third and the fourth methods. For this purpose I shall survey briefly the kinds of cases that I believe would be dealt with in much the same way under either method.

A. *Common Ground for the Third and Fourth Methods*

First among these kinds of cases are those in which the conflict would be found to be false since, when the laws involved in such a case are scrutinized, the purpose of only one of them would be advanced by its application in the case.[1] The conflict may be found false in other cases because both laws are the same[2] or would yield the same result.[3] Cases posing conflicts which appear to be true can sometimes be resolved, and the conflicts avoided, by a careful evaluation of the facts which reveal connections with the laws involved that are so significant in terms of one law's purposes and so inconsequential in terms of the other's purposes that the application of the former is plainly called for.[4] In cases of this sort, the factor of fairness to the parties in the light of expectations that they may have reasonably entertained may be important.[5] In still other situations, the terms or the plain purpose of the forum's law will be found to require its application.[6] The converse may appear: situations in which the benefits to be derived from the application of the forum's law are so attenuated, and the detriment to the parties or to

[1] E.g., Grant v. McAuliffe, 41 Cal. 2d 859, 264 P.2d 944 (1953); Schmidt v. Driscoll Hotel, Inc., 249 Minn. 376, 82 N.W.2d 365 (1957); Babcock v. Jackson, 12 N.Y.2d 473, 191 N.E.2d 279 (1963).

[2] E.g., Booth v. Milliken, 194 N.Y. 553, 87 N.E. 1115 (1909); Marie v. Garrison, 13 Abb. N. Cas. 210 (N.Y. 1883); *cf.* Waynick v. Chicago's Last Dep't Store, 269 F.2d 322, 324 (7th Cir. 1959).

[3] E.g., Scheer v. Rockne Motors Corp., 68 F.2d 942 (2d Cir. 1934) (on the assumption that it is found that the defendant merely gave the driver possession of the car).

[4] E.g., Bernkrant v. Fowler, 55 Cal. 2d 588, 12 Cal. Rptr. 266, 360 P.2d 906 (1961); Shanahan v. Landers Construction Co., Inc., 266 F.2d 400 (1st Cir. 1959).

[5] See Cavers, "Oral Contracts to Provide by Will and the Choice-of-Law Process: Some Notes on *Bernkrant*," in PERSPECTIVES OF LAW: ESSAYS FOR AUSTIN WAKEMAN SCOTT 38, 48-53 (Pound, Griswold & Sutherland, eds. 1964).

[6] Zogg v. Penn Mutual Life Ins. Co., 276 F.2d 861 (2d Cir. 1960).

the purposes of the other state's law are so substantial, that justice can be served only by the application of the latter law.[7]

The decisions reached in such cases would tend, I suspect, to be particularized to a considerable degree. As precedents, therefore, they would become the core of quite specific rules of relatively narrow application, yet, I need scarcely add, recourse to such rules would not be inconsistent with "equal justice under law," the ideal invoked by Griswold, J., in *Knickerbocker*. These rules would not always be seen as rules for choice of law, though choice of law would be the result of their application. Probably they would often be viewed as rules for the construction and interpretation of the forum's law, precluding or permitting the choice of another state's law.[8]

To shift from abstract methodologies to living conflicts scholars, I believe there would be relatively little difference in the way cases like the foregoing would be handled by that growing group of contemporary Americans whose writings, to quote Paul Freund's comment on the *Seeman* case,[9] are "noteworthy for renouncing a geographical test in favor of a teleological one in the choice of law."[10] Let me make it plain that I should not expect complete uniformity in the results the members of this group would reach in such cases. There is too much room for individual differences in the assessment of the purposes of laws and of the significance of facts to assure this, especially in an area where, as I have just pointed out, particularization is to be expected. And I do not assume that all

7 Lauritzen v. Larsen, 345 U.S. 571 (1953); Green v. Northwestern Trust Co., 128 Minn. 30, 150 N.W. 229 (1914).

8 E.g., in Schmidt v. Driscoll Hotel, Inc., *supra* note 1. The decision was cast in terms of a construction of the forum's dramshop act, holding it to be applicable; in Lauritzen v. Larsen, *supra* note 7, the same process led to a holding that the Jones Act was not applicable.

9 Seeman v. Philadelphia Warehouse Co., 274 U.S. 403 (1927).

10 Freund, "Chief Justice Stone and the Conflict of Laws," 59 Harv. L. Rev. 1210, 1214 (1946).

scholars, any more than all judges, will be immune to the appeal of laws which they esteem when these are pitted against laws which they deplore.

If I were to be more specific in my allusion to conflicts scholars who, I believe, would adopt much the same approach to my garland of cases, I could marshall a substantial array. Without attempting to exhaust the constituency, I would include, in addition to Professor Currie and myself, the list which follows: Professor Freund of Harvard, from whose 1946 article on "Chief Justice Stone and the Conflict of Laws" I have just quoted, perhaps the first among American scholars to articulate the choice-of-law problem in terms of the "interests and policies of the two states";[11] John H. C. Morris of Oxford University, who may be surprised to find himself drawn into this American company but whose suggestive article on "The Proper Law of a Tort,"[12] written during his stay at Harvard in 1951, compelled reexamination of that monolithic solution to choice between competing tort laws which the "place of injury" rule had provided, however varied the laws; Professor Albert Ehrenzweig, who, when he pauses in his reiteration of the "basic rule" of "the proper forum," demonstrates a readiness to examine in terms of fact and purpose the claims of the other state's law to application;[13] Professor Moffat Hancock of Stanford, who has ranged in recent writings far beyond his well-known earlier work, *Torts in the Conflict of Laws,* and lately

[11] *Id.* at 1217-19.

[12] 64 HARV. L. REV. 881 (1951), in which he would have the court arrive at "the proper law of a tort" by examining the particular issue before it in the light of "the social factors involved," (*id.* at 893), "balancing the interests of the states whose law is involved," (*id.* at 890).

Dr. Morris, Fellow and Tutor, Magdalen College and All Souls Lecturer in Private International Law, is General Editor of Dicey's *Conflict of Laws.*

[13] See, e.g., the treatment of charitable institutions in EHRENZWEIG, CONFLICT OF LAWS § 221 (1962), and of product liability in *id.* § 223. See Cavers, "Some of Ehrenzweig's Choice-of-Law Generalizations," 18 OKLA. L. REV. 238 (1965).

has rejected what he terms "the package deals" imposed by jurisdiction-selecting rules;[14] Professor Russell Weintraub of Iowa, who has followed the teachings of Professor Currie up to the point of the latter's acceptance of the law of the forum in the true conflicts case where he then advances a number of suggestions for its resolution;[15] Professor William F. Baxter of Stanford, who also has recently advanced a principle for resolving not only such cases as the foregoing but also true conflicts;[16] and, latest but not least, my colleagues, Professors Arthur von Mehren and Donald Trautman, whose views, though foreshadowed in prior writings, have been developed much more fully through the medium of a course book, *The Law of Multistate Problems,* which appeared not long before publication of these lectures[17] and in which they have identified in considerable detail techniques for the resolution of choice-of-law problems, drawing in the process on multistate policies. Finally, the latest article by Professor Edwin W. Briggs of Montana persuades me that, despite his fidelity to "legislative jurisdiction," he would not only approach cases of the sort that I have described in much the same way as would the others but that his approach could contribute to the development of the fourth methodology.[18]

14 Hancock, "The Rise and Fall of *Buckeye v. Buckeye* 1931-1959: Marital Immunity for Torts in the Conflict of Laws," 29 U. CHI. L. REV. 237, 267 (1962); "In the Parish of *St. Mary Le Bow* in the Ward of *Cheap,* Choice-of-Law Problems Resolved by Statutory Construction: The Charitable Testamentary Gift Cases," 16 STAN. L. REV. 561 (1964).

15 Weintraub, "A Method for Solving Conflict Problems," 21 U. PITT. L. REV. 573 (1960); "The Contracts Proposals of the Second Restatement of Conflict of Laws—A Critique," 46 IOWA L. REV. 713 (1961); "A Method for Solving Conflict Problems—Torts," 48 CORNELL L.Q. 215 (1963).

16 Baxter, "Choice of Law and the Federal System," 16 STAN. L. REV. 1 (1963).

17 The volume includes much more text by the authors than is customary in more conventional casebooks.

18 Briggs, "An Institutional Approach to Conflict of Laws: 'Law and Reason' versus Professor Ehrenzweig," 12 U.C.L.A.L. REV. 29 (1964).

That, despite differences in doctrinal statement, such a substantial array of scholars should exhibit such a substantial degree of agreement as to the ways in which a number of choice-of-law problems should be handled is ground for encouragement; the area of agreement might, if it could be put to the test of actual application, prove greater than the area of disagreement. Perhaps, moreover, as discussion continues, some of our differences will be eroded away or may even prove to have posed false conflicts.

At what point would this concurrence in a method end? Where would the differences in doctrinal statement be translated into significant differences in method? As I see it, division is encountered when courts confront cases that lie beyond the ambit of the relatively easy cases which are covered in my survey. At that point, the alternatives seem to be (1) recourse to the law of the forum (hopefully an interested forum) as the third methodology would require, or (2) a resolution of the conflict by an *ad hoc* decision evaluating, on the basis of choice-of-law considerations, the claims to application of the conflicting laws in the light of the circumstances of each case, or (3) where generalization seems possible, the formulation of a rule or principle of preference on choice-of-law grounds and its application to choose the preferred law. Those faithful to Professor Currie's methodology would stop with the first alternative; those not so inhibited would go on to the second alternative, and, one may hope, some would venture the generalizations contemplated by the third alternative. The fourth methodology includes both the second and third alternatives, but its emphasis is on the latter.

Although primarily an extended review of the Ehrenzweig treatise, this article indicates Professor Briggs' approach to choice-of-law problems. At page 54, he divides choice-of-law cases into four categories, the first two of which would embrace cases of the sort under consideration in this section. His "institutional approach" to the harder cases in his fourth category looks to "an emerging recognition by all or most states of certain *common* interests." *Ibid.* (Italics in original.)

Of the scholars listed above, none appears ready to join in Professor Currie's stern rejection of all choice-of-law rules (statutory rules excepted).[19] Professor Ehrenzweig at times seems prepared to accept this view in principle. Though he resignedly accepts some choice-of-law rules that are both "formulated" and, in his opinion, good and would also create "true" rules by reformulating decisions to reflect their "true motivations,"[20] nevertheless he too appears to view the decision of cases not covered by those rules as posing simply a matter of construction and interpretation by the forum of its own laws and the relevant laws of the other state or states.[21]

Professors von Mehren and Trautman have been developing a technique for choice of law which they term "functional analysis." For them the multistate transaction will always in theory and often in fact confront the court in a choice-of-law case with the need not only to analyze the respective purposes

[19] Currie, "Notes on Methods and Objectives in the Conflict of Laws," 1959 DUKE L.J. 171, 177, in SELECTED ESSAYS 177, 183, (1963): "We would be better off without choice-of-law rules. We would be better off if Congress . . . were to legislate concerning the choice between conflicting state interests in some of the specific areas in which the need for solutions is serious." See also Currie, "Comment on *Babcock* v. *Jackson*, A Recent Development in Conflict of Laws," 63 COLUM. L. REV. 1212, 1233, 1241: ". . . must all choice-of-law problems be solved on an *ad hoc* basis, or will new generalizations be possible? My response is that, for the time being, at least, new efforts to find short cuts and syntheses should be sternly discouraged."

[20] EHRENZWEIG, CONFLICT OF LAWS 352-3 (1962). The concepts of "formulated" and "true" rules are subjected to criticism in Currie, Book Review, "Ehrenzweig, *Conflict of Laws*," 1964 DUKE L.J. 429. (Some rejoinders by the author reviewed are included in footnotes.)

[21] "And where the available material does not even suffice [for "formulated" or "true" rules], we shall have to be satisfied with interpreting each domestic rule as to its applicability to those foreign facts for the sake of which that rule is claimed to be displaced." EHRENZWEIG, CONFLICT OF LAWS 308 (1962). See also *id.* at 353. Though these statements are cast in terms of the forum's law only and though Professor Ehrenzweig would reject renvoi as a doctrine, he would, nevertheless, allow the forum to consider the other state's law in an appropriate case. *Id.* at 336.

of the conflicting laws in the light of the transaction's connections with those laws but also to examine the bearing on the case of a number of policies developed for multistate transactions, for example, the policy of facilitating interstate transactions.[22] From cases in which multistate policies are invoked, they have identified certain choice-of-law rules or principles for their implementation that have already been developed, and they anticipate the development of others.[23] However, the authors are concerned at this juncture in their work to identify the approach that they believe courts should adopt in choice-of-law cases. Until that approach achieves more widespread recognition in the case law, they might well view as premature any scholarly efforts to formulate additional choice-of-law rules or principles.

Professor Baxter, like Professors von Mehren and Trautman, has been interested in the development of a choice-of-law technique which not only could resolve true conflicts but also could foster choice-of-law rules and principles.[24] Moreover, I am not at all convinced that Professor Ehrenzweig's approach would actually dispense with the development of choice-of-law rules or principles in those areas where acceptable, settled rules do not now exist. Professor Briggs sees their development as the result of the institutionalization of the interests involved.

I shall have more to say of some of these authors in a later chapter after I have developed my own conception of the kind of choice-of-law doctrine that I believe is needed to

[22] Von Mehren & Trautman, The Law of Multistate Problems 76, 240-54; see generally *id.* 257-304 (1965).

[23] *Id.* at 395-406; *cf. id.* at 551-52. "In a fully developed system of functional choice-of-law rules, . . . these rules would be relatively particularized and nuanced; they should state fairly precisely whether the jurisdiction wishes to regulate a given issue at all, and, if so, under what conditions." *Id.* at 551.

[24] Baxter, *supra* note 16. His "comparative impairment" method will be discussed briefly in Chapter VIII *infra*.

resolve conflicts which are neither false nor readily avoided in one or another of the various ways indicated by the cases surveyed above. Now, however, I wish to give further consideration to certain problems which are suggested by the "ordinary processes of construction and interpretation."

The first few of these problems are terminological. Even if each of us were to reserve to himself the terminological freedom asserted by Humpty Dumpty,[25] there would be need of mutual tolerance for, and an effort at understanding of, each other's terminologies lest the hope of a working consensus should be frustrated in a succession of logomachies.

B. *Terminological Questions: Herein of "Policies" and "Interests"*

(1) *"The Ordinary Processes of Construction and Interpretation."* It is in this spirit that I find it possible to refer to a court's decision in a choice-of-law case to employ or not to employ a common-law rule of the forum or of another state as an "interpretation" of that rule though the processes whereby common-law precedents are extended or contracted in application do not fit easily with my own notion of the interpretative process.[26]

With respect to statutes, the terminology is easier to employ —up to a point. When a court has before it a statute of its own or of the other state, it should seek for evidence of legislative intent bearing on the applicability of the statute to the facts before it and, when this guide to decision proves

25 See Carroll, THROUGH THE LOOKING GLASS, ch. VI: "When *I* use a word," Humpty Dumpty said, in rather a scornful tone, "it means just what I choose it to mean—neither more nor less."

26 Resort to the term is sometimes hard to escape for our methodological vocabulary does not seem to have achieved a satisfactory and distinctive term to identify the process. In Levi, "An Introduction to Legal Reasoning," 15 U. CHI. L. REV. 501 (1948), the distinctive characteristics in the development of rules in case law is illuminated, yet the author refers to "the interpretation of case law, statutes, and the constitution of a nation" in calling attention to "important similarity and difference" among them. *Id.* at 505.

unavailing, there remains, as Professor Currie has recently observed, the process of identifying "the general objectives . . . the legislators sought to attain by enactment of the legislation" and then of reaching a decision which would advance those objectives.[27] Certainly such legislative purposes can sometimes be recognized with confidence and found to point rather plainly to a decision on applicability, especially to a court which has taken pains to consider the other state's law. Incidentally, a good example of this process is provided by Mr. Justice Jackson's opinion in the case of *Lauritzen v. Larsen*,[28] where the Supreme Court held the Jones Act not applicable to a Danish seaman employed in New York by a Danish ship and injured in Havana.

The difficulties I see in identifying the process as "construction and interpretation"—especially when the adjective "ordinary" is added to modify "process"—arise when the considerations which determine the court's decision are chiefly drawn from sources derived from the interstate situation and have no specific relation to the statute before the court. To be sure, even in such a case, the court must wind up with a decision to apply or not to apply the statute and so in that sense is "construing" it. But to accept the adequacy of this label for the process is to conceal the emergence of rules and principles distinctive to choice of law, a matter I shall consider in the last section of this chapter.

(2) *"Policy."* This is a key term in Professor Currie's method of resolving conflicts by employing the "ordinary processes of construction and interpretation." He would have the court faced by apparently conflicting laws first "inquire into the policies expressed in the respective laws."[29] This

[27] See Currie, "The Disinterested Third State," 28 LAW & CONTEM. PROB. 754, 762n (1963), quoting Jones, "Statutory Doubts and Legislative Intention," 40 COLUM. L. REV. 957, 973 (1940).

[28] 345 U.S. 571 (1953).

[29] Currie, "Comment on *Babcock v. Jackson*, A Recent Development in Conflict of Laws," 63 COLUM. L. REV. 1212, 1233, 1242 (1963).

objective, in the opinion of Dean Kramer, a sympathetic critic, requires pushing inquiry on to another level, to an ascertainment of the "reasons and interests" behind the "policies."[30] Moreover, there surely are laws which help to further broad policies but can scarcely be said to have "expressed" them. All states have certain rules which, when complied with, render transactions legally binding and, when disregarded, render transactions legally unenforceable. These rules do not express a state policy in favor of security of transactions when they result in enforcing a transaction and against the security of transactions when they frustrate one. Yet, an emphasis on certain objectives in the application of the rules or the preponderance of conditions conducive to the enforcement of transactions (or to the reverse) may reveal a basic policy. Such policies relate to the employment of rules or the structure of rules; they are not policies to be found in the particular rules themselves.[31]

In the light of these considerations, I believe it is more helpful to refer, not to the "policies" of the apparently conflicting laws, but to their "purposes," a concept that will embrace that inquiry into the underlying reasons and interests which Professor Kramer calls for. I would utilize the term "policy" for those broad plans of action implemented by law which are not specific to the rules being construed though their effectuation may be advanced by an appropriate choice of law. However, this terminological preference is personal; I have no substantial objection to Professor Currie's use of "policy." I think it can coexist peacefully with my use of "policy" and "purpose."

(3) *"Governmental Interest."* Professor Currie would have

30 Kramer, "Interests and Policy Clashes in Conflict of Laws," 13 Rutgers L. Rev. 523, 531-32 (1959). This use of "interests," a familiar one, differs from Professor Currie's own use of that term, as will appear in the text below.

31 There are, of course, not a few rules which have purposes so relevant to the problem of their application that there is no need to look beyond their terms for multistate policies bearing on applicability.

the forum which has ascertained the policies expressed in the apparently conflicting laws next "inquire into the circumstances in which it is reasonable for the respective states to assert an interest in the application of those policies."[32] When the inquiry produces an affirmative answer with respect to a state, that state is said to have an "interest" in the application of its law.[33] This interest Professor Currie terms a "governmental" or "state" interest; indeed, he terms his methodology the "governmental interest analysis."[34] His use of "governmental interest" has aroused vigorous objection. The reality of any interests derived in this way has been questioned. It is sometimes denied that rules of private law produce "governmental interests" and asserted that only public laws create interests in the state itself, private laws having simply the function of doing justice between private parties.[35] I understand Professor Rheinstein takes essentially this position, and Professor Ehrenzweig has recently referred to these interests as "fictitious."[36] Now that Professor Currie has put "pseudo-

[32] Currie, *supra* note 29, at 1242. [33] *Ibid.* [34] *Id.* at 1241.

[35] See Ehrenzweig, Conflict of Laws 350 (1962). A forthright assertion of this position appears in the following passage which I have been permitted by its author, Dr. Gerhard Kegel, a leading German scholar in the conflict of laws, to quote from his as yet unpublished lectures on "The 'Crisis' of Conflicts of Laws" delivered at the Academy of International Law at The Hague in the summer of 1964: "The state uses private law rules, not in order to serve its own goals, but rather to search for *justice* in the relations of individuals. [Exceptions are conceded for private law rules which are closely related to public law.] It seeks to find a substantively just solution to conflicting private interests. This goal cannot produce a basis for the *spatial* application of private law rules. A new question is at issue here. Different interests, namely, the interests of the parties, of commerce, and of legal order present themselves . . . . Governmental interests are the own interests of the state. . . ." (Italics in original.)

[36] See Ehrenzweig, "Comment on *Babcock v. Jackson*, A Recent Development in Conflict of Laws," 63 Colum. L. Rev. 1212, 1243, 1246 (1963): "The solutions in such cases must be found by considering the interests of the *parties* in the light of forum policy (as opposed to fictitious 'governmental interests')." (Italics in original.)

juridical mumbo-jumbo" into circulation,[37] the epithet in the hands of his critics may reveal homing tendencies. The makings of logomachy are at hand.

I find it hard to join in the objections to the term wholeheartedly. As I see it, Professor Currie has felt a need for a word in which to embody a conclusion that the purposes of a statute or common-law rule would be advanced by its application to a particular set of facts. He has used the word "interest" to meet that need. Since the rule emanates from the state, I believe the rule's purposes may reasonably be ascribed to the state even though the rule is simply a legislative or judicial determination that it represents the best way to achieve justice between litigating private parties. However, few rules can be held to so narrow a function. Even within the sphere of private law, they generally represent norms for the ordering of behavior, not merely for dispute settlement, and today public-law objectives are coming increasingly to infiltrate private law.

Even in the case of laws with the most limited public objectives, I think it reasonable to ascribe to the state a desire to have the purposes of its laws effectuated in situations where this would appear to advance those purposes, absent countervailing considerations. To identify that desire in such a situation by modifying "interest" by "governmental" or "state" does not seem to me inapt, though the resulting term is not without its hazards.

The chief hazard, as I see it, may spring from the misleading air of substantiality that the term "interest" exudes. It suggests that the state's concern (which may be the belated product of a highly speculative and attenuated attribution of purposes to a given law) is comparable to the state government's interest in the achievement of public objectives it is actively pursuing or would vigorously defend. Perhaps equally important is the tendency for this "interest" concept to obscure the often-

[37] Currie, *supra* note 27, at 789.

noted fact that the purposes of a given domestic rule are not the only policies of the state that may bear upon the choice-of-law question before the court.[38] To be sure, Professor Currie would doubtless declare that, if such other policies do exist, the court may properly take them into account in determining whether the forum's interest should be given a "moderate and restrained interpretation." But the scales in which this delicate weighing process is to be conducted may have been unbalanced by the use of the loaded concept of "governmental interest."

There is another difficulty that becomes apparent when one compares the use of "interest" by Professors von Mehren and Trautman. They seek to contrast "state interests" with "individual interests."[39] Thus they contrast policies which relate to the concerns of a state as a member of the world community of states or of a federation of states with policies which reflect the state's concern for the individual. They, for example, note a "state interest in facilitating out-of-state transactions" and an "individual interest in being able to rely on commitments entered into on the assumption that they are binding."[40] Obviously state policies having these objectives might in a given case produce "governmental [or state] interests," in Professor Currie's sense, reflecting both purposes. However, the blanketing of the differences in the values involved by the use of the single "governmental interest" label may discourage discriminating analysis.

The same difficulty may be posed by another contrast, that between public and private law. Unlike the critics who would

[38] When these policies derive from the fact that the types of acts, events, or transactions to which they relate involve two or more states, they are termed "multistate policies" by Professors von Mehren and Trautman in whose work, *op. cit. supra* note 22, at 237-304, more careful attention is devoted to their identification than in most writings on choice of law.

[39] Von Mehren & Trautman, *op. cit. supra* note 21, at 237, see generally 237-304.

[40] *Id.* at 285.

confine the use of "governmental interest" to the public-law field, I would deny the wisdom or feasibility of drawing such lines in an effort to differentiate these two categories of laws. However, the extent to which a given law furthers the purposes of the public as a whole as distinguished from the purposes of individuals under particular conditions ranges over a spectrum. At one extreme are laws governing the organization and functions of the state and its subdivisions which have little pertinence to the individual save as a member of the community and at the other are laws enabling competent persons to enter into contractual and property arrangements with one another which have little concern to the public except as the public is composed of individuals, any one of whom may take advantage of a given law's provisions. Again, the blanketing of the entire spectrum by a concept which is more aptly used to denote one end of it may tend to discourage analysis. At the least, it has excited the critical expostulations already noted.

For these various reasons, though I do not reject the term "interest," as Professor Currie has used it, I shall take advantage of the fact that I find it dispensable. The decisive factor in Professor Currie's method is the finding that the application of a law is reasonable in the light of the circumstances of the case and the policies the law expresses. Obviously the idea that such a finding has been, or can be, made can be conveyed without using the term "interest" to label that conclusion. Of course, a label can be a convenience, but not if its use incites much disputation, and, even if explanations were to succeed in quieting criticisms of "governmental interest" based on misunderstanding, there would remain the risks of distorting judgment that I have noted. Accordingly, I shall try to do without it.

C. *The Other State's Choice-of-Law Rules*

Insofar as I am correct in my belief that, under either the third or the fourth method, the forum would often have to examine not only its own law but also the law of the other state involved in the controversy, the latter task would create difficult problems for the forum in certain cases which the ordinary processes of construction do not ordinarily pose. Suppose we assume that the case is one in which Professor Currie would have the forum consider whether, for the purpose of accommodating potentially conflicting state interests, it should give to its own law a "moderate and restrained interpretation" and thereby eliminate any conflict between that law and the law of the other concerned state. Should a court in State X, finding itself in that situation, arrive at that "moderate and restrained interpretation" of its own law independently of the interpretation given to the potentially conflicting law of State Y, and, if not, how should State X court determine the interpretation to be given the State Y law?

Case 5 will provide an example: the case of the Massachusetts citizen who has been negligently injured in New York by the Massachusetts charity that was teaching him nature lore. The suit against the charity is brought in New York. Should the New York court give a "moderate" reading to the New York law denying the charity immunity by holding it not to apply to a Massachusetts charity when the beneficiary victim is also from Massachusetts? New York plainly has the constitutional power to apply New York law to compensate people hurt in New York State, but ought its courts to assert that power? Consulting Massachusetts law may help. Suppose a Massachusetts case had held that its immunity law did not extend to torts by Massachusetts charities outside Massachusetts, at least in states denying charities immunity. For the New York court the conflict would thereupon have been avoided, and it would apply its law denying immunity.

Suppose, however, that the Massachusetts courts are silent as to immunity for extra-state torts, though cases can be found there invoking the place-of-injury rule to select a law to govern other issues of tort liability. New York is the place of injury. Ought, therefore, the New York court to view that Massachusetts choice-of-law rule as having avoided the conflict and so as being decisive of its problem? This would enable the court to avoid the question whether it should give a "moderate" reading to its own law.

This problem could become serious if the approach that Professor Currie and I join in advocating, despite our differences, were to be widely employed. There is a deposit of old jurisdiction-selecting choice-of-law decisions in the law reports of every state; in the older, larger states, a very big deposit. How seriously must they be taken?

Consider the problem confronting a forum which is considering the applicability of a rule of law of State X. The court's attention is called to certain X cases which, by means of a jurisdiction-selecting rule, would automatically apply the law of another state to cases in which the latter state is the site of the contact that the X rule prescribes. Despite these cases, the forum might well conclude that State X might in the future insist on applying its own law where its application would advance the purpose of the X rule. Reappraisals would occur as courts came increasingly to choose between specific laws rather than legal systems and so had to confront the questions of purpose and value that competing laws pose. Yet, the very fact that State X had been ready to apply a law other than its own, even by the medium of a mechanical choice-of-law rule, does raise some doubt as to the commitment of State X to its relevant domestic law. It also suggests a possible readiness in X to construe that law moderately. The forum might act on the basis of that suggestion.

A like situation might present itself in Case 5. The New York court in that case would be entitled to give the suggested reading to the Massachusetts law where, at least, other factors render a moderate reading by Massachusetts not unrealistic. Among these, for example, might be not only choice-of-law cases but also domestic cases in which the Massachusetts court had astutely applied the local rule restrictively when the occasion arose.[41]

Suppose the forum finds that the other state's choice-of-law cases point to that state's domestic law. The forum should be less confident then of predicting the other state's readiness to reach a different conclusion if it were to reexamine the problem. The choice-of-law rule might have been acceptable because it brought the domestic law into play. It would, therefore, be harder to infer a readiness to give a "moderate" reading to that law.

I have been speculating concerning a forum's appraisal of the other interested state's application of its own law. Why, however, should the forum be so "other-directed," to borrow David Riesman's phrase from *The Lonely Crowd*? Suppose the forum deemed a moderate interpretation of its own law wiser than an interpretation pressing to the full extent of its constitutional power. Suppose the forum were to find that the other state, State X, has also been shrinking back. Perhaps, the forum would conclude that X's choice-of-law rule or X's own "moderate" interpretation, would lead X not to apply its own law to this situation. As translations of some recent foreign writings have put it,[42] the forum finds that the X law doesn't "want" to be applied. What then? If each law defers to the other, have we a gap in the law—a case fallen between the stools of two legal systems?

This has created problems for conflicts scholars on occasion,[43] and, although I do not recall his having discussed it, I should think it would do so for Professor Currie's

[41] My example is not a happy one; the Massachusetts court has shown no such tendency.

[42] See, e.g., De Nova, "New Trends in Italian Private International Law," 28 LAW & CONTEMP. PROB. 808, 818, 820 (1963), where the verb is aptly put in quotation marks.

[43] In the choice-of-law methodology developed more than twenty years ago by my colleague, Professor Louis Sohn, the problem of how best to fill the gap was thoughtfully examined. See Sohn, "New Bases for Solution of Conflict of Laws Problems," 55 HARV. L. REV. 978 (1942).

"governmental-interest analysis."[44] State X appears to have disclaimed a governmental interest of its own, and how could the forum have a governmental interest in the application of X's law? Perhaps the forum should simply deny that X knows its own interest or that its conventional choice-of-law rule identifies that interest. The forum could then proceed to its own definition of the X interest.

For me, the question seems to be easy of solution, and I note that Professor Ehrenzweig is of the same opinion.[45] Why ought the forum not adhere to its own self-restricting interpretation and apply the law of the other state, even though that law doesn't want to be applied? Useful as it is to take into account the way the other state would apply its own rules, the forum has the responsibility of adjudicating the case. If the forum is satisfied that its domestic rule should not be applied and that the X rule provides an appropriate norm, given its purposes and the connection of the event or transaction with State X, then why should the forum refrain from using the X rule?[46] If my indifference to the question whether the X law

[44] It is of interest that Judge Currie in Case 3 faced without blenching the possibility that the governmental interest analysis would lead to disclaimers by both states. See p. 39, *supra*. For Judge Cavers' reaction, see pp. 41–42, *supra*.

[45] EHRENZWEIG, CONFLICT OF LAWS 336 (1962).

[46] I can accept in part the thesis reiterated and elaborated over many years by Professor E. W. Briggs of Montana, most recently in "An Institutional Approach to Conflict of Laws: 'Law and Reason' versus Professor Ehrenzweig," 12 U.C.L.A.L. REV. 29 (1964), that there are certain situations where the forum should follow the choice-of-law rule of State X, recognizing X as the state of "paramount interest," to use the term *Restatement Second* applies to the state of the parties' domicil in marriage cases. RESTATEMENT (SECOND), CONFLICT OF LAWS, Topic 1 Introductory Note, at 94 (Tent. Draft No. 4, 1957). The situs of property is conventionally accorded this position in recognition of its power over the *res*. Yet, when it has this power, no other state is in a position to accord it the recognition that is said to be its due, so atypical cases must be found in which the property has left the situs after the legally critical event at issue. This fact should tend to cause a court to defer to the way the situs would handle the case, but surely this would not always

wants to be applied seems bold, I hasten to remind you that it is pure orthodoxy from which the original *Restatement* deviated at only two points.[47]

Perhaps I should also add for any conflict-of-laws student whom it may have eluded that what I have been discussing for the past few pages is a subject that has excited several generations of conflicts scholars—the problem that is usually introduced under the mystery-making label of *renvoi* although it also embraces the companion mystery of characterization or qualification.[48] I see it simply as the question how much attention the forum should pay to the choice-of-law rules of another state, their analytical and conceptual apparatus included. That these should not be ignored and that these should not be controlling are propositions on which I am in accord with my colleagues, Professors Freund and von Mehren.[49] My prosy approach to the subject lacks the glamour of the *circulus inextrabilis* and precludes an opportunity knowingly to

---

be desirable. *Cf.* Shanahan v. Landers Construction Co., Inc. 266 F.2d 400 (1st Cir. 1959), where the movable might have been either in transit at the time of the transaction or transiently in Vermont before removal to the contemplated situs, New Hampshire. See Cavers, "The Conditional Seller's Remedies and the Choice-of-Law Process: Some Notes on *Shanahan*," 35 N.Y.U.L. Rev. 1126, 1135 (1960).

[47] Restatement, Conflict of Laws §§ 7, 8 (1934), permitting the inclusion of choice-of-law rules in the law of the state to which the *Restatement* requires reference to be made only in cases involving title to land and divorce. In all other cases, reference is to be made to the local law.

[48] The question may arise because the choice-of-law rule of State X differs from that of the forum and refers either to the forum or to a third state (renvoi) or because the corresponding choice-of-law rule in State X, though the same in terms as the forum's rule, is not viewed by State X as applicable to the question before the forum because State X has characterized that question differently from the forum. Therefore, X would apply a different choice-of-law rule to its solution.

[49] See Freund, *supra* note 10, at 1218; von Mehren, "The Renvoi and its Relation to Various Approaches to the Choice-of-Law Problem," in XXth Century Comparative and Conflicts Law 380 (von Mehren, Nadelmann & Hazard, eds. 1961).

let fall such terms as *Rückverweisung* and *Weiterverweisung*, but choice of law for this nation of fifty states has real problems aplenty without fabricating or importing any artificial ones.

D. *The Emergence of Choice-of-Law Rules and Principles*

My own efforts and my observation of the efforts of contemporary courts and scholars to extract guidance for choice of law from the purposes of the forum's and the other state's laws have convinced me that the process is more difficult than Professor Currie's advocacy would lead one to believe. The trouble does not always spring from an inability to identify any specific purpose whatever. On the contrary, speculation as to the purposes of statutes and common-law rules has an inconvenient tendency to yield multiple purposes, and the two or more specific purposes of a given law which have been identified by the analyst's probings may point in quite different directions when the question is raised as to that law's application in situations involving another state. Naturally this compels an attribution (often of dubious authenticity) of primacy to one purpose or another.

Where evidence or reasonable inferences of specific purposes are wanting and recourse must be had to the legislature's general purpose, this may not afford the court much guidance when the question is whether to press the application of a statute to its logical extreme or to exercise moderation; indeed the statute's domestic purpose may throw little light on the basic question whether that purpose would be materially advanced in any out-of-state situation. And where the forum finds the teaching of its own legislature's general objectives hard to decipher, it may have at least as much trouble in reading the sibylline leaves of the other state's law. In addition to deciding what that law's domestic purposes may be, the forum may have to cope not only with the problem we have just considered—what effect to give to the choice-of-law rules of the other state—but also with the more difficult problem created by spatial conditions on that state's internal law (a matter which, though tempting to take up at this point, must be deferred to a later chapter).

Naturally, a perplexed court, finding no guidance in the specific laws before it, yet seeking a rational resolution of its difficulty, will, as I have already suggested, turn to considerations bearing on multistate transactions generally. It will also look for policies for resolving conflicts that are not specific to the particular laws before the court but are germane to broader categories of laws in which the laws in controversy are included. An able court that had earlier tried to articulate its reasons for a choice-of-law decision would almost inevitably have had something to say that would be relevant to a later case involving a different though analogous domestic statute or case-law rule. If, in that later case, the court were to draw on the earlier reasoning, a rule or principle would begin to emerge that could, with accuracy, be called a choice-of-law rule or principle.

Perhaps, as I have suggested, this would initially be viewed as simply a rule or principle for construing statutes or for interpreting case law, but in the course of time it would achieve an autonomous existence. The principle would have relevance not only as to the conditions under which the forum's law would be employed but also as to the conditions that would lead to the use of the other state's law. Courts might still say in a case involving a domestic statute that their task is to determine its scope "in the light of the applicable principles of the conflict of laws," as Justice Traynor wrote not long ago in *Bernkrant v. Fowler*,[50] but, as a result, the "applicable

[50] *Supra* note 4 at 594, 360 P.2d at 909. Professor Currie, who has repeatedly and justifiably applauded this decision, does not appear to have entered into an examination of the principles that Justice Traynor found applicable. I shall assume the reader's acquaintance with the case. On both hypotheses as to the promisor's domicil, the main principle invoked appears to have been the protection of the reasonable expectations of the

principles" would gain in significance as a guide to choice. The principles would also come to aid the lawyer wanting to know what, if any, choice of law he could expect when his client's interests seemed likely to turn on a choice between other laws of the same general type as those that the court had "construed." And, now and then, a good case lawyer could gain clues to future rulings by observing the kinds of considerations that had moved the courts in cases involving quite different laws.

The emergence of choice-of-law principles by these familiar common-law processes would, of course, aid the purely disinterested forum and also the forum which, though not bereft of all interest, realizes that its own law has less claim to recognition than the conflicting laws of two other states, a situation neatly illustrated by a federal case in Maryland that Professor Currie has lately brought to our attention.[51]

On rare occasions, a case involving an unavoidable true conflict between the laws of two interested states might come before a disinterested third state in circumstances precluding dismissal as *forum non conveniens*.[52] Such a conflict might also confront an independent federal forum if the *Klaxon*

---

parties: on the first hypothesis, against giving retroactive effect to a post-agreement change of domicil; on the second, against frustrating a transaction centered in one state by invoking the contingent concern of another state, the promisor's then domicil. These considerations, though taking the policy of the relevant statutory provision into account, have a significance for future decisions that reaches well beyond the particulars of the case before the court.

51 LaChance v. Service Trucking Co., 215 F. Supp. 162 (D. Md. 1963), discussed in Currie, *supra* note 27, at 768-72 (third-party complaint against a Maine husband in suit brought by his wife in U.S. District Court in Maryland against the Service Trucking Co. for injury in North Carolina where, unlike Maine and Maryland, interspousal immunity has been abolished; motion to dismiss denied).

52 Or where circumstances render a *forum non conveniens* dismissal very unlikely as, e.g., in the *LaChance* case, *supra* note 51, where the defendant was a corporation of the forum state.

rule[53] should be done away with in interpleader and in multiparty, multistate diversity cases.[54] As I have already noted, in the United States Professor Currie would view as at least permissible an independent choice of law by a disinterested state court.[55] Since the power to control choice of law by legislation has been vested in the Congress and since, for good reason, it has not exercised that power, he would have the state court, confronted by the necessity of decision, ask itself, "What interest would Congress subordinate if it were to consider the conflict from the viewpoint of the national interest?"[56]

Here "the ordinary processes of construction and interpretation" would be applied to a nonexistent statute. The difficulty in the state's serving in this way as surrogate for the Congress is illustrated by the fact that, in the hypothetical case he posed to illustrate his problem, Professor Currie thought that the court might find either way.[57] When, however, he postulated a federal forum, which had been rendered independent, de-

[53] I.e., the requirement stemming from Klaxon Co. v. Stentor Electric Mfg. Co., 313 U.S. 487 (1941), that a federal court in a diversity case apply the conflict-of-laws rules of the state in which it sits.

[54] See ALI, Study of the Division of Jurisdiction Between State and Federal Courts 21-32, 33-34, (Tent. Draft No. 1, 1963), for a proposal to adhere to the *Klaxon* rule in diversity cases except in federal interpleader and in multiparty, multistate cases involving recourse to a nation-wide extension of federal process proposed for such cases. For a favorable comment on these proposals, see Cavers, "The Changing Choice-of-Law Process and the Federal Courts," 28 Law & Contem. Prob. 732, 743-50 (1963); for a mixed reception, see Currie, *supra* note 27, at 785-90.

[55] *Id.* at 778.

[56] The quoted question is my own; Professor Currie wrote for the court in State F the following: "Our task is simply to place ourselves in the position of Congress, and to reach the decision we think Congress would reach if it were to consider the matter." *Ibid.*

[57] *Ibid.* The imaginary opinion he provided chose a law permitting unlimited recovery for wrongful death as against a ceiling, the reasons stated indicating the court's view that the no-ceiling rule was the better one. Presumably the contrary choice would be fortified by reasons showing the ceiling rule to be the better.

ciding an interpleader case, like *Griffin v. McCoach*, long a target of the commentators, he found the task easier. He would, for example, have a federal court in Texas in that situation apply New York law rather than the Texas law which the Supreme Court held mandatory in *Griffin*.[58] The Texas law denied recovery to New York and New Jersey plaintiffs (assignees of an insurance policy delivered in New York), who lacked an "insurable interest" in the life of the Texas insured. He finds a clear national interest in not undermining interstate insurance transactions by allowing Texas to indulge its "cynic fear" for the life of its insured citizen. Success in the court's search for a "national interest" in such a situation might well be the seed of a new choice-of-law principle.

When, moreover, either an interested or a disinterested forum seeks guidance which the laws before it do not provide, the findings of the past need not be disregarded. Professor Ehrenzweig has insisted that, underneath the language of "vested rights" and territoriality, the courts have often been reaching results that he finds quite defensible.[59] If his evaluations come to be widely shared, perhaps they will form the core of principles which, if less comprehensive than his "Basic Rule of Validation,"[60] will at least have more guidance value

[58] 313 U.S. 498 (1941). Professor Currie's preference is stated in Currie, *supra* note 27, at 789. Absent an independent power in the federal interpleader court, he would have the court apply Texas law. Currie, "Change of Venue and the Conflict of Laws: A Retraction," 27 U. Chi. L. Rev. 341, 345-46 (1960), in Selected Essays 431, 437 (1963).

[59] See Ehrenzweig, "Choice of Law: Current Doctrine and 'True Rules,'" 49 Calif. L. Rev. 240, 241 (1961): ". . . however confused by bad theory and language, our courts, skilled and unskilled, have produced in their unique laboratory many a 'true rule' of choice of law which relieves, and indeed prohibits, us from engaging in a search for interests."

[60] Ehrenzweig, Conflict of Laws 465-90 (1962). The "Basic Rule" calls for the application of the law upholding a consensual transaction where the law of one of the states with which it has a connection would regard it as valid. In the chapter on torts, he has proposed solutions for a number of problems in terms which seemed broader than the particular points at issue. Unfortunately these have sometimes been stretched unwisely in order to widen the reach of the *lex fori*. For a comment on both tendencies, see Cavers, *supra* note 13.

than the individual cases from which they were drawn.

I find unpersuasive the argument which Professor Currie has drawn from separation-of-powers doctrine for confining all judicial choice-of-law thinking to the process of construction and interpretation. This argument, with which I shall deal in a later chapter, has not won general acceptance and of this I am glad, for, as I see it, the problem we face today is not how to exorcise choice-of-law rules and principles but how to develop them. We are agreed that we should not resort to *cadi* justice. We are also agreed, I believe, that mechanical rules will not give proper guidance to courts and counsel once the resources of construction and interpretation have been exhausted. Ought we to divide and subdivide problems on the theory that little problems are easier to solve than big problems? I doubt it, though, of course, one must expect that distinctive situations will on occasion produce correspondingly specific rules. Granting this, however, I have come to believe that in the area with which we are here concerned, that is, where the legislatures of the states involved have not spoken and the conflict is neither false nor readily avoided, agreement upon a limited number of principles of preference that are broader than the specific conflicts posed by particular cases may be easier to reach than agreement upon a set of particularized solutions. Moreover, if such an agreement were attained, the resolution of specific conflicts would become less difficult. Before I advance some examples of choice-of-law principles of these dimensions, I must explain my conception of the principle of preference and its functions.

V

PRINCIPLES OF PREFERENCE IN RESOLVING TRUE CONFLICTS

A. *Today's Characteristic Choice-of-Law Problems*

Before I enter upon the main theme of these lectures, the development of principles of preference as guides to judicial decision in choice-of-law cases, it may be useful to comment on the character of the cases that give rise to choice-of-law problems, especially in American courts, and also to note briefly the distinctive task with which those courts have been confronted and its significance for choice of law.

I believe each age in the history of our subject has been characterized by certain problems recurring in the intercourse between the societies of the age, problems typical of its culture. Thus, in the intercourse between the medieval Italian city-states which were the seed-bed of our earliest doctrines, problems arising out of limitations on capacity to contract and convey seem to have been especially consequential. In Renaissance France, with its many provincial legal systems, problems posed by dealings in land came to the fore. As people became more mobile, problems of marital property regimes multiplied. As trade between nations grew not only in volume but in distances spanned, the involvement of transactions in quite different legal systems led to a greater diversity of questions. It also exerted pressure on the parties to try to insulate themselves from unexpected consequences by choosing the governing law by agreement. In nineteenth-century America, the development of a credit economy on the shaky foundations provided by our collapsible banking system led to a special stress on conflicts within the zone of commercial law and in the flow of funds from the capital-rich East to the capital-poor West. In the latter half of the century, the uneven emergence among the states of statutes designed to remove anachronisms in the common law, such as restraints on married women as property owners and traders, the denial of actions for wrongful death, and the fellow-servant rule, created the potentiality of many conflicts.

What are the conflict areas of the future now that progress in the unification and modernization of commercial law has accompanied the stabilization of our credit institutions and, at the same time, the business of removing common-law anachronisms nears completion, with only limited room left for conflict in the differences among the modernizing statutes? In my effort to answer this question of mine, I must depend in part on my impressionistic observation of the flow of cases and in part on my personal powers of prophecy; I have no statistics to offer.

I believe that, in the United States at least, the principal sources of conflict—apart from the problems of family disintegration—will arise out of two trends. One is the ever-growing network of regulatory laws which are diverse in their terms and their incidence and which, though imposing governmentally sanctioned requirements, also have an impact on private rights and obligations. The other source of conflicting laws is the uneven response of our state laws to the risks of injury to which modern technology has exposed us. The problems posed by varying safety measures, varying schemes for distributing risk, and varying procedural mechanisms for implementing these measures, all are giving rise to questions of choice of law that are accentuated by the mobility not only of people but also of those products of technology on which the safety of people has come so largely to depend.[1]

[1] The automobile and the airplane are responsible for many of the choice-of-law cases in which important departures from received doctrine have been made. The automobile also first inspired the "long-arm"

Interestingly, our problems of conflicting laws as to property appear to be withering away, despite the coexistence of two great systems of property law within this country, neither of which is uniform within the states that comprise it.[2] The area of conflicting laws which has given rise to most difficulty for the American family comprises problems of divorce, judicial separation, and annulment, together with the related problems of alimony, support, and child custody. For the American conflict-of-laws scholar these problems represent an embarrassing array, whether one views the problems as solved or unsolved. The answers our courts have worked out are far from satisfactory, but they appear to be the best that is compatible with that deep division in our mores which makes it seem preferable in this field to provide ways of evading the issues than to seek rational solutions for them. However, for

---

statutes, permitting a suit to be brought in the state in which harm was done, despite the fact that the person causing it could not be served with process within that state. The scope of these statutes is now being extended to business litigation and to cases involving tortious injuries of all kinds, including product liability suits against manufacturers of commodities and their components. For a detailed evaluation of the long-arm statutes and the chief Supreme Court decisions concerning their constitutionality, see Briggs, "Contemporary Problems in Conflict of Laws: Jurisdiction by Statute," pt. 1, 24 OHIO ST. L.J. 223 (1963), pt. 2, 24 MONT. L. REV. 85 (1963). The substantive law of product liability is itself in process of rapid change, and, since the rate of that change is uneven among the states, choice-of-law cases relating to product liability can be expected to increase in number. Another factor that is influencing substantive, jurisdictional, and choice-of-law developments is the great expansion in the volume and varieties of liability insurance.

2 For a detailed comparison of the relevant features of the marital property laws of the United States, together with a thorough consideration of the choice-of-law problems they present, representing conventional methodology at its best, see MARSH, MARITAL PROPERTY IN CONFLICT OF LAWS (1952). As the author's analysis makes plain, the marital property laws of the community property states must not be treated as homogeneous; there are important differences among them. Legislation has caused almost as much diversity among the laws of the common-law property states.

the conflicts scholar whose concern is choice of law, most of this troubled area can be bypassed. In American law the principal questions here go to other branches of the subject: jurisdiction of courts and the recognition and enforcement of the judgments and decrees of other courts. Only with respect to the question of the validity of marriage does choice of law loom large and, as a practical matter, the crucial issue in answering that question is often whether a prior divorce decree or annulment is invalid and open to attack.

In common with most American scholars concerned with choice of law, I have been preoccupied with choice-of-law problems arising in American courts out of conflicts between the laws of the states of our union. I have never been satisfied that these conflicts posed questions so different from the conflicts between national laws that the latter required a significantly different methodology. However, I have had to take account of four distinguishing factors.

One, of course, is the Constitution of the United States, with its Full Faith and Credit, Due Process, Equal Protection, and Privileges and Immunities Clauses—all potentially relevant to a choice-of-law ruling by a state court or legislature.[3] So loose is the Supreme Court's rein in exercising the powers to control

[3] The literature of the constitutional law of choice of law is extensive. Among recent contributions are Currie, "The Constitution and the Choice of Law: Governmental Interests and the Judicial Function," 26 U. CHI. L. REV. 9 (1958); Currie, "The Constitution and the 'Transitory' Cause of Action," 73 HARV. L. REV. 268 (1959); Currie & Schreter, "Unconstitutional Discrimination in the Conflict of Laws: Equal Protection," 28 U. CHI. L. REV. 1 (1960); Currie & Schreter, "Unconstitutional Discrimination in the Conflict of Laws: Privileges and Immunities," 69 YALE L.J. 1323 (1960), all in CURRIE, SELECTED ESSAYS ON THE CONFLICT OF LAWS (1963); Leflar, "Constitutional Limits on Free Choice of Law," 28 LAW & CONTEMP. PROB. 706 (1963); Weintraub, "Due Process and Full Faith and Credit Limitations on a State's Choice of Law," 44 IOWA L. REV. 449 (1959). For a valuable early treatment of the problem, see Dodd, "The Power of the Supreme Court to Review State Decisions in the Field of Conflict of Laws," 39 HARV. L. REV. 533 (1926).

state choice of law conferred on it by these clauses that I can complete these lectures with relatively few references to this source of supra-state authority. Nonetheless, it is important to keep in mind the fact that states which have been able to exercise judicial jurisdiction within the expanding bounds permitted by the Due Process Clause are armed by the Full Faith and Credit Clause with the authority to compel the recognition of their judgments within all the sister states and this regardless of how unpalatable to those states may be the purposes of the laws which the adjudicating state has chosen to apply.[4]

The authority thus to override objections based on a state's public policy would doubtless have been found intolerable but for the second distinguishing factor: the pressure exerted by the ever-growing cultural homogeneity of the nation, reinforced by the restraints imposed by the Constitution, to keep the laws of the several states and their exercise of legal power within generally accepted bounds of reasonableness and fairness. The occasions for a state to reject on grounds of public policy a claim based on the law of a sister state are, as a consequence, likely to be less frequent than are the corresponding occasions for a nation to reject on like grounds a claim arising in another nation since the social and economic institutions of the latter may be quite different from the forum's. Moreover, the fact that the Constitution's application to choice-of-law cases is seldom required may be due to the very existence of its inhibitions against unreasonable and discriminatory state action. They have doubtless operated to deter the states from indulgence in inequitable, self-regarding measures which a nation free of such restraints might not hesitate to adopt.

The third factor is in a sense the obverse of the second:

[4] Fauntleroy v. Lum, 210 U.S. 230 (1908). State judgments for unpaid taxes must be accorded "full faith and credit," Milwaukee County v. M. E. White Co., 296 U.S. 268 (1935), but, as yet, state judgments based on claims which the Supreme Court would consider "penal in the international sense" need not be. Huntington v. Attrill, 146 U.S. 657 (1892).

the legal hazards which arise because of the homogeneity that I have just noted. Though our nation is divided into fifty-one separate legal systems, our people act most the time as if they lived in a single one. In contrast, when people or their transactions cross national border lines, I suspect the legal significance of the action is much more likely to be observed. However, the consequence of our people's chronic failure to take account of differences in state laws means that any method of choice of law must be prepared either to protect people against the hazards of their heedless behavior or to impose harsh consequences upon them.[5] I suspect the European nations, especially those forming the Common Market, will have to face up to a comparable phenomenon as increasing intra-community trade and travel tends to erase the significance of national boundaries. I doubt that the current effort to harmonize national laws can do more than mitigate the difficulty.

The fourth factor may rest more on hope than experience. Be that as it may, I think it reasonable to assume that, in a closely-knit federation of states in which a common legal tradition coexists with innumerable common economic, social, and political needs, goals, and values, the courts will come increasingly to strive to accommodate the conflicting laws of the several states in ways that will optimize the working of the federation.[6] This potentiality has not as yet been tested:

[5] The method must also be alert to the risk that one of the parties to a transaction may be fully aware of the differences in the laws of the states involved and may be trying to exploit his superior knowledge unfairly.

[6] The existence of a federation gives rise at once to a special opportunity and to a special need for accommodation, but both the opportunity and the need exist within looser combinations of nations, and one may hope that a growing sense of world community will encourage a similar concern for accommodation between nations having no special ties to each other. Although the cases discussed and cited in these lectures are drawn almost exclusively from the great store of American precedents, I do not consider the methodology I am proposing as one which is appropriate and useful only in the context of the American or similar federal systems.

past doctrines have left little room for such an effort; the courts' methodology has not helped them to pursue this objective.

B. *The Task of Accommodating Conflicting State Laws*

An effort to "accommodate the conflicting laws of the several states in ways that will optimize the working of the federation" is easier to formulate as a goal than to translate into action. Accommodation itself is a rather euphemistic term which tends to conceal the fact that, while one state's law is being applied, another state's law is being rejected, and this despite the fact (which the postulated true conflict presupposes) that there is a reasonable basis for the rejected law's application. How I believe accommodation might best be achieved will be the burden of several of the succeeding chapters, but at this point it might be useful to note some negative points, four propositions that accommodation in the sense noted above does *not* mean, namely:

(1) Accommodation does not mean that in all cases involving interstate conflicts, federal or multistate considerations should be controlling. This would subvert one of the advantages of a federation over a centralized state. The courts of a member state should have freedom to advance the purposes of the state's own laws by applying them in certain cases where their application would be important to the realization of an important state purpose, even though this might be disadvantageous from a federal or multistate standpoint.

(2) Accommodation does not mean that all cases should be decided on the basis of the forum's preference for its own laws. This would subvert an advantage of a federation over a group of wholly independent states. The courts of a member state should recognize that the federation also has its purposes and that their realization may call for another state's law to be applied in situations where the claim of the forum's own law to application is not exigent.

(3) Accommodation does not mean that the problem of accommodating conflicting state laws in cases involving private claims is merely a problem of advancing or restraining state purposes: the claims of the parties to the litigation (and other persons who may be similarly situated) to fair treatment must be kept in mind. Choice between rules reflecting conflicting governmental purposes should not expose people to entrapment, surprise, or exploitation. To echo a phrase quoted earlier in these lectures, the court in formulating a rule or principle to govern its choice should seek one that will do "justice in the particular case."

(4) Accommodation does not mean that it should be viewed simply as an abstract goal, a general desideratum. On the contrary, I believe that, so far as practicable, the ways in which it should be achieved ought to be embodied in rules or principles. As Judge Griswold reminded the court in *Knickerbocker*,[7] a court making a choice of law should seek equal justice under law, and this implies an obligation to render judgment in accordance with a rule or principle. I suspect it is the fear that today's pioneering courts and scholars may be turning their backs on that obligation which leads to appeals, sometimes nostalgic, sometimes vehement, for a return to the orthodoxy of the first *Restatement*.

If we are to avoid slipping into a chaos of essentially meaningless *ad hoc* decisions[8] or, instead, reverting to our inherited

[7] See p. 20, *supra*.

[8] "Meaningless" in the sense that they do not provide guidance for either courts or counsel confronting subsequent cases which present analogous but not identical patterns of fact and law. The opportunity to impose generalizations on a considerable number of *ad hoc* choice-of-law decisions which are deficient in this respect is limited in choice of law by the scatter in the law-fact patterns presented by the cases. On the other hand, it does not follow that because a choice-of-law decision is *ad hoc*, it must therefore be meaningless in the sense noted. The court may develop the considerations which it has taken into account in resolving the specific issue in such fashion as to be helpful to a court that is later faced by a similar, if distinguishable, issue. The type of decision to be

apparatus of mechanical, jurisdiction-selecting rules, I believe courts and scholars must recognize that there is need for the development of rules and principles of appropriate breadth to resolve the hard cases, those cases in which legislative purposes are unclear or conflicting, cases which cannot be disposed of as posing either false conflicts or situations in which the claims of one state's law to application are plainly preponderant. We may have to accept the adequately articulated *ad hoc* decision as an interim substitute, but we should persevere in the search for rules or principles which would determine when the law of a state which served one purpose should be preferred to the law of another state which served a different purpose. Such a rule or principle of preference would, of course, have to delimit the range of circumstances under which the choice it called for would be made. Its protagonists would have to justify it not only as a desirable accommodation of the conflicting laws of the states involved but also as fair to the parties affected by the choice.

The choice which a principle of preference would call for would not be "result-selective," as Professor Hancock has used the term, that is, the choice of "the [domestic] rule that best accords with present-day ideas of justice and convenience."[9] Though, as I conceded long ago, one cannot expect judges in choice-of-law cases always to close their minds to a conviction that one of the competing domestic rules is intrinsically superior to the other, avoidance of that ground of preference, with its constant invitation to parochialism, should constitute

---

feared—and in the absence of more general guides, to be expected—is the one that simply lists contacts or invokes the policy of the forum without revealing the factors that have led the court to prefer the policy embodied in its law over the conflicting law of the other state involved in the controversy.

9 Hancock, "Three Approaches to the Choice-of-Law Problem: The Classificatory, The Functional, and the Result-Selective," in XXTH CENTURY COMPARATIVE AND CONFLICTS LAW 365, 374 (von Mehren, Nadelmann & Hazard, eds. 1962).

one of the chief claims to recognition of principles of preference.

Even though that kind of value judgment is avoided and the court refuses, say, to choose its strict liability law as against State Y's "due care" standard because it considers the latter standard outmoded, nonetheless principles of preference, operating as I have suggested, would involve other value judgments, and, as Professor Rheinstein has properly asked of such a value judgment, "From what point of view is it to be made?"[10] From the standpoint, for example, of the state imposing the regulation involved in a case? Or from the standpoint of the state allowing the activity in question to go unregulated?

If this question is posed by a case that involves a true, unavoidable conflict, we are prone to assume that, given the chance, each interested state will prefer its own law, even though the forum has no special reason to advance the purpose of its own law by applying it in the case before it. Therefore, both Professors Rheinstein[11] and Reese,[12] with Professor Currie in vehement dissent,[13] have suggested that the ideal forum to formulate a choice-of-law rule would be a disinterested one. But may not the interested forum's tendency to apply its own law simply attest the absence of a rational alternative?

Suppose the interested forum were to seek a broader base for its decision than the immediate conflict confronting it. Let us suppose, by way of example, that that conflict was between a rule of law in force in one state designed to protect a class of people who engage in a given type of activity and the law of the other state having no such protective rule. I

[10] Rheinstein, "How to Review a Festschrift," 11 AM. J. COMP. L. 632, 657 (1962).

[11] *Ibid.*

[12] Reese, "Conflict of Laws and the *Restatement Second*," 28 LAW & CONTEMPT. PROB. 679, 692 (1963).

[13] Currie, "The Disinterested Third State," 28 LAW & CONTEMPT. PROB. 754, 766 (1963).

suspect that the forum might seek a principle of preference that would apply to all protective laws of the same general type as that in issue. The court should inquire how the purposes of regulating states could best be accommodated to the purposes of nonregulating states and vice versa.

C. *The Supreme Court of State* X *Adopts a Principle of Preference*

Let me try to give greater concreteness to this suggestion by resorting once more to an imaginary case. This time I shall go behind the scenes and take you to the conference table in the Supreme Court of X. Unfortunately, I cannot call upon the same bench I previously conjured up since the jurists whom I exploited in my series of charitable immunity cases have not had occasion to engage in colloquies of the sort that I am about to present.[14]

In my new case the X tribunal has before it an appeal from a judgment applying a protective rule of X law to a transaction in Y involving an X resident, the defendant. If the transaction had been wholly domestic to X, the defendant would plainly have come within the class of persons the X rule is designed to protect. State Y has no such rule, and, if its local law had been applied below, the plaintiff, a Y resident, would have prevailed. This X rule is judge-made and of long standing, but the case law involving it has related only to X situations. Neither the briefs nor the researches of the justices' law clerks have revealed anything specific in the rule's history, purpose, or terms which throws light on its application to transactions outside X.

By the time the conferring justices have satisfied themselves

[14] For the reader of these lectures who will read the three opinions by the Oregon Supreme Court in the very recent case of Lilienthal v. Kaufmann, 395 P.2d 543 (1964), the task of re-creating a colloquy of the sort imagined here would not seem too difficult. Parochial counsels prevailed in that case. It is discussed in Chapter VII at p. 189 *infra*.

on this score, Mr. Justice A has grown impatient. "This case strikes me as an easy one," he says. "When our state has adopted a rule, we ought to apply it to any case which is connected with X. Here the defendant is one of our own citizens."

"But," objects Mr. Justice B, "we can't look just at our own rules. As you know, Y has a protective rule analogous to ours, but it covers transactions that we in X leave to the free choice of the parties. How would you decide a case growing out of a transaction which doesn't fall within the terms of our rule but does come within the terms of that Y rule? Ought we to say that our citizens when in Y should be free to disregard the Y rule?

"Don't we also have to consider the case of the Y citizen who comes over here to X and engages in the type of transaction that only Y regulates? If we decide the case now before us on the ground that we should apply X law to protect X citizens when they act in Y, doesn't consistency require us to apply Y law to protect Y citizens when they act in X? But, if so, isn't that going to undermine our policy of leaving these latter transactions free from regulation?"

At this Mr. Justice C remarks, "I'm inclined to think that, when a state has deliberately adopted a protective policy, that policy ought to be preferred, so I would apply whichever is the protective law not only in the case before us but in both of B's hypotheticals."

Mr. Justice D bridles at that. "You're being paternalistic as usual, C. My view is directly the opposite of yours; I'm for preferring freedom to regulation whenever they conflict."

"Aren't we forgetting the parties to these cases?" asks Mr. Justice E reprovingly. "The question in this case is not simply whether the State of X has a reason to be concerned; we have to try to be just to both plaintiff and defendant. Moreover, the question we must answer is not whether having protective laws is a better or worse policy than having none. X believes in some forms of protection; Y, in others. I'd like to find a rule that would make room for both kinds of policies and at the same time be fair to the parties."

At this Chief Justice F speaks up. "E is on the right track, and I don't think his objective is unrealistic. We need a rule or principle which will declare in what circumstances a state's protective policy will be preferred to the nonprotective policy of other states. Plainly such a rule ought to prevent the protective policy from being undermined by persons seeking to avoid it, and at the same time we must not stretch it so far as to impair a free enterprise policy whether it is in our own law or in our neighbors'. Finally, we have to do this in a way that will not take people by surprise and upset reasonable expectations."

Mr. Justice A mutters, "Counsel of perfection again."

"Not at all," returns the Chief Justice, who has come to expect A's *sotto voce* observations. "To begin with, I think we can properly decide that our law should not be applied in the case before us. This case grew out of a Y transaction. There was nothing evasive about the deal. To be sure, the plaintiff knew that the defendant was from X. Maybe he knew the X law; the record as to the actual transaction isn't as clear as one would have wished. But why shouldn't he be able to do business in his own state under its own rules without having to check the rules of X or any other state or country? Our protective system won't fall apart if we don't cover a deal of this sort. If out-of-state operations or even in-state evasions of our own rule had been a problem of any real consequence here, I think we would have turned up some facts evidencing a recognition of this hazard which might well have justified our taking a tougher stand. But we didn't."

"I'm sympathetic with what you and E are trying to work out," Mr. Justice B tells the Chief Justice, "but what you've just said seems to me only to call for a sensible interpretation—one might say, a restrained and moderate interpretation—of our common-law rule. We would interpret it not to apply to a Y transaction."

"What is more important," Mr. Justice D interjects rather tartly, "is that, if we did so, we'd be cutting down the reach of our own law and denying protection to our own citizen while getting nothing for it in return."

At this juncture, Mr. Justice E returns to the discussion: "If I have understood the Chief correctly," he says, "we would have accomplished very much more than simply restricting the application of an X rule. I take it that the Chief would have us rest our decision on a broad principle, one that would assert our intention to prefer protective rules of law to non-protective rules of the type we're dealing with here but only when the transaction involving such a rule was centered in a state having the protective rule in its law. Applying that principle to this case, we should not hold the X rule applicable and therefore should reverse."

Mr. Justice G is troubled. "This sounds like a throwback to the old *Restatement's* place-of-contracting rule. And doesn't it matter where the defendant was domiciled?"

The Chief Justice is patient. "As to your first point, G, the answer is, 'Clearly not.' The principle I am proposing is not designed to pick a law out of a hat by pulling on the string labeled with the proper 'contact' but rather to guide courts in determining when, as between conflicting protective and non-protective laws, we should prefer the protective.

"Surely a choice-of-law case should never turn on when and where, according to local rules of offer and acceptance, the last act necessary to make a contract had taken place. What does that circumstance have to do with the problem of protection versus no protection which is here at issue? It is the transaction which the parties have carried out—or which they had proposed to carry out—that gives rise to the claim for protection and hence to our problem. Ordinarily that transaction is centered in one state. If the transaction were rather evenly divided between two states, I suppose we should have to decide whether to prefer the protective rule to the nonprotective rule in that situation and elaborate our principle accordingly.

"Now, as for the residence of the parties, G, your question is a good one; in groping for the principle which I think we should formulate, I said nothing at all about that very relevant point. Suppose, for example, the transaction is squarely centered in X but the party who is claiming the benefit of X's protective rule lives in Y, having come into X on business. I think you would agree that he is not a proper beneficiary of the X rule. This is what the modern conflicts writers call a 'false conflict.' No, I think an X rule of this type is for the protection of people engaging in X-centered transactions if they live in X or, I suppose, if they live in other states having like protective laws. How settled their residence must be in X or in the other state is a specific which, in formulating the general principle, we don't now have to resolve. However, I would certainly question giving to a resident of Y the benefit of a protective X law simply because the Y resident had retained a technical domicil in X."

Mr. Justice C breaks the silence that ensues as the six justices digest Chief Justice F's remarks. "I find this explanation helpful, and I think what you propose is just, but here we sit, the Supreme Court of only one of the fifty United States, not to mention the hundred-odd nations that exist in the world around us. Outside of X, what difference does it make what our preferences may be? Our preferences reflect our own values. There is nothing to prevent the courts in Y or Z or in any other state from reflecting different values and disregarding our decisions completely. If we decide to apply Y law here, a Y court could still refuse to allow an X resident to recover from a Y resident for a transaction centered in X if the deal happened to fall within that protective rule of Y's which X has refused to adopt."

"Granted," replies the Chief Justice. "Except where the United States Supreme Court is prepared to intervene or the Congress or our own legislature, to prescribe a rule, each state supreme court is, of course, free to make its own rules. However, that puts a special responsibility on us to satisfy ourselves as to the justice of the choice-of-law rules and principles we declare. As to this, let me make two points:

"First, if we believe that the principle I have proposed is just and if we commit ourselves—as far as a *ratio decidendi* can commit a court—to be guided by that principle whether the next case involves an X law or a Y or Z law, or an X resident or a Y or Z resident, then I submit we have acted justly.

"Second, if what we have proposed has seemed reasonable to us, may it not seem reasonable to other courts? We have addressed ourselves to the real problem in our case and in all other cases like it. We have advanced a principle which is both definite and inclusive enough that other courts, including our trial courts, can apply it in a range of future cases without great difficulty. At the same time, the principle is sufficiently flexible that it can be adapted to meet those unusual facts which crop up now and then in choice-of-law cases. Surely, G, other courts have been as perplexed as we have been in trying to escape from mechanical choice-of-law rules that do not seem to be concerned with what really is at issue. Aren't those courts likely to be grateful for the guidance that a principle of preference can give them?

"Moreover, we have tried to retain no special advantage for X law or X residents. We have taken the Y law into account, and indeed in this case we would be giving effect to it. If the courts of Y and Z and other states can recognize the benefits to all states and their peoples which can be realized by making such accommodation mutual, then I should not be surprised to find them following in our footsteps. At least, this effort seems to me wiser than merely consulting what appears to work to the immediate advantage of an X policy or an X resident."

Mr. Justice D requires further assurance. "But you do agree that when the X legislature or even the X decisions show an intention that X law should be applied extraterritorially, then the duty of this court is to apply X's law, however much some of us may want to be accommodating to other states?"

"I agree," replies the Chief Justice, with the comfortable sensation that the battle has been won and the uncomfortable realization that a difficult and important opinion remains to be written.

D. A *Test for the Justice of a Principle of Preference*

The adoption by the X Supreme Court of the principle which its Chief Justice has broadly sketched would be a concrete manifestation of that oft-repeated aspiration that states in a federation or nations in the world community pursue the common good by recognizing the interests they share with the other states or nations, and, in so doing, exercise not only restraint in asserting their individual policies and laws but also liberality in accepting the different policies and laws of the other jurisdictions. Moreover, the courts proceeding in this way could claim that their course reflected the conception of justice as fairness that the Harvard philosopher, John Rawls, has been developing in a number of recent essays.

"A practice is just," writes Professor Rawls, "if it is in accordance with the principles which all who participate in it might reasonably be expected to propose or to acknowledge before one another when they are similarly circumstanced and required to make a firm commitment in advance without knowledge of what will be their peculiar condition."[15] Rawls

15 "Justice as Fairness," in JUSTICE AND SOCIAL POLICY 80, 98 (Olafson ed. 1961), reprinted from 67 PHILOS. REV. 164 (1958). In converting Professor Rawls' thesis to my own uses, I have taken the liberty of using his test to generate actual working principles of some degree of specificity.

further specifies that "each person participating in an institution or affected by it has an equal right to the most extensive liberty compatible with a like liberty for all," a specification with which I believe Chief Justice F's approach was consistent.[16]

This test of the justice of a practice Professor Rawls holds to be applicable to nations as well as to human beings,[17] but presumably, when a nation acts as surrogate for the people subject to its decision, as takes place when a court adopts a

---

The reader who examines Professor Rawls' work will note that he uses his "analytical construction" of mutually self-interested, rational and approximately equal persons proposing for unanimous acceptance principles for judging their institutions in order to generate only the most general principles, i.e., the principle of equal liberty and the principle that inequalities must work to everyone's advantage. These general principles are then applied as criteria of the justice of institutions. Professor Rawls, it appears, requires the participants in his analytical construction to remain at this level of abstraction so that none can hope to provide any special advantages for himself by proposing a principle favorable to his known position. The principles are so general and a firm commitment is required so that "no one can be given the opportunity to tailor the canons . . . to fit his own special condition, and then to discard them when they no longer suit his purposes." *Id.* at 87. See also Rawls, "Constitutional Liberty and the Concept of Justice," in JUSTICE, NOMOS VI 98 (Friedrich & Chapman, eds. 1963); "The Sense of Justice," 72 PHILOS. REV. 281 (1963). The application of his text to the generation of specific choice-of-law principles which I have undertaken is, I submit, justified by reason of the approximation of the forum's situation in that problem to the situation of the participants in Professor Rawls' "analytical construction" as they are forced to choose general principles of justice. The court knows, of course, how the state in which it sits and the parties would be affected by the application of the principle to the case before it, but the principle relates to a category of cases which in the future will or will not lead to the application of the forum's law, since, as the principles in the next chapter indicate, the results they work will depend on the varying law-fact patterns which a succession of cases over time are certain to yield.

[16] See Rawls, *supra* note 15, in JUSTICE, NOMOS VI at 100. The "persons" in the application of Professor Rawls' test which I am seeking to make are the states which, through their courts, are participants in the choice-of-law process.

[17] *Id.* at 101.

principle of choice of law in a case before it, the proposition that is advanced must be formulated with a view to its fairness to the individuals affected by that action as well as to the states or nations whose interests are involved. The test does not depend on the mutual acceptance in fact of the principles proposed or acknowledged, but the character of the principles likely to be evolved in conformity to the Rawls specifications should be conducive to such acceptance. The "firm commitment" of which he writes would, of course, have to be diluted in the complex field of judgment in which courts operate; as Chief Justice F conceded, a decision based on such principles could at best have no greater weight than the *ratio decidendi* of any precedent. Certainly, in the field of choice of law, such principles, if rigidly conceived and applied, would not survive. However, Professor Rawls's test of a just practice suggests an answer to Professor Rheinstein's question: "From what point of view are value judgments to be made?" The answer, I take it, would be the following: "From the point of view of any forum—the more interested the better—which undertakes to propose, and to adhere to, a principle of preference in the hope, but not on the condition, that it will provide a mutually acceptable scheme of accommodation for laws of the same general type as are involved in the case before it."

In referring to states proposing and states accepting principles of preference, I am not, of course, employing operational terms. Reduced to such terms, what I am suggesting is only that a court seeking to ground a choice of law on a principle of preference make plain its position in its opinion. It would thereby both attest its readiness to recognize the claims of other states' laws whenever the principle worked to their advantage and also aid judges of other courts in employing the principle if it should appeal to them as offering a fair and sensible solution. Other courts, of course, may have the same opportunity with respect to a different but comparable set of conflicting laws. One of the benefits derived from a principle's breadth is that cases contributing to its development can be expected to recur with some frequency—in marked contrast to the long intervals that are likely to elapse between reported decisions involving a conflicts rule applicable to an issue that has been narrowly defined.

E. *The Origin of (My) Principles of Preference*

Before I turn to the seven principles I am submitting for your consideration in the next chapters, I believe I should explain their source. Those principles, as well as my belief that other affirmative principles like them may be developed, have sprung from my own efforts to arrive at choices between conflicting laws and to provide a rational basis for each choice. My forum has been the classroom. In contention or in cooperation with my students, I have sought reasonable grounds for preferring one state's law to another's in situations where their conflict could not be held false or readily avoided. Often our starting point was one of these recent decisions in which a court has broken away from conventional rules but, with instinctive caution, has held its *ratio decidendi* close to the particular facts of the event or transaction. Sometimes the classroom solution had to be limited to those particular facts, but, for a substantial fraction of the remaining cases, the solution that seemed "right" rested on considerations that were broader than the particular laws in conflict or the particular circumstances of the controversy. This characteristic meant that the considerations which justified a particular solution in one situation would serve to justify a comparable solution in another. In short, they could be generalized into principles.

This was not the goal of the classroom analyses; it has been the result. I would doubtless have viewed this broadening tendency askance when, back in 1933, I called for "the development of standards for the evaluation of the facts" which the new nonjurisdiction-selecting choice-of-law rules would render significant.[18] We were very fact-minded in the 30's and

[18] Cavers, "A Critique of the Choice-of-Law Problem," 47 HARV. L. REV. 174, 196 (1933).

liked even our principles narrow. However, I have come gradually to the belief that it is this very breadth of application which makes it possible to invoke a principle in order to prefer one result to another (the effect of preferring, in the circumstances, to advance the purpose of one kind of law to that of another) without having to demonstrate that one state's domestic rule is superior to the other's.

As I have reviewed the principles I have formulated and the facts that have seemed to me significant as connecting links, I have found in my thinking what I suspect some of you will consider a territorialist bias. Today the tendency is to lean in the opposite direction. An inquiry into the purposes of conflicting laws—and the formulation of principles of preference necessitates that inquiry—leads naturally to an emphasis on the persons on whom laws have their impact when, at least, it is mainly the interests of the parties to a relationship or a controversy that appear to be at stake. It becomes easy in such situations for one to ascribe to the state or states with which those persons are connected a paternalistic concern for them, wherever they may be, thereby rendering the place of their actions "fortuitous" and even irrelevant to the process of choice.

To quote anew Judge Cardozo's words in *Loucks v. Standard Oil Co. of New York*, written to reject a contention which he found inconsistent with "the territorial system": "The suggestion sounds like an echo of the theory of the statute personal, a body of national law which the citizen carries about with him."[19] I believe that there are circumstances where the citizen may properly, if metaphorically, be considered to carry a law of his state about with him. However,

[19] 224 N.Y. 99, 109, 120 N.E. 198, 201 (1918). The "suggestion" to which Judge Cardozo alluded was "that if [in a wrongful death action against a New York corporation for a death caused in Pennsylvania] the defendant [had been] a nonresident the restriction [on damages in New York law] would not apply." The court applied the New York ceiling. Wooden v. Western N.Y. & P.R.R., 126 N.Y. 10, 26 N.E. 1050 (1891).

I also agree with Judge Wyzanski that "departures from the territorial view of torts ought not to be lightly undertaken,"[20] and I would not confine his admonition to the law of torts. Our states and nations are territorially organized; the legal order that each has created impinges on actions and affairs which, in a very high proportion of all instances, are wholly domestic to the state where they take place. To withdraw like actions and affairs from the reach of domestic law because the persons participating in them are not domestic to the state causes a wrench away from customary attitudes toward law that may lead the disadvantaged party to "regard the distinction as involving a personal discrimination against him rather than as a step toward comity between states," to quote Judge Wyzanski once more.[21]

The hazard is accentuated by two other considerations. First, the attribution to a state of a purpose to protect or otherwise advance the interests of its inhabitants which would lead to the application of that state's law to out-of-state events or transactions is a determination that may often be questionable; *ex hypothesi*, we are not here dealing with cases in which the lawmaker has revealed a relevant purpose. Second, in the United States today as distinguished from, say, the Italian cities of the fourteenth century, the Dutch states of the seventeenth century, or even the nations of contemporary Europe,[22] the

[20] Gordon v. Parker, 83 F. Supp. 40 (D. Mass. 1949).

[21] *Id.* at 43. The prevention of too gross a difference between the law applicable in the forum by virtue of a choice-of-law rule and the law applicable to domestic cases has been suggested by Professor Wilhelm Wengler as a function of the "public policy" doctrine in choice-of-law cases; the author's extensive discussion is under the subheading, "Public Policy as a Manifestation of the Principle of Equality." See Wengler, "The Significance of the Principle of Equality in the Conflict of Laws," 28 LAW & CONTEMP. PROB. 822, 851 (1963).

[22] My colleague, Professor Henry J. Steiner, finds much more frequent justification for the use of nationality as the basis for the application of the national's law in international choice-of-law problems than he finds for the corresponding use of domicil in interstate choice-of-law problems.

individual's link with a particular community and the identification of his rights and privileges with its laws is attenuated not only by our ever-accelerating mobility but also, I suspect, by the need for a considerable sophistication to enable a citizen to differentiate the state laws that govern him as the citizen of a state from the federal laws that govern him as a citizen of the United States.

F. *The Form and Use of the Principles*

Although, despite these considerations, I believe territorial law should yield to the personal law in circumstances in which the case for preferring the latter is strong, there remains a sufficient territorial cast to my seven principles that the results which certain of them would indicate would not differ in many cases from those called for by that document which, for a generation of its critics, has epitomized mechanical rules, the first *Restatement*. This circumstance may render it wise for me to add some words of explanation as to the form into which I have cast my seven principles. In terms and in style, they are painfully reminiscent of the *Restatement* black letter. I have adopted this mode of presentation for expository purposes on this occasion and not with the hope that courts or even commentators would also employ it in case they too sought to formulate such principles. Moreover, despite the formality with which these principles are stated and their false air of precision, I see them only as guides for decision, leaving ample room for independent judgment to any courts that resorted to them. All of them contain terms that are obviously in need of a gloss which I have not attempted to provide save to a very limited extent.

The seven examples I have provided are illustrative; they do not form a system. The fact that a situation falls short of conditions specified in a given principle does not mean that a contrary choice of law must be made; the question is left open for decision on a narrower base. Its solution could lead to the formulation of another principle, but the court might prefer to leave the problem to *ad hoc* determination until a trend in the relevant case law could be ascertained. Another possibility, indeed, a probability, is that, in the course of decision, the principles which I have stated in very broad terms—again, more for purposes of exposition than from conviction—would be subjected to fission as distinctions were drawn on grounds that I have not attempted to identify and consider. This process of fission could continue for some time before what had begun as a principle would be converted into a set of specific rules, although it is certainly possible that now and then such a rule might be declared to govern a particular situation within the compass of the original principle or one of its successors.

I must reiterate that the principles I am submitting and others having the same function are intended to be invoked only when a question of choice has not been foreclosed by a valid statute of the forum and when it is evident from an inspection of the laws in conflict, in the light of their purposes and the circumstances of the case, that the conflict is neither false nor readily to be avoided. This fact will, I hope, be recalled by those who, as they read the principles, may feel that they defeat that particularization of inquiry into laws and facts which some have regarded as a virtue of the position I presented in my 1933 article. Hopefully, the most fruitful place for particularization would be in advance of the employment of the principles. Scrutiny of the particular legal policies and facts then either might lead to a conclusion that the apparent conflict was false or might afford grounds justifying the non-application of one of the conflicting laws. It is my belief that opportunities for thus disposing of conflicts without recourse to principles of preference are likely to be less frequent than some may suppose. If their calculation were to prove more accurate than mine, this would not invalidate the principles or condemn them to desuetude; it would mean only that their contribution to the choice-of-law problem, quantitatively viewed, was less than arguably might have been expected.

Accompanying each principle is a comment noting some of

the reasons that lead me to believe that it might achieve mutual acceptance if ever courts were moved to seek principles of this sort. I have also discussed some cases which may help to put flesh on the principles' bare-boned statements, and in some instances, I have commented on the disposition of cases that do not fall within a principle.

Now for the principles themselves.

VI

PRINCIPLES OF PREFERENCE EXEMPLIFIED: TORTS

I have drawn on the field of tort law for the five principles of preference that I shall present and discuss in this chapter. As these lectures have already disclosed, that field is one in which the new methodologies of choice of law have been manifesting themselves clearly, perhaps most clearly. Tort cases have provided occasions aplenty for the classroom controversies in which, as I have just confessed, these principles had their origin. Moreover, the difficult problems of choice that the tort cases, real or imagined, so often present lead me to trust that you will keep in mind the limitations on the use of these principles that I have indicated in the preceding pages.

1. *Where the liability laws of the state of injury set a* higher *standard of conduct or of financial protection against injury than do the laws of the state where the person causing the injury has acted or had his home, the laws of the state of injury should determine the standard and the protection applicable to the case, at least where the person injured was not so related to the person causing the injury that the question should be relegated to the law governing their relationship.*

This is one of the propositions that may be set down to the territorialist bias I mentioned in the previous chapter. I accept a territorialist attribution here without apology. Our territorially organized governments undertake by means of laws and regulations governing conduct to provide for "the general security," to use Dean Pound's term,[1] to safeguard the health and safety of people and property within their bounds. As a second line of defense against violators, they prescribe modes of financial protection for those endangered. These range from providing a cause of action for damages to elaborate schemes for compulsory insurance and even government indemnity.

This system of physical and financial protection would be impaired if a person who enters the territory of a state were not subject to its laws requiring conformity to legally prescribed health and safety standards. Impairment would also result if actions outside the state but having foreseeable effects within it were not also subject to its law. A visitor or outsider violating the rules of the state of injury may be liable to criminal sanctions. If the state's plan of financial protection for the victims of violations of its standards includes the civil liability of the violator, the fact that he would be held to a lower standard of care or of damages back in the state where he had his home (or in the state where he acted) or, indeed, the fact that he enjoyed an immunity there, all would ordinarily seem matters of little consequence to the state of the injury. (I refer to the defendant's "home" with a facility that conceals the slipperiness of the term and ignores the fact that many defendants are corporate. However, I shall soon take further note of these trouble-making facts.)

The need to maintain physical and financial protection against injury-causing conduct is not the particular concern of one or a few states or a need relating to one or a few special laws. All states experience this need and do so with respect to all—or nearly all—of their laws establishing standards of conduct and remedies to protect against physical and financial haz-

[1] Quoted by Judge Friendly from POUND, INTRODUCTION TO THE PHILOSOPHY OF LAW 87 (1953 ed.), with reference to a rule imposing strict liability on manufacturers. George v. Douglas Aircraft Co., 332 F.2d 73, 76 (2d Cir. 1964).

ards. Therefore, if general recognition is given to this principle, all states will on occasion benefit by it.

The defendant who is held to the higher standard is not an apt subject for judicial solicitude. He cannot fairly claim to enjoy whatever benefits a state may offer those who enter its bounds and at the same time claim exemption from the burdens. If he has not entered the state but has caused harm within it by his act outside it, then, save perhaps where the physical or legal consequences of his action were not foreseeable, it is equally fair to hold him to the standards of the state into which he sent whatever harmful agent, animal, object, or message caused the injury.

This principle extends to so many cases that illustrations may seem superfluous. However, let me instance one: a hypothetical variant of the much-discussed California case of *Grant v. McAuliffe*.[2] In that casebook favorite, the California Supreme Court, *per* Traynor, J., applied California law to permit the survival of a personal injury action brought by a Californian against the personal representative of a deceased Californian. The injury had occurred in Arizona, and, by Arizona law, personal injury actions do not survive the tortfeasor's death. The decision, criticized as a departure from the place-of-injury rule,[3] was vigorously defended by Professor Currie who pointed out that Arizona had no interest in applying its nonsurvival rule, since it was not the domicil of the deceased tortfeasor nor was it administering his assets in this action.[4] Hence, the conflict was false.

My hypothetical case changes the tortfeasor's domicil to

[2] 41 Cal. 2d 859, 264 P.2d 944 (1953).

[3] See Sumner, "Choice of Law Governing Survival of Action," 9 HASTINGS L.J. 128 (1958), based on a study for the California Law Revision Commission recommending corrective legislation.

[4] See Currie, "Survival of Action: Adjudication versus Automation in the Conflict of Laws," 10 STAN. L. REV. 205, 209, 227-28 (1958), in CURRIE, SELECTED ESSAYS ON THE CONFLICT OF LAWS (hereinafter cited as SELECTED ESSAYS) 128, 132, 151-52 (1963).

Arizona and the place of the accident to California. The resulting conflict is a true one: obviously there is a reasonable basis to apply Arizona law to protect (in theory at least) the estate of its domiciliary from personal injury claims. I should hope, however, that if an Arizona court were to be seised of the case and its statutes permitted, it would refuse to provide a haven in which the beneficiaries of its deceased citizen could be sheltered from claims for the injuries he had done in California and for which California's financial protection plan would hold a decedent's estate liable. Californians should not be put in jeopardy in California simply because an Arizonian, mounted in one of those death-dealing four-wheeled mechanical contrivances that are made in Michigan, had come into California from a state whose law provides a lower standard of financial protection than does California's.[5]

A harder case may be conceived where the defendant's conduct causing an injury in State X took place in State Y which, to advance interests of its own, had declared such conduct privileged. To be more concrete, suppose the defendant, A, in the course of a political campaign in Y, had libelled B, an X public official. Suppose, further, that the libel was absolutely privileged in Y whereas X had granted the defendant only the qualified privilege which the United States Supreme Court regards as his constitutional minimum.[6] Would

[5] Professor Currie, in a comment on this hypothetical case, "The Disinterested Third State," 28 Law & Contemp. Prob. 754, 759-61 (1963), examined a series of possible "interests" in California which might justify an Arizona court in recognizing the California interest as superior to its own. He found none, nor was his failure surprising since he conceived the problem in terms no broader than the particular statutes in conflict and assumed no concern on the part of the Arizona court to find a rational basis for accommodation. Nevertheless, he concedes that an Arizona court might have accorded its law a "moderate and restrained interpretation." But why? Even an *ad hoc* decision should have a rationale. And his preference for the *ad hoc* decision over a decision based on a broader principle is rested on a fear that legislative correction would be inhibited by the latter pronouncement. This concern seems artificial and implausible.

[6] New York Times Co. v. Sullivan, 376 U.S. 254 (1964).

this principle of preference operate to render A liable for his broadcast by calling for the application of X law, malice being provable? Probably a court in Y would never reach this principle, finding its own rules applicable "by construction and interpretation." An X court might impose liability. On the other hand, it might well conclude that an exception to the principle should be drawn whenever the state where the defendant had acted had seen fit to encourage the free exercise of conduct of the kind in question by granting absolute protection against liability. The X court might therefore impose a "moderate and restrained interpretation" on its own law of defamation and deny liability.[7] However, a principle delimiting the bounds of such an exception could scarcely be formulated at this time; particularization would doubtless be necessary here.

Suppose, in a personal injury case, that the person injured is a visitor from out of state. In his suit he is seeking the protection of the higher standard of conduct or of financial protection of the state in which he has been injured. Should the out-of-state plaintiff be denied the benefit of the state of injury's laws to the extent that these are more protective to plaintiffs than those to which he would have been subject at home?

Ordinarily an easy negative can be given in answer to this question when a standard of conduct or a basis of liability is involved, since their regulatory function can properly be invoked to justify their application whenever the defendant acts in the regulating state. But when the measure of damages is at

[7] The circumstances of the particular case could easily be controlling. Thus, if B's activities to which A had maliciously referred had had no bearing on public affairs in Y but had been singled out by A because of personal animosity and B's party affiliation, there would be little reason for X to give recognition to the privilege. But, of course, B's official activities might have been related to Y affairs. Incidentally, the first RESTATEMENT, § 382 (2), recognized the defense of privilege by the law of the place of the defendant's conduct, a surprising departure from its pattern of jurisdiction-selecting rules.

issue and it does not purport to be punitive, one may ask wherein would the policy of the state of injury be advanced by according the plaintiff a more liberal recovery than that to which he would have been entitled if he had been hurt in his home state. Indeed, where the recovery permitted by the latter state's rule would assure funds enough to meet medical and hospital costs in the state of injury, then, arguably, the state of injury has no interest whatever in providing its more liberal compensation to the out-of-state plaintiff at the expense of its own citizen, the defendant.

This contention neglects the consideration that the financial protection a state has prescribed, being a part of its provision for the general security, is in part a sanction for wrongfully causing harm. As a consequence its purposes include elements of deterrence and retribution even though it may be couched in essentially compensatory terms. When the laws of the state of injury are viewed in this light, the restrictive laws of the plaintiff's home state tend to fade into irrelevance. Furthermore, at least as important a consideration is concern for equal protection of the laws. Ought not the injured stranger to receive the same measure of protection that the citizen is accorded? I submit that an extension of the principle to support his claim is amply justified—and may be constitutionally requisite.[8]

As the qualification I have appended to this principle of

[8] An affirmative answer to this question seems called for not only by the Equal Protection Clause but, in the case of the citizen of a sister state, by the Privileges and Immunities Clause. Clear-cut cases are not easily found. Careful scrutiny of the case law under the latter clause led to the following conclusion in Currie & Schreter, "Unconstitutional Discrimination and the Conflict of Laws: Privileges and Immunities," 69 YALE L.J. 1323, 1377 (1960), in CURRIE, SELECTED ESSAYS 445, 508 (1963): ". . . on the basis of the situations that have been considered it appears that, when the law of a state provides benefits for its residents generally, the same benefits should be extended to citizens of other states unless there is some substantial reason, in addition to the fact that the governmental interests of the state do not require extension of the benefit to foreigners, for limiting the benefit to residents." In a companion

preference reveals, there may be some few cases where it should not be applied, where the parties to the litigation have such a relationship to each other and to the state in which they live that the application of its laws to certain issues in a damage suit between them may be justified. The case for this is strongest when that state's laws have specific purposes that would be frustrated by the application of the laws of the state of injury. This, however, is a problem to be considered below under my fifth suggested principle of preference.[9]

---

article, the authors state: "It will hardly be doubted that a rule denying the benefits of the wrongful death statute in the three cases supposed [involving, respectively, a decedent who is a citizen of a sister state, a resident alien, and a nonresident alien] solely on the ground that the deceased was an alien or a nonresident, would violate the equal protection clause." Currie & Schreter, "Unconstitutional Discrimination in the Conflict of Laws: Equal Protection," 28 U. CHI. L. REV. 1, 12 (1960), in CURRIE, SELECTED ESSAYS 526, 538 (1963).

Should a distinction be drawn when the defendant is also from out of state? A divided Court of Appeals recently held in a diversity case from Indiana that failure to prove dependence, as required by Indiana law, barred recovery by Indiana beneficiaries of a Kentuckian killed in Illinois by Indiana defendants. Indiana was said to have "a more significant relationship on the issue of recovery," Illinois, to lack "a sufficiently substantial interest." Watts v. Pioneer Corn Co. Inc., 342 F. 2d 617, 620 (7th Cir. 1965). One judge concurred, holding Illinois law applicable but finding it the same as Indiana's. Kentucky law, not mentioned by the court, does not require dependency. KY. REV. STAT. ANN. § 411. 130 (Baldwin, 1963). The beneficiaries' domicil does not seem an apt basis for protection that properly should be viewed as having been accorded the decedent. See Currie, "The Constitution and the 'Transitory' Cause of Action," 73 HARV. L. REV. 36, 46 (1959), in SELECTED ESSAYS 283, 293. Doubtless the court's choice could withstand constitutional attack.

[9] See p. 177, *infra*. An example of a case where application of the law of the state of injury would have frustrated a purpose of the state of the relationship is Stacy v. Greenberg, 9 N.J. 390, 88 A.2d 619 (1952): an action by employees against fellow employees for injuries sustained in an automobile accident in New Jersey through which the parties were passing en route to New York, their place of employment. The New York workmen's compensation act, to which all were subject, specifically bars actions against fellow employees. The New Jersey court applied the New York law.

2. *Where the liability laws of the state in which the defendant acted and caused an injury set a* lower *standard of conduct or of financial protection than do the laws of the home state of the person suffering the injury, the laws of the state of conduct and injury should determine the standard of conduct or protection applicable to the case, at least where the person injured was not so related to the person causing the injury that the question should be relegated to the law governing the relationship.*

Here again we are concerned with a state's provision of standards of conduct and financial protection for people within its bounds. However, now we must recognize that the state's plan has been drawn, not merely for the benefit of the endangered public, but also with concern for the people whose activities may cause the harm.[10] Therefore, the state has refrained from imposing what its lawmakers would view as an unreasonably exacting standard of conduct or an unduly burdensome duty to provide financial protection upon people and corporations engaged in activities within the state.[11]

Consider the response that would be accorded a proposal that was the opposite of this principle if it were advanced against a person living in the state of injury on behalf of a

[10] A state's law may reflect, for example, a belief that recoveries of damages, if unlimited or permitted to include certain speculative elements, would unfairly allocate the economic burden of accidents, that the right to sue certain categories of defendants, such as charities, spouses, and parents, should be denied entirely or allowed, as in the case of auto guests, only where the defendant's conduct has been seriously below the usual norm.

[11] Occasionally, as in the case of the privilege accorded critics of public officials, a law's purpose may be to free conduct from the risk of liability in order to encourage desired behavior. However, when liability is based on a higher degree of fault, this is seldom on the supposition that activity involving a lower degree of fault is to be encouraged. *Cf.* Halpern, J., dissenting, in Babcock v. Jackson, 17 App. Div. 2d 694, 696, 230 N.Y.S.2d 114, 118 (1962); Cavers, "Comment on *Babcock v. Jackson*, A Recent Development in Conflict of Laws," 63 COLUM. L. REV. 1212, 1219, 1226 (1963).

person coming there from a state having a higher standard of care or of financial protection. The proposal thus advanced would require the community the visitor entered to step up its standards of behavior for his greater safety or lift its financial protection to the level to which he was accustomed. Such a proposal would be rejected as unfair. By entering the state or nation, the visitor has exposed himself to the risks of the territory and should not expect to subject persons living there to a financial hazard that their law had not created.

The principle is one that I believe would be likely to achieve acceptance, apart from its coincidence with conventional doctrine. Indeed, this conclusion might have seemed too obvious for mention but for the spreading notion that a state as forum has the duty of asserting its own policies for the benefit of its own citizens, regardless of the claims of other states and the people who rely on their laws.[12] Though each state would re-

[12] Such a decision may have been reached in a case applying the New York no-ceiling rule to a wrongful death caused in a Massachusetts automobile accident killing a New Yorker, the home of the defendant not being disclosed. Bopp v. Bell, 18 App. Div. 2d 914 (1963) (one-line opinion citing *Kilberg;* facts noted above stated in Gore v. Northeast Airlines, Inc., 222 F. Supp. 50, 54 (S.D.N.Y. 1963)). The problem was resolved in June 1965 in a case brought in the District of Columbia by American plaintiffs for the wrongful deaths of 18 U.S. Navy bandsmen by a Brazilian plane which crashed into the Navy plane in which the bandsmen were flying. The Brazilian ceiling (100,000 cruzeiros) amounted to $170. Tramontana v. S.A. Empresa de Viacao Aerea Rio Grandense, 33 U.S.L. WK. 2666 (D.C. Cir. 1965). The court refused to apply the law either of the forum or of the decedent's domicil.

In view of the past fidelity of the French courts to the *lex loci delicti,* it is surprising to find the 1st Chamber of the Court of Appeal of Paris invoking "*le but social affirmé par le loi*" and "*lois de police*" to justify as a matter of "*l'ordre public international français*" the imposition of "*dommage moral*" pursuant to French law on a French defendant who had negligently killed the French plaintiff's son in an auto collision in Germany, the law of which would permit only the recovery of economic damage. Kieger v. Amigues, (1963) 2 Gazette du Palais 355, questioned in a note in 91 J. DROIT INT. 103 (1964) by the Editor-in-chief, Professor Berthold Goldman. The Court of Appeal, unlike the court below ((1963) 1 Gazette du Palais 373), did not mention the defendant's

nounce the possibility of applying its higher standards for the benefit of its citizens who were injured outside the state, it would gain in the protection accorded its citizens by preventing their exposure at home to the more exacting laws of another state.

I have a favorite hypothetical case to illustrate this principle, a variation of the famous *Kilberg* case[13] where, as you may recall, New York refused to apply the Massachusetts $15,000 ceiling on wrongful death damages in a suit brought by a New Yorker's personal representative for the decedent's death in an airplane crash on Nantucket. The New York court viewed the Massachusetts ceiling as contrary to its strong public policy, embodied in its constitutional ban on such ceilings.

In my hypothetical, a Nantucket bank president, while bicycling to work one morning, carelessly runs down and kills a New York tourist. Some months later, the victim's executor sues the bank president in New York for $100,000, getting service upon the banker when he was attending a convention at the Waldorf. In my opinion, the New York court should limit the damages recoverable to the Massachusetts ceiling.[14] Inhabitants of Massachusetts should not be put in jeopardy of liabilities exceeding those which Massachusetts law creates

---

nationality; apparently the result would have been the same had he been a German. Yet the Court prefaces its holding by affirming that, "whatever the nationality of the parties to a case, it is the law of the place where the wrongful actionable fact had its effect that governs the conditions of civil responsibility, as well as the mode and extent of the reparation to which the victim can lay claim." (1963) 2 Gazette du Palais 1963, p. 356.

13 Kilberg v. Northeast Airlines, Inc., 9 N.Y. 2d 34, 172 N.E.2d 526 (1961).

14 I rest my view on the principle of preference, not on the circumstance that the case did not involve airplane travel. Thus far, the New York Court of Appeals has not extended the Kilberg rule to other types of accidents, and the hypothetical case above might be rested on this fact. But *cf.* Davenport v. Webb, 11 N.Y.2d 392, 183 N.E.2d 902 (1962); see Bopp v. Bell, *supra* note 12.

simply because persons from states with higher standards of financial protection choose to visit there.

I may have picked an easy set of facts. Let me pose a much harder one. The bicyclist who ran down and killed the New York tourist was not the local banker but another tourist, a lady who is also from New York. She is sued in New York and pleads the Massachusetts statute.

Here one cannot say that she had molded her mode of behavior and her insurance plans in conformity to Massachusetts requirements. If she was aware of the content of any body of law (road signs apart), it was probably New York law. Maybe, if asked what law she thought she was subject to in Nantucket, she would have said, "Massachusetts law"; maybe not.

Surely this New York lady could have relied on the Massachusetts view of what constitutes negligent cycling if that were more indulgent than the New York view. A lady coming to the Bay State should be free to ride as Bay Staters ride. Moreover, if the decision I proposed in the case of the Nantucket banker is correct, then, in the lady's encounters with Massachusetts people, she is to be denied the benefit of her own state's higher standard of financial protection. But should she be subjected to its burden?

I submit that, if the New York lady had run down a native of Nantucket, his executor should not be free to recover unlimited damages against her in either Massachusetts or New York. It is fair to hold him to the standards of the community of which he is a part. His home state has no affirmative policy to assure full protection to him and his dependents. Fairness also requires that the visitor be given the benefit of the defense available to Massachusetts citizens.[15] However, when we turn

[15] In the state of injury at least, the Constitution may require this result. See the position reported in note 8, *supra*. The denial of a "benefit" to the out-of-state party may take the form of the denial of a defense. If Massachusetts is constitutionally required to apply its own

to the case brought by the New York tourist's executor, we confront the New York lady with a claim based on the law of a state which has a full-recovery policy, one to which it is deeply committed.

A "*Personal Law*" *of Torts? The Case Between Two Out-of-State Parties*

This hypothetical case, an action brought against one New Yorker for the death in Massachusetts of another New Yorker, confronts the conflicts scholar today—and will confront some courts tomorrow—with a choice between two difficult routes: one calls for the pursuit of an analysis based on the purposes of the laws in conflict which threatens to create what a statutist would call a "personal law" of torts, with an attendant host of complexities; the other would beat a full retreat to territoriality, to the application of the territorial law even when doing so seems to serve no purpose of that law. Between these alternative routes, no obvious *via media* appears.

There are a few possible modes of escape that merit consideration. I propose to examine in some detail both the dilemma and ways of avoiding it. This should throw light on the difficulties that one must anticipate as one moves away from those situations in which the purposes of state laws are open to reasonably clear identification and the conditions that lead one or the other purpose to be preferred can also be identified with some confidence. There remains a residue of hard cases, of which tort cases involving two out-of-state parties contribute more than their share. Yet their existence does not, I submit, impugn the validity or destroy the usefulness of those principles of preference which can be formulated for the more common, more tractable problems.

---

law, it would seem anomalous for New York to be free to disregard it. If the plaintiff as well as the defendant came from a no-ceiling state, the difficult choice-of-law problem discussed below would be created, but the refusal to apply the local ceiling would not seem open to constitutional attack.

Before seeking ways of escape from the dilemma, let us take a good look at the first horn: rigorous insistence on making the choice which will advance the purpose of the law chosen without frustrating or seriously impairing the purpose of the law that is rejected. New York has a measure of damages for wrongful death which is designed to give full financial protection to the dependents of New Yorkers wrongfully killed.[16] The Massachusetts law limiting recovery does not reflect a preference that widows and orphans should be denied full recovery; plainly its law seeks only to shield defendants from exaggerated claims. Therefore, in a case where both decedent and defendant are from New York, New York should not adopt a self-denying principle that would limit the protection it would accord the decedent's dependents while at the same time holding the New York defendant to no greater financial risk than he has customarily assumed in his New York activities. This analysis leads to the conclusion that the case of the two out-of-state parties poses a false conflict, and, if this is so, then there is no occasion to invoke the principle since, as was noted above,[17] the principles of preference do not come into play in false-conflict cases.

This analysis is most persuasive when presented in support of unlimited recovery for wrongful death—and not merely because the ceiling appears unfair and anachronistic in these days when far higher recoveries are a commonplace in actions for personal injuries that create no greater financial hardships. Being a rule of damages, the statutory maximum is not a primary rule to regulate conduct and so does not trench on the

[16] One obvious purpose of the New York law is to accord financial protection to New Yorkers by assuring them that, in the event of their wrongful death, full compensation will be available to their dependents. Its realization does not require that the dependents themselves be New Yorkers. Surely the requirement to this effect in Gore v. Northeast Airlines, Inc., *supra* note 12, is erroneous, especially denying recovery under *Kilberg*, *supra* note 13, to the New York decedent's widow because she moved her domicil to another state two months after the accident.

[17] See p. 137, *supra*.

domain ordinarily reserved to the state of injury. If the route we are pursuing stopped at this point, the specter of a "personal law" of torts would arouse relatively little concern. But does not the logic of the analysis carry much further?

Consider rules establishing bases of liability and determining what conduct is wrongful. One's first reaction is that, of course, these are matters for the state of injury. But suppose its laws have not been transgressed. Its laws may reflect a purpose to encourage risk-taking by relieving activities in a certain field from the hazard of civil liability either entirely or at least until the case against the way they are conducted is a clear one.[18] Then, even though both parties are from another state which would impose liability on conduct of the sort the state of injury wishes to encourage, the defendant should have the benefit of the state of injury's law. The out-of-state plaintiff should be precluded from imposing on the defendant's activity a legal burden from which the state of that activity sought to relieve it.

Thus far, we have encountered no difficulty. But, though such privileges as I have attributed to a law of the state of injury do exist, I suspect that, when a state sets or maintains a lower standard of conduct or financial protection than its neighbors, its usual purpose is simply to protect potential defendants from exposure to burdens of liability that it regards as unfair or excessive. Thus, when a state relieves an auto driver from liability for harm to his guest-passenger in the absence of gross negligence, it is not doing so to relieve drivers of financial inhibitions and encourage them to take risks short of gross negligence. Accordingly, where the purpose of the law of the state of injury is thus limited, there would seem to be no conflict with that purpose in holding a defendant from another state to the more exacting or burdensome standard of liability which the latter state imposes, provided this is done on behalf of the defendant's fellow citizen. The injured fellow citizen in

18 For example, the privilege of fair comment and the recognition of truth as an absolute defense in defamation cases.

turn receives no more protection than his own state's law confers upon him. What end would be subserved by denying this protection to him?

The question appears to be rhetorical, yet, if the answer to it is "None," then a foundation may indeed have been laid for what that statutist would term a "personal law" of torts. Let us explore the implications of that answer with respect to my wrongful-death hypothetical of the New York lady cyclist who runs down and kills another New Yorker in a chance encounter on Nantucket. Does the answer not lead to the conclusion that New Yorkers in Massachusetts remain subject to the tort laws of New York as to each other (except to the extent that Massachusetts tort law is more exacting than New York law or instead seeks to encourage risk-taking which New York law would inhibit)? Moreover, we cannot stop with the claims of New Yorkers *inter se*.

Assume that a difference between more exacting New York tort laws and less exacting Massachusetts tort laws would pose a false conflict in a case arising from a Massachusetts injury involving two New Yorkers. Assume next that the law of New Jersey is the same as the law of New York. Surely, then, the conflict remains false when an action arises between citizens of New York and New Jersey. Moreover, if the laws of New York and New Jersey differ, then, though both are more exacting of the defendant and more beneficial to the plaintiff than the law of Massachusetts on the point at issue, presumably the law of the less exacting of the two states should control. In this situation the analysis we have been pursuing should entitle the plaintiff to claim only when, and to the extent that, the law of his own state would permit; similarly the defendant should be obligated to pay only when, and to the extent that, his state requires.[19]

[19] To the extent that the plaintiff in a wrongful death action can justly claim an amount greater than that allowed by the law of the state of injury, it is because the decedent's home state's law had sought to afford the decedent greater protection. The fact that the wrongdoer's

These conclusions produce a disturbing phenomenon: a tort action between two out-of-staters would be governed by an issue-by-issue amalgam of laws of the state of injury, of the plaintiff's state, and of the defendant's state, with the laws of the state of injury setting the minimum as to each issue (if my first principle of preference is to be respected) and with the less exacting of the other two laws applying to every issue as to which both laws exceed the state of injury's minimum.[20]

Disconcerting though the practical problems of litigation thus presented would be, my exposition has thus far avoided another source of difficulty that would manifest itself in many actual cases. The principle refers to a party's "home state,"

---

state uses a more liberal measure for its wrongful death cases should not enlarge the plaintiff's recovery. Similarly, to the extent that the wrongdoer can justly be held liable in an amount greater than that allowed by the law of the state of injury, it is because his home state's law had subjected him to the higher level of liability. The fact that the victim's state uses a more liberal measure than the wrongdoer's should not enlarge the latter's liability. Accordingly, on the assumption that recovery for a Massachusetts wrongful death involving two out-of-state parties is not to be limited to the Massachusetts ceiling (now set at $30,000), then, if the decedent came from a state with a $50,000 ceiling and the defendant from a no-ceiling state, the plaintiff's recovery should be limited to $50,000. Conversely, if the decedent came from a no-ceiling state and the defendant from a state with a $50,000 ceiling, the recovery should still be limited to $50,000.

20 Consider this case, unlikely but by no means impossible: A driver, A, from State X picks up a friend, B, at the latter's home in State Y, and they drive together in A's car to State Z where B is killed in an auto accident caused by A's negligence. State X has no ceiling on damages for wrongful death; it holds drivers liable to guest passengers for "willful and wanton" conduct; it has a comparative negligence rule which it applies even in wrongful death cases. State Y has a $50,000 ceiling on wrongful death damages; it holds drivers liable to guest passengers for failure to use due care; it puts the burden on the defendant to prove contributory negligence. State Z has a $20,000 ceiling on wrongful death damages; it holds drivers liable to guest passengers for "gross negligence"; and it puts the burden on the plaintiff to disprove contributory negligence. B's executor sues A. If it is clear that the actual loss caused by B's death exceeded $50,000 and uncertain not only whether the defendant's negligence met the standards for liability to guest passengers of States X and Z

a term used in a deliberate effort to avoid the complexities of greater precision.[21] When is New Jersey a "home state"? Like all hypotheticals, my cases are also over-simplified. Who is a New Yorker? A person technically domiciled there but resident in Massachusetts, for example, the Harvard graduate student in history who will never return to his native New York unless he is offered a more enticing teaching post there than universities in other states offer him? A Columbia graduate student from Massachusetts? A freeholder of Nantucket who lives five months a year on the island, seven months in New York? The problem is especially serious when it is the defendant whose association with the state of injury is more than nominal, for example, the New York director of a boys' camp on Cape Cod. Still greater difficulties are conceivable when

---

but also whether the decedent was contributorily negligent, how should the trial court instruct the jury as to the applicable laws? An answer can be worked on the basis of the formula noted in the text, but, even with the procedure proposed in Chapter XI *infra*, the court's task would be unenviable. For those who wish greater complexity, I recommend adding two different "built-in" statutes and one general statute of limitations, with appropriate assumptions as to the plaintiff's delay.

[21] Unfortunately, it invites some conflict with the *Restatement*'s conception that "home" is a basic ingredient of "domicil." See RESTATEMENT (SECOND), CONFLICT OF LAWS §§ 9.12, 13 (Tent. Draft No. 2, 1954). However, the *Restatement* recognizes that a person may have more than one home. *Id.* § 9, Comment *a*. Hence, I feel free to detach "home" from "domicil" and use it as the equivalent of "settled residence." Of course, the term will not mean the same thing to all courts in all cases. Moreover, lesser connections with a state may sometimes seem significant. Thus, in refusing to apply Babcock v. Jackson, 12 N.Y.2d 473, 191 N.E.2d 279 (1963), to a suit between two New Yorkers attending summer school in Colorado, where one injured the other, a guest-passenger in his car, the Appellate Division seemed to attach some importance to the parties' "temporary residence" in Colorado. See Dym v. Gordon, 22 App. Div. 2d 702, 253 N.Y.S.2d 802, 803 (2d Dept. 1964), *reversing* 41 Misc. 2d 657, 245 N.Y.S.2d 656 (1963). Even the lower court recognized that "residence of a more substantial, though still not permanent, nature" might have created a "sufficient interest" in Colorado to warrant application of its law. For a discussion of the *Dym* case as affirmed in the Court of Appeals, see appendix, *infra* p. 293.

the party is a corporation—as defendants often are—for example, a company with a place of business in New York from which it conducts some operations in Massachusetts. The possible variations on this theme are manifold.

In all the situations where it is the tie to Massachusetts that is in question, I believe the proper question to ask is whether the party's connection with Massachusetts is sufficiently close to justify subjecting him (or it) as plaintiff to the less protective standards of Massachusetts or to justify giving the benefit to him (or it) as defendant of the less exacting standards of Massachusetts. Once the Massachusetts law is found to have a reasonable basis for application, the conflict can no longer be considered false, and the principle of preference can be invoked (unless the existence of a relationship between the out-of-state parties gives rise to the qualification noted in the statement of the principle, a matter to be considered later).

Plainly the tests I have suggested would call for nice judgments, judgments that might well vary with the issues to which they related. If these complexities were to be added to the problems of conducting litigation under the amalgam of laws that I have just noted, it would not be surprising if courts were to shrink from incurring them. They might turn to the alternative route which leads to a reassertion of territoriality.

This alternative can be simply stated. It would proffer, as a basis of accommodation, a multistate policy pursuant to which each state would maintain its own system of tort law intact as the source of law in cases where out-of-state defendants had acted and caused injury within the state, regardless of the fact that the home states of the out-of-state parties set more exacting standards than the place of injury. This was essentially the position, if not the rationale, of the first *Restatement*. In the light of more recent decisions and commentaries, it seems scarcely credible that we can go all the way back to that simple allocation of authority.

At this point, the search for *via media* begins. Certain issues have a minimal bearing on conduct and a closer tie to matters of special concern to the domicil; let the source to govern them be found in the out-of-staters' law or laws. On this basis, wrongful death damages and survival of tort claims seem matters that could more readily be relegated to the out-of-staters' state laws than could, say, the laws governing bases of liability.[22] By restricting reference to the out-of-staters' laws to a few issues only, certain of the complications I noted above would be materially reduced, though the problem of determining who was an "out-of-stater" would remain.

Acceptance, with respect to certain issues, of a limitation on the applicability of the less exacting law of the state of injury in cases involving parties from another state or states having more exacting laws would, of course, require a restrictive amendment of the foregoing principle of preference. One or more additional principles should indicate affirmatively the scope of the exception to be made in cases involving out-of-state parties. Thus, if it were thought wise to carry this exception beyond wrongful death cases to the measure of damages for personal injuries, a new principle might be formulated as follows: "*If both plaintiff and defendant have their homes in a state or*

[22] Except under the odd Massachusetts statute which measures damages by the degree of the defendant's fault, damages for wrongful death are designed simply to provide compensation for the decedent's wife and family; they are not ordinarily available for the decedent's debts or even for his medical and funeral expenses. As Professor Currie has noted, they cannot be availed of to satisfy claims in the state of injury. Currie, "Conflict, Crisis, and Confusion in New York," 1963 DUKE L. J. 1, 13, in CURRIE, SELECTED ESSAYS 690, 702 (1963). Laws abolishing the common-law rule abating causes of action on the tortfeasor's death were doubtless designed to make his liability insurance available to persons injured by him, but they also expose other assets of his estate to these claimants. The principal administration will ordinarily be at the tortfeasor's domicil where usually any persons dependent on those assets will also be domiciled. Such considerations are reflected in Grant v. McAuliffe, 41 Cal. 2d 859, 866, 264 P.2d 944, 949 (1953): "Basically the question is one of the administration of decedents' estates, which is a purely local proceeding."

states other than the state of injury and if the measure of compensation under the law of the state of injury affords a lower degree of financial protection than that afforded by the law or laws of the parties' home state or states, the measure of compensation under the law of that home state which affords the lower degree of financial protection should be applied."

A second intermediate course should be noted, one that could be used in conjunction with the narrow middle route just described. This second course was foreshadowed in the qualification appended to the second principle of preference. That qualification, it will be recalled, recognized that the person injured might be so related to the person causing the injury that the question at issue should be relegated to the law governing their relationship.

This proviso will be embodied in a separate principle of preference, the fourth principle to be discussed in this chapter. The question this principle poses is whether the existence of a relationship created in another state should constitute *a condition* to the application of that state's law in place of the law of the state of injury, even though analysis in terms of purpose might fail to demonstrate that applying the state of injury's law would advance a purpose specific to that law.

Such a condition presumably would reflect a multistate policy to restrict the scope of a "personal law" of torts by confining resort to the "personal laws" of out-of-staters in controversies between them to those cases in which they had formed a relationship before entering the state of injury, plus, perhaps, some additional cases of the sort noted above, cases where the matter at issue (e.g., damages for wrongful death and survival) had a peculiarly close relation to the parties' home state—or states.

That a prior relationship may be important in providing a basis for denying the application of the less exacting or less protective law of state of injury is suggested by the fact that in none of the trail-blazing cases in this area—*Kilberg*,[23]

[23] Kilberg v. Northeast Airlines, *supra* note 13.

Griffith,[24] and *Babcock*[25]—has the court been content to rely simply on the circumstance that both the parties had a substantial connection with the same state; in each case the court has also taken account of the relationship that had been created *between* the parties in that state. Moreover, in the recent New York guest-passenger case of *Dym v. Gordon,*[26] the lack of a prior relationship appears to have been a factor of some consequence in leading the Appellate Division to refuse to apply New York law simply on the basis of a false-conflict analysis. However, further examination of the role of the prior relationship will be deferred till another principle limiting resort to the lower standard of the place of injury is considered.

3. *Where the state in which a defendant acted has established special controls, including the sanction of civil liability, over conduct of the kind in which the defendant was engaged when he caused a foreseeable injury to the plaintiff in another state, the plaintiff, though having no relationship to defendant, should be accorded the benefit of the special standards of conduct and of financial protection in the state of the defendant's conduct, even though the state of injury had imposed no such controls or sanctions.*

This is not a principle of general applicability; it is designed for the implementation, in multistate situations, of a specialized scheme of regulation imposing greater requirements or liabilities on a particular activity than would be provided by the general law of torts.

Let me give you two cases: one easy and one hard. The easy

[24] Griffith v. United Air Lines, 416 Pa. 1, 203 A.2d 796 (1964). In this case the Pennsylvania Supreme Court applied the forum's no-ceiling damage rule to a claim for the wrongful death of a Pennsylvanian killed in Colorado, a ceiling state, in the course of a flight beginning in Pennsylvania.

[25] Babcock v. Jackson, *supra* note 21. In the Appellate Division, the brilliant dissent by the late Judge Halpern repeatedly notes the fact that the parties' relationship was created in New York. See Babcock v. Jackson, 17 App. Div. 2d 694, 230 N.Y.S.2d. 114 (1962).

[26] *Supra* note 21.

case is a dramshop case like the much-cited Minnesota case of *Schmidt v. Driscoll Hotel, Inc.*,[27] where the Minnesota court held a Minnesota saloonkeeper (operator of the Hook-Em Cow Cafe) to liability under a Minnesota statute for the injury sustained in Wisconsin by the Minnesota passenger of a Minnesota auto driver who had inbibed too freely at the Hook-Em Cow, the sales to him being in violation of Minnesota law. My case is just the same except that the plaintiff is a Wisconsin pedestrian run down in Wisconsin by the Minnesota driver. Wisconsin, I should add, is assumed to have neither a dramshop act nor a common-law rule imposing liability on the saloonkeeper.

Where a state has chosen to regulate a particular line of activity by special rules, reinforced by the imposition of liability, for the purpose of rendering the persons engaging in that conduct more careful, more skillful, or more responsible than they would otherwise be, I think the principle most likely to achieve mutual acceptance if proposed would be to extend the benefits of the protection thus accorded to persons injured outside the enacting state, provided at least that the causing of injury there was foreseeable. The conduct is just as bad when the victim is an outsider as an insider. The law's admonitory and deterrent values would be impaired by denying the outsider protection. The need of the dramshop owner to protect himself against financial risk would not be greatly diminished if he were relieved of liability to outsiders, except perhaps in the case of a state-line dramshop. Plainly it would be unjust—and quite possibly unconstitutional—for Minnesota to protect Minnesotans hurt in Wisconsin and not to protect Wisconsinians.[28] Moreover, to sustain the projection of Minnesota law to Wisconsin, I see no need to resort to the special concept of the "altruistic interest," as Professor Currie would

[27] 249 Minn. 376, 82 N.W.2d 365 (1957).

[28] Presumably the Wisconsinian could complain of violation of the Privileges and Immunities Clause. See note 8 *supra*.

term Minnesota's interest in applying its dramshop act for the benefit of a Wisconsinian. His concern that the regulating state not impose its liability where to do so would represent an intrusive meddling with interests of the state of injury may be valid, but surely it would rarely be invoked.[29]

Now for my hard case. State X has passed a statute imposing strict liability for damage caused by blasting. State Y continues to require proof of negligence. The A Co., blasting in X near the state line, does damage to B's home in Y. No negligence can be shown. Should B be permitted to recover without proof of negligence, relying on the State X statute?[30]

Why, if the dramshop case was easy, should this be hard? Aren't they basically alike?

I do not think so. I see the dramshop act as essentially a law concerned to regulate the dramshop owner's conduct, with the civil damages allowed in part as compensation to the injured but in part as an effective deterrent. In the blasting statute, there is, I am sure, some element of regulation: a

[29] Professor Currie has to invoke the special concept of the "altruistic interest" here because he sees Minnesota's primary interest as restricted to the compensation of its own citizens. (For the purposes of this analysis, he excludes consideration of the deterrent policy also involved in his dramshop act.) By giving a lower status to the protection of Wisconsinians, he achieves a conceptual objective: he can envisage the subordination of the Minnesota interest to the Wisconsin interest in case of "an intrusive meddling" without having to recognize the "weighing" of competing state interests. For Professor Currie's treatment of the "altruistic interest," see Currie & Schreter, "Unconstitutional Discrimination and the Conflict of Laws: Privileges and Immunities," *supra* note 9, at 1361, in CURRIE, SELECTED ESSAYS at 489 (1963). The view that the Minnesota legislature gives a higher status to the claims of a Minnesota victim than of a Wisconsin victim of a Minnesota dramshop operator's wrongdoing strikes me as more appropriate to a tribal system of law than to that prevailing in the American Union.

[30] Readers of conflicts casebooks will recognize this hypothetical case as reversing the law-fact pattern of Dallas v. Whitney, 118 W. Va. 106, 88 S.E. 766 (1936), where the West Virginia court applied the Ohio absolute liability rule to the claim of an Ohio plaintiff whose property in Ohio was damaged by blasting in West Virginia.

blaster who knows that he must proceed at his peril is probably going to take even more pains to be careful than if he knows he won't be held unless he can be shown to have been negligent. However, blasting is a socially useful and often necessary occupation which is difficult to conduct without sometimes injuring other people's property. The primary purpose of the X statute, which prescribes no rules to govern the conduct of blasting operations, is probably to assure the collection of damages by the people whose property is hurt. It can, therefore, be argued that the X legislature is concerned chiefly in protecting X property owners when it imposes liability on X blasters. If Y wants to protect its people, let Y pass a similar law.

Given X's concern to keep its blasters liability-conscious as a stimulus to great care, I see little social gain to X in depriving the Y victim of an X blast of the financial protection that would be freely accorded an X victim. Unless a breed of blasters developed who were state-line specialists, the cost to X blasters of protecting themselves against liability would be much the same, whatever the rule. The fact that their counterparts in Y would sometimes escape liability for Y damage does not harm X blasters in any way. It should be noted, moreover, that, under our first principle, Y blasters would be held strictly liable for damage caused in X by their Y operations. Finally, the principle that would dictate the liability of X blasters in this case might operate to X's advantage in some other situation where Y was the state imposing the stricter standard of liability.[31]

I recognize, of course, that my "easy" case, the variant of *Schmidt*, might be explained as a simple example of the "ordinary processes of construction and interpretation," the court having concluded from the legislative purpose—though

[31] This would not justify a choice that was unfair to the private parties involved. However, the consideration should comfort a court fearful that it was sacrificing local interests. The basic problem is discussed in Chapter V, *supra*.

not the terms—of the Minnesota dramshop act that it was intended to apply to injuries inflicted on Wisconsinians in Wisconsin, thereby yielding a false conflict. If so, there would be no occasion for the Minnesota court to have recourse to a principle of preference.[32] However, even in *Schmidt*, the court's application of the Minnesota act ran counter to precedent, and my variant, adding a plaintiff from Wisconsin, is a little harder. What considerations moved the court in *Schmidt*? Perhaps they were broader than those the court articulated.

Without resolving this question, let us assume that Minnesota had subsequently passed a statute imposing absolute liability on blasters. Suppose now that the Minnesota court were to be confronted by a case caused by blasting in Minnesota, the damage done in a neighboring state where liability was based on negligence. The court might distinguish the new case from *Schmidt* for the reasons noted above and simply apply the law of the place of injury. But if it found *Schmidt* helpful in deciding to apply Minnesota law, this, I take it, would be because the court had generalized the significance of that decision beyond the bounds set by its facts and the particular laws involved. By applying the Minnesota blasting liability law, the court would be laying foundations in precedent for a principle of preference along the lines I have suggested. If this were so, then the court could aid other courts by identifying, along with the specifics of the statute and the facts, the considerations of principle that had moved it to prefer the Minnesota statute.

My own statement of the principle gives rise to a question

[32] Having found a direction from its own legislature to apply its own statute, the Minnesota court would be bound by that discovery. Suppose, however, that the same case had been brought before a Wisconsin court or the court of a third state. The forum should take both the relevant principle of preference and the Minnesota interpretation of the Minnesota statute into account. Since, in the case supposed, the statute and the principle both point to the same law, no difficulty is created. If the contrary were true, the Wisconsin court should re-examine the solution proposed by the principle in the light of the Minnesota ruling but should consider itself bound by neither.

of meaning—and also one of purpose—when it limits the principle's application to cases where the defendant's state had adopted "special controls." What is a "special control," and why should it make a difference? I see it simply as an instance where a legislature (rarely, a court) has identified a particular calling or other activity as giving rise to more than ordinary hazards and has therefore laid down special rules regulating its conduct or simply subjecting it to a higher standard of liability or financial protection. When the implied warranty was extended to noncontracting third parties, the courts moved cautiously within a few commodity areas, such as food and drugs, in which danger to the user from a defective product would be considerable and his ability to protect himself was slight. This could be viewed as an instance of a special control. The affected manufacturers and processors had to recognize that they had been singled out for special responsibilities and that only through a combination of care and insurance (or self-insurance) could they protect themselves.

When a legislature or court has thus subjected to this special discipline a business or other activity that is not entirely localized, I do not think it valid to attribute to the law-maker a purpose to benefit only those persons who happen to be injured by the regulated activity within the state or in states having similar laws. The protection is accorded "consumers" or "the public," wherever they may be.

When, however, only the general body of tort law is involved, there is less reason to invoke it for the benefit of persons injured in other states having laws which in certain respects prove less protective than the general tort laws of the place of conduct. Each of the states involved has provided by its general tort laws for its general security. If noncompliance with its norms of conduct causing harm to persons or property within the state is sanctioned as the state's tort laws prescribe, this will give adequate protection to the general security there without reaching out to invoke the more exacting norms of another state where the harm-causing conduct has occurred. In the latter state, there is no incentive to advance a regulatory scheme by holding a regulated industry or activity to compliance with special rules of liability.

Yet the line is not, I confess, a wholly satisfactory one. How, for example should the doctrine of implied warranty be classified where, as in a rapidly increasing number of states, it is being extended to cover all commodities when "unreasonably dangerous to the user or consumer" and is not being confined to certain types?[33] Fortunately, however, the concept of the principle of preference as a guide to decision makes decisions as to inclusion and exclusion less consequential than at first they might seem. The fact that a tort rule was not considered "special" and therefore not within the principle, would still allow a court to consider the contention that that tort rule should in a particular situation be applied to an injury in another state having a less exacting rule.

Before we leave this principle, I ought to acknowledge that sometimes a state may refuse to subject an industry or activity to special rules of liability and that this refusal may indicate its preference as plainly as legislation, in this instance a preference to relieve participants in the industry or activity from the inhibiting financial hazards of the higher standards of care or of financial protection that other states are adopting.[34]

[33] RESTATEMENT (SECOND), TORTS § 402A, Special Liability of Seller of Product to User or Consumer (Tent. Draft No. 10, 1964). Responding to "the most radical and spectacular development in tort law during this century" (prenatal injuries excepted), *id.* at 2, the Institute in 1964 dropped a provision, approved in 1962, restricted to products "for intimate bodily use" and adopted the broad provision cited. A caveat covers harms to other persons, goods processed after leaving the seller, and components.

[34] For an example of a state's refusal to follow a statutory trend and its adherence instead to the common-law standard of due care, which was given weight by the court in the state where this refusal had occurred, see Babcock v. Jackson, 12 N.Y.2d 473, 482, 191 N.E.2d 279, 284 (1963), wherein the Court of Appeals took note of the legislature's repeated refusal to diminish the common-law duty of care owing to automobile guests.

This legislative position, though negative, might be viewed as binding upon the courts of the state adhering to it when that state is the state of the defendant's conduct. When, however, that position is considered by the courts of the state of injury, they might well persevere in the application of the first principle stated in this chapter; they would hesitate to sacrifice the values embodied in their own law in order to encourage risk-taking that their own legislature had denied to their domestic industry.

4. *Where the law of a state in which a relationship has its seat has imposed a standard of conduct or of financial protection on one party to that relationship for the benefit of the other party which is* higher *than the like standard imposed by the state of injury, the law of the former state should determine the standard of conduct or of financial protection applicable to the case for the benefit of the party protected by that state's law.*

This is an antiterritorialist principle that has been foreshadowed by the possible exception to the second principle that I noted. As you may recall, the latter principle would allow the person who caused an injury which was not actionable where it was inflicted or which was subject to a lower measure of damages to be protected from the higher standards of the plaintiff's state. However, I noted that the existence of a relationship arising elsewhere between the parties to the case might afford grounds for an exception. (To associate the relationship with the other state, I have referred to its "seat" as being there. The term is reminiscent of Savigny; I am employing it as a stopgap and am not prepared to defend it against all comers.)

To exemplify applications of this principle, I am tempted to cite *Haumschild v. Continental Casualty Co.*[35] applying the law of the spouses' domicil, Wisconsin, and denying interspousal immunity to a California injury, despite the latter

[35] 7 Wis. 2d 130, 95 N.W.2d 814 (1959).

state's rule granting immunity. Or I might refer to that recent luminary among the New York decisions deviating from the first *Restatement*'s doctrine, *Babcock v. Jackson*.[36] However, those inter-spousal immunity and guest-passenger cases might seem too readily disposed of as posing false conflicts for them to serve as very satisfying illustrations. Let me try a harder example: a variation of *Kilberg v. Northeast Airlines, Inc.*,[37] the only difference from the original being the fact that the suit is in a forum other than New York or Massachusetts. This hypothetical case has already been used by Professor Currie to exemplify that *rara avis*, a case of a true conflict in a disinterested forum.[38] He believes the forum may solve it simply by applying its own law. As an alternative he would allow the forum to assert an authority to fill the vacuum left by Congress's failure to enact choice-of-law statutes by deciding which law Congress would think the better and then applying that law.[39] Which law that would be, Professor Currie declines to decide. My principle would allow the forum to prefer the New York law without having to brand it superior.

The purpose of the Massachusetts limitation on wrongful death recoveries could reasonably be viewed as being advanced by applying the limitation for the benefit of Northeast Airlines, a Massachusetts corporation with its principal office in Boston. But Northeast also operates out of New York City, and there it entered into a relationship, carrier and passenger, with a New York citizen, undertaking to carry him to Massachusetts, a venture that exposed him to the risk of death if Northeast failed to complete the trip successfully. For New York to assert that the purpose of its constitutional ban on wrongful death recovery ceilings extended to this journey seems to me plainly reasonable. New York's concern with the relationship does not stop when the New York State

36 *Supra* note 34. 37 *Supra* note 13.

38 See Currie, *supra* note 5, at 775.

39 *Id.* at 778 (with three reservations).

boundary is crossed. Yet, if New York cannot continue the financial protection it prescribes when the plane leaves New York, then the state's effective control over the relationship is seriously impaired.

Let us view the situation from the standpoint of Professor Rawls' test: could the principle I have stated reasonably be proposed for mutual acceptance by states in a position of equal liberty? By acceptance, each state would gain the advantage of being able to impose more exacting legal consequences on a relationship it had undertaken to regulate even though the parties to the relationship had gone to a state that imposed less exacting consequences. Each state, when the place of injury, would surrender the power to apply its own lower standards of conduct or financial protection to a relationship arising in, and regulated by, another state.

(The preference which would be accorded the more exacting rules of the state of the relationship, even in a case of true conflict, ought not to be stretched beyond those rules which can reasonably be considered incidents of the relationship.[40] A carrier-passenger relationship created by, say, motor-bus carriage from New York to Massachusetts does not include among its incidents all the rules which New York has developed to define due care in driving, even when these are more exacting than those of Connecticut and Massachusetts.[41] That the

40 Of course, the relationship should not be so localized in function that it is no longer of consequence when the parties to it have left the state.

41 This limitation does not have a logical counterpart when the requirement of a relationship is dropped for the alternative of a "personal law" of torts. Under the latter, if the primary purpose of the New York law is viewed as the protection of New Yorkers against the substandard conduct of other New Yorkers, it is easy to determine what is the standard and what is substandard conduct by New York rules and to label the place where the substandard conduct occurs as "fortuitous." In *Babcock*, the court denies an intention to apply New York law so inclusively. See Babcock v. Jackson, *supra* note 34, at 483, 191 N.E.2d at 284. Of course, certain of New York's behavior-regulating rules—maximum per-

measure of damages for wrongful death may properly be regarded as an incident of the carrier-passenger relationship is attested by the New York case holding invalid under New York law a contractual limitation on recovery for wrongful death in an airplane flight from New York to New Jersey.)[42]

How important to the state of injury is the imposition of its lower legal consequences on a relationship which had been created in another state? In our variation of *Kilberg*, the concern of Massachusetts would seem confined to one party to the relationship, the airline. Though that party would lose the benefit of the Massachusetts ceiling, giving preference to the law removing the ceiling would still leave the ceiling on wrongful death recoveries intact in most Massachusetts cases. Under my second principle, directly or by implication, the ceiling would continue to apply to nearly all actions based on in-state wrongful deaths: it would apply not only to all such actions involving Massachusetts persons but also where either the person causing the death or the person killed had a home in, or a close business connection with, Massachusetts, except where the existence of an out-of-state relationship justified resort to the other state's more protective rules.[43] The relationship would provide an objective basis for differentiating the

---

missible speeds, for example—are so plainly localized that no one would propose their extrastate application. Professor Currie has explained the forum's unwillingness to use its own rules of this type on the ground that they are not "rules of decision" but rather "rules of conduct" which apply "only to conduct within the territorial limits of the state." See Currie, "On the Displacement of the Law of the Forum," 58 Colum. L. Rev. 964, 1021 (1958), in Selected Essays 3, 69 (1962). The distinction is not easily drawn.

[42] Conklin v. Canadian-Colonial Airways, Inc., 266 N.Y. 244, 194 N.E. 692 (1935).

[43] To be sure, the exception could not be restricted to an out-of-state relationship in any case in which both persons are from a more protective state if, as suggested above, p. 157 *supra*, certain rules (such as wrongful-death damages and survival) are to be drawn from their home state laws, even in the absence of any prior relationship.

cases involving it from other cases arising within the state of injury and thus relieve the problem of discrimination. What the forum would be concerned with would be a special case, one carrying with it a special justification. In sum, I believe the proposed preference could be advanced for mutual acceptance with good prospects of success.

Incidentally, I have long thought that the element of the carrier-passenger relationship in *Kilberg* has been underappreciated. Especially since *Kilberg's* procedural rationale was disavowed by the New York Court of Appeals,[44] the tendency has been to rest the case solely on the decedent's domicil. But suppose the wrongful death had resulted, not from the crash in landing but from the negligent handling of the plane at the Nantucket airport where the plaintiff's decedent was not a passenger but one of several sightseers who were killed. The coincidence that he was also a New Yorker creates a much more difficult case for recovery of full damages than that presented by *Kilberg*. Since Northeast is a Massachusetts corporation, with its principal office there, the removal of the carrier-passenger relationship renders the case rather close to my hypothetical case of the Nantucket banker-cyclist who runs down and kills the New York tourist.

Ought the existence of a relationship to be significant for

[44] Davenport v. Webb, *supra* note 14, refusing to extend the *Kilberg* procedural rationale to justify the application of New York's rule permitting pre-judgment interest to be recovered on tort claims for unliquidated damages when the deaths complained of were caused in Maryland, a state denying the recovery of such interest. The case arose out of a collision between the car of the New York decedents and a truck operated by a Virginian. (Facts reported by Halpern, J., dissenting, in Babcock v. Jackson, *supra* note 25, at 698, 230 N.Y.S.2d at 121.) The Court of Appeals did not have to consider whether the *Kilberg* rule would have been applicable to this auto accident if a ceiling on damages had been at issue. Maryland, the place of injury, has no wrongful death ceiling. Virginia, however, does have a $30,000 ceiling. Understandably, a claim to the application of its law does not appear to have been pressed.

choice-of-law purposes if the deceased airline passenger were from New Jersey, a state which has no wrongful death ceiling? If so, this would enable the New York law to be applied, contrary to the ruling of the Federal District Court that decided *Pearson v. Northeast Airlines, Inc.*,[45] the case that held the *Kilberg* ruling constitutional? I recognize that the case of the New Jersey passenger poses a distinguishable question since New Jersey's choice-of-law decisions, not having anticipated *Kilberg*, would doubtless point to Massachusetts law. Moreover, New Jersey had not asserted its no-ceiling rule as solemnly as had New York.[46] Yet, as I contended in Chapter IV, one state should not be constrained always to adopt another state's choice-of-law rules or always to have to find expressions of strong policy predilections in the substantive rules of another state in order to justify their use. Plainly, the unlimited recovery would advance the purposes of the New Jersey law in the case of the New Jersey widow just as much as it would advance the purposes of the New York law in the case of the New York widow. New York's concern to prescribe the terms of financial protection of the carrier-passenger relationship for air carriers operating out of New York can scarcely be considered a tribal one, restricted solely to its own citizenry. A New York court's refusal to accept the Massachusetts rule in the case of the New Jersey decedent would therefore seem reasonable enough.[47] Much harder would

[45] The District Court decision in Pearson v. Northeast Airlines, Inc., 199 F. Supp. 539 (S.D.N.Y. 1961), *rev'd* in 309 F. 2d 553 (2d Cir. 1962), *cert. denied,* 372 U.S. 912 (1963), was accompanied by a decision (unreported) denying recovery above the Massachusetts ceiling to the widow of a New Jersey citizen killed in the same Nantucket crash that killed Kilberg. Trauth v. Northeast Airlines, Inc., Civil No. 149-256, S.D.N.Y.

[46] New Jersey had not embodied its no-ceiling rule in its state constitution.

[47] Professor Currie approves the District Court's ruling in the *Trauth* case, *supra* note 45. He believes it was correct in respecting New Jersey's place-of-injury choice-of-law rule, and that the application of New York law would "probably be a denial of full faith and credit to the law of the

be a case involving a Massachusetts decedent: should the principle be denied application here in view of the concentration of factors supporting recourse to Massachusetts law?[48]

An instance in which preference ought to have been given to the law governing a relationship which imposed a liability not imposed by the law of the place of injury is the venerable case of *Alabama Great Southern Ry. v. Carroll.*[49] In it a railroad operating in Alabama and Mississippi escaped liability by reason of the Mississippi fellow-servant rule. The injury was caused there by the negligence of the Alabama plaintiff's fellow-servant in Alabama (which had abolished the rule). Here plainly the rule at issue formed a term in a relationship created and subsisting in Alabama. I think Mississippi had as much basis for applying its rule as Massachusetts had for applying its rule in *Kilberg,* yet surely a disinterested third state—and even Mississippi itself—might

---

only state having an interest in the matter: Massachusetts." See Currie, *supra* note 22, at 31, in SELECTED ESSAYS at 719. An interesting sidelight on his method is cast by his difficulty in justifying the recovery of unlimited damages in New York despite an assumption that New Jersey would make the same choice of law as New York. Since Professor Currie would deny the New York court the use of choice-of-law rules and would view its own no-ceiling rule as intended only for the benefit of New Yorkers, he would leave the court with no tool to resolve the case. In this predicament, he grudgingly concedes the court the privilege of using its own law. *Id.* at 33 and 720. For an alternative mode of decision, suggested more recently, see Currie, *supra* note 5, at 778.

[48] With the airline a Massachusetts corporation, with its principal office in Boston, with the decedent a citizen of the Commonwealth, and with the place of injury there, a justification for refusing to apply that state's ceiling on recovery must rest on the circumstances involving the relationship: the carrier's operation out of New York and the passenger's embarkation there. However, their significance is weakened by the fact that the New York rule permitting full recovery for wrongful death does not have a purpose that is specific to the carrier-passenger relationship, even in the sense that retention of the common-law rule of negligence to govern the New York driver's liability to his guest-passengers represents a purpose specific to that relationship.

[49] 97 Ala. 126, 11 So. 803 (1892).

reasonably have recognized this principle and so have given Alabama law a claim to preference on the strength of the relationship.

I might add that I do not think that, in the case of a relationship arising out of contract, it is necessary in order to invoke the relationship to convert the plaintiff's case into a contract claim by some feat of characterization.[50] I believe the Pennsylvania Supreme Court in its counterpart of *Kilberg*, *Griffith v. United Air Lines*,[51] was wise to reject a contract classification as justification for the application of its own unlimited measure of wrongful death damages while at the same time noting Pennsylvania's interest in a flight starting in Pennsylvania by an airline operating out of Pennsylvania.

Does it matter that the relationship have its "legal seat" within the state whose law is being invoked? Suppose a New York passenger is killed at the end of a flight on a Northeast Airlines plane to Massachusetts from Maine. Like Massachusetts, Maine has a ceiling on wrongful death damages. I submit that the New York executor of the decedent should not have the benefit of *Kilberg*. Despite Northeast's connection with New York, there are countervailing concerns in the other two states, and New York had no basis for regulating the carriage in the course of which the accident occurred.

This brings us to the difficult case I have already discussed: the case where the parties are from the same state (or from states having the same laws on the point at issue) and it is difficult to find countervailing concerns in the state of injury. The paradigm for this problem has already been noted, *Dym v. Gordon*,[52] where the plaintiff guest-passenger sought un-

[50] For the classic example of this operation, see Levy v. Daniels' U-Drive Auto Renting Co., 108 Conn. 333, 143 Atl. 163 (1928), applying to a Massachusetts injury a Connecticut statute imposing liability on the renter of automobiles there for injuries done by his lessee's negligence. The plaintiff's claim was upheld because he was viewed as a third-party beneficiary of a contract into which "the law inserted" its liability rule.

[51] *Supra* note 24. [52] *Supra* note 21.

successfully to impose New York common-law liability on a negligent New York automobile driver for a Colorado motor accident, the parties to the accident having met while attending summer school in Colorado, a state which holds the host-driver liable only for "willful and wanton disregard of the rights of others."[53] Though the Appellate Division in a brief memorandum opinion, blanketed the grounds of its decision by resting it on a finding that Colorado had "the dominant contacts and the superior claims to the application of its law," the court took note of the fact that the relationship between the parties was confined to Colorado.[54] Indeed, the fact plainly afforded the most consequential distinction differentiating *Dym* from *Babcock* to which the court duly attorned. [The discussion that follows had been in type for some weeks when, on the last day of the term, the New York Court of Appeals affirmed the decision below by a vote of 4 to 3. What I had written seemed sufficiently pertinent to the opinions that I decided not to attempt to revise this section but instead to add a comment devoted to the case in the Court of Appeals. My comment appears as an appendix to these lectures.]

In this case, where the rule at issue is specifically concerned with the relationship, the contention is most persuasive that the relationship itself, and not merely the parties to it, should have a substantial connection with the state whose liability-imposing law is being invoked. Obviously, in its adherence to the common-law rule of liability to auto guests, New

[53] See Colo. Rev. Stat. Ann. § 13-9-1. A host-driver is also liable for injuries inflicted intentionally or while intoxicated.

[54] The opinion notes that the parties were "temporarily resident" in Colorado, a fact I have already remarked as evidencing the difficulty of identifying parties with particular states. See note 21 *supra*. There is a suggestion that the decision was influenced by the fact that the Colorado guest-passenger act, *supra* note 53, was cast in terms of a standard of care and so was a conduct-regulating rule of the place of injury. This would represent a serious misunderstanding of *Babcock*. See Cavers, *supra* note 11, at 1226-27.

York is not trying to prescribe rules for the host-guest relationship in motor cars the wide world over. I also find it hard to accept the idea that New York has sought to determine the legal consequences of the relationship wherever in the world New Yorkers happen to create it. It is when a host-guest relationship has begun in New York between New Yorkers that a decision to subject it to New York law wherever the motorists may later go seems a reasonable assertion of New York's concern.

Note that, in the foregoing proposition, there are two elements in the condition to the application of New York law: the creation of the relationship within New York and the fact that it is between New Yorkers. Is the latter necessary? Suppose a citizen of a state which, like New York, adheres to the common-law rule of liability becomes a guest-passenger of a New York driver in New York. I see no objection to according him the protection of the New York rule when they go elsewhere, nor would I argue against the imposition of its burden if the driver-passenger roles had been reversed. I should think the same conclusion should be reached if both driver and passenger came from another state or states adhering to the common-law rule.

Suppose, however, that one or both of the parties came from the state of injury or from another state with a guest-passenger statute. Does the fact that the relationship was created in New York override this circumstance? Ought New York law still to be viewed as controlling a guest-passenger relationship created in New York between two Ontario citizens in view of that province's refusal to allow a guest to recover under any circumstances?[55] I should think an affirmative answer to that question very doubtful, despite the fact the principle may in terms appear to cover it.[56] More, however, can be said for

[55] Ontario was the place of injury in Babcock v. Jackson, *supra* note 34.

[56] The concept of the principle of preference, it will be recalled, does not bind a court proposing a principle to treat it as a rigid prescription

applying New York law to a New York driver who injures an Ontario guest in Ontario or even for giving its benefit to a New York guest who is injured in Ontario by his Ontario driver, the relationship having in both cases begun in New York. Perhaps the ultimate destination of the trip or still other factors should be taken into account.[57] Plainly, at least in the formative stage of a principle of preference in this area, choice of forum is likely to be significant.

Despite these uncertainties, I believe time may demonstrate that the instincts of the Appellate Division in *Dym v. Gordon*[58] were sound in refusing to apply the New York rule governing the host-driver's liability to his guest-passenger when the relationship had not been created in New York. This decision, if it were to stand, might provide a basis for confining the "personal law" of torts mainly to relationships which had their inception in the home state or a state having the same law.[59]

---

covering all cases falling literally within its scope. Circumstances which undermine the reasonableness of a principle in its application to a peripheral situation may therefore be heeded. However, such a departure must not be designed to advance only the individual interest of the state whose court is proposing the departure; the duty of mutuality which applies to he principle ought also to apply to the exception, though obviously it is more difficult of application.

[57] The possibility of excepting certain laws from this principle is suggested in the text at note 22 *supra*.

[58] *Supra* note 21.

[59] The state of relevant European law is reported in a thoughtful comment in English on Babcock v. Jackson and its methodology by a Dutch lawyer, Dr. Huibert Drion, who once studied at the Harvard Law School. See Drion, "The Lex Loci Delicti in Retreat," in FESTSCHRIFT FÜR OTTO RIESE 225 (1964). He notes the discriminatory Article 12 of the Einführungsgesetz which denies recovery for foreign torts committed by Germans above the limit allowed by German law; the 1942 German decree (RGBl. 706), still in force, applying German law to foreign torts between Germans; the application (under Swiss Road Traffic Act of 1958, art. 85, para. II) of the Swiss rule of absolute liability to foreign motor accidents if the plaintiff is a Swiss domiciliary (or a passenger carried for hire from or to a point in Switzerland) and the accident was caused by

5. *Where the law of a state in which a relationship has its seat has imposed a standard of conduct or of financial protection on one party to that relationship for the benefit of the other party which was* lower *than the standards imposed by the state of injury, the law of the former state should determine the standard of conduct or financial protection applicable to the case for the benefit of the party whose liability that state's law would deny or limit.*

This, it will be observed, is the converse of the preceding proposition: the relationship is used as a basis to avoid the full application of the liability-creating law of the state of injury. In my first principle of preference, calling for the application of that law, I recognized this principle as a possible exception. However, I disapprove of this as a principle, though quite possibly some cases falling within its pattern might justly be resolved by the choice it proposes. I present it here as a principle because my purpose in this chapter is illustration, a goal that may be pursued by the negative example as well as by the affirmative.

The most obvious example of a case that might fall within this principle is one where a spouse, domiciled in State X which has retained inter-spousal immunity, is injured by the other spouse in State Y which has abolished it. Several recent

---

a Swiss motor vehicle; and a Dutch decision (in accord with the unratified Benelux Treaty, art. 18, para. 2) applying Dutch law to a case "on all fours with the Babcock case," though, where the common Dutch nationality and domicil of the parties were "more or less accidental," lower courts have more often kept to the *lex loci delicti*. Dr. Drion cites 1 LUNZ, INTERNATIONALES PRIVATRECHT 164 (1961), for the propositions that, under Soviet law, a foreign *lex loci* "may only be applied when the defendant's act was also illicit" under Soviet law and that "the *lex loci delicti* does not apply at all to claims between Soviet citizens." In Belgium, France, and Austria, the author finds that in a *Babcock*-type case the courts would apply the *lex loci*. *Id.* at 228-31. But see, as to France, note 12, p. 147 *supra*. England would, of course, reach the *Babcock* result by virtue of its long-established choice-of-law rule for torts. *Cf.* McLean v. Pettigrew, [1945] 2 D.L.R. 65 (1944).

cases have applied the law of the domicil of the spouses when that law had abolished inter-spousal immunity.[60] The state of injury which had retained immunity would not serve the purpose of its law by applying it to the claim of an out-of-state spouse whose domestic relations and liability insurance would both be the concern of the state of domicil. The case with the law-fact pattern before us is less often litigated, however.[61]

By its denial of inter-spousal immunity, the state of injury has determined to afford the injured spouse the financial protection of a claim against the negligent spouse. No doubt the trend in this direction reflects a recognition of the likelihood that the only private funds adequate to meet the financial costs of a serious injury would be those provided by liability insurance. By enabling those funds to be tapped, the state of injury protects its public and charitable agencies against the cost of medical care whenever it must be provided at the scene of the accident and the other spouse lacks the money to meet the bills. But a negligent, uninsured husband would not infrequently be able to meet the costs of the injury from his private means and medical insurance, and even a severely injured spouse might return home and incur the expenses of recuperation there. Accordingly, the financial hazard of the state of injury may seem too erratic or too narrow

[60] Haumschild v. Continental Insurance Co., *supra* note 35 (but the court casts its decision in terms of a jurisdiction-selecting rule); Thompson v. Thompson, 105 N.H. 86, 193 A.2d 439 (1963) (but Massachusetts gross negligence standard of care for guest passengers to be applied); *cf.* Pittman v. Deiter, 10 Pa. D. & C.2d 360 (1957) (suit after husband's death). *Contra*, Shaw v. Lee, 258 N.C. 609, 129 S.E.2d 288 (1963).

[61] *Cf.* LaChance v. Service Trucking Co., 215 F. Supp. 162 (D. Md. 1963). In Forbes v. Forbes, 226 Wis. 477, 277 N.W. 112 (1938), the Wisconsin Supreme Court had applied to spouses from an immunity state the law of Wisconsin, the place of injury, which denies immunity, but in *Haumschild, supra* note 35, its adoption of the domicil as the controlling factor in a jurisdiction-selecting rule led it to overrule *Forbes* along with five other cases. Its failure to differentiate is criticized in Hancock, "The Rise and Fall of *Buckeye v. Buckeye*, 1931-1959: Marital Immunity for Torts in Conflict of Laws," 29 U. Chi. L. Rev. 237, 267 (1962).

a basis for applying its law.[62] If a base were sought for disregarding the immunity that did not depend for its justification on the particulars of the case, it should be found in the basis for the first principle I have proposed: a preference for the law of the state which has established general standards of conduct and of financial protection against the hazards of life in that state.

Whether an exception to that broad principle should be admitted with respect to inter-spousal claims poses a question that is hard to answer without taking into account the intrinsic merits of the competing rules. Ought a court to disregard the fact that one basis for the immunity rule—fear of causing marital disharmony—has been rendered fictitious by the great spread of liability insurance in the past generation? And, when it takes account of the other basis, the risk of collusion between the spouses to bilk the insurer, with higher losses and higher premiums (in theory at least) resulting to drivers in the spouses' domicil, ought it not also to consider the advantage to the insurers of third-party defendants in being able to implead the insured spouse?[63] Should it note the fact that the difference in the loss experience in the domiciliary state owing to the adoption of one rule as against

[62] In a letter to me, John H. C. Morris of Oxford University, the general editor of *Dicey*, remarked, anent the notion of a state interest in protection from the burden caused by uncompensated injuries within its bounds, ". . . it seems to me reminiscent of the Writ of Quominus, the fiction whereby our old Court of Exchequer extended its jurisdiction from Crown debts to debts owed to a subject. The plaintiff alleged that the defendant refused to pay his debt, 'by which the less' he (the plaintiff) was unable to pay his debt to the King!" The point is telling, but my correspondent's reaction may reflect the fact that he writes from a land where medical care has long been socialized.

[63] By rejecting the interspousal immunity granted by the law of the domicil, the court in LaChance v. Service Trucking Co., *supra* note 61, enabled itself to permit the husband to be impleaded by the defendant in the wife's personal injury action.

the other would almost certainly never show up in that state's liability insurance rates?[64]

There are other relationships posing similar problems in cases involving injuries in states not according the parties to such relationship any special protection: for example, the guest-passenger-host-driver relationship when created in states having statutes that relieve the driver of liability, absent proof of gross negligence or willful and reckless driving; the charity-beneficiary relationship in jurisdictions retaining the immunity, as illustrated by Case 5 in the *Knickerbocker* series where the plaintiff is the Massachusetts beneficiary.[65] Each of these poses distinctive problems, and I suspect would encounter doubts comparable to those that I have raised with respect to inter-spousal claims. Probably, therefore, this principle would not achieve general acceptance. Certain states would give effect to the exception it poses to the first principle for certain relationships and not for others. Some states would reject it out of hand. In the course of time, generalizations reflecting these decisions would be possible, even though unanimity might not have been achieved. But how often, among comparably difficult problems in our law, have our fifty jurisdictions achieved unanimity?

[64] A study of the effect on insurance premiums of a change from contributory to comparative negligence was unable to detect any difference. The experience in neighboring states also produced negative results. See Peck, "Comparative Negligence and Automobile Liability Insurance," 58 Mich. L. Rev. 689 (1960).

[65] See p. 50, *supra*. What is the bearing of the five principles on Cases 1-4? All four would fall under the second principle on the charitable immunity issue but for the false conflict permitting New York law to be applied. In Case 3, the first principle would call for Massachusetts' strict liability rule, absent a "public policy" or penal law defense. In Case 4, the New York widow might escape the wrongful death ceiling under the fourth principle, the relation between decedent and defendant having its seat in New York. So, too, if an exception to the second principle were made for wrongful death damages in suits between out-of-staters. Neither ground would be open to the other widow.

VII

PRINCIPLES OF PREFERENCE EXEMPLIFIED: CONTRACTS AND CONVEYANCES

Thus far I have been concerned with conflicts arising in tort litigation. In the fields of contract and property law, one of the main sources of conflict springs from the efforts of states to interpose protective barriers to curb the free exercise of economic power in situations where its use can have socially undesirable effects. Conflicts in this area can be avoided when the protective state gives a restricted reading to the reach of its law, confining its application to intrastate transactions, as, for example, has been the tendency in the case of general usury laws. For application in absence of such abnegation by the state with the protective law, the following principle is proposed:

6. *Where, for the purpose of providing protection from the adverse consequences of incompetence, heedlessness, ignorance, or unequal bargaining power, the law of a state has imposed restrictions on the power to contract or to convey or encumber property, its protective provisions should be applied against a party to the restricted transaction where (a) the person protected has a home in the state (if the law's purpose were to protect the person) and (b) the affected transaction or protected property interest were centered there or, (c) if it were not, this was due to facts that were fortuitous or had been manipulated to evade the protective law.*

This principle is a formidable proposition. Before attempting to illustrate its operation, I should provide some further gloss for its terms. The laws that would be embraced by this category would range from rules restricting the capacity of married women, infants, and other persons subject to protective disabilities[1] to rules protecting insured persons from harsh provisions in the fine print of insurance policies, to rules limiting the creditor's right to repossess chattels sold on credit, and so on to those fountainheads of litigation, the statutes of frauds. Some of these protective laws are designed to shield a class of persons; others, to interpose safeguards in classes of transactions or for types of property interests. Where the person is the object of protection, the domiciliaries of the state having the protective law might seem the persons whom that law was designed to protect, but, where domicil is dissociated from a settled residence, it then becomes a technical concept designed to meet legal needs other than those with which this principle is concerned. Consequently, for the purpose of this principle, settled residence rather than domicil seems the apt concept where these differ. However, it is a clumsy term without precise meaning and so, as in certain of the principles proposed in the preceding chapter, I have used an equally loose but neater term: "a home."[2]

Before turning to the cases, some comment on the rationale of the principle is in order. The conflicts that occasion it are often difficult. Once a state has reduced its protective laws to a minimum in order to foster free and secure transactions,

[1] A recent choice-of-law case has furnished an example: Lilienthal v. Kaufman, 395 P.2d 543 (Sup. Ct. Ore. 1964), in which the defendant was asserting (successfully) the protection of an Oregon law under which he had been declared a "spendthrift" to defeat the claim of a lender who had advanced him money in California to finance a joint venture.

[2] As in the previous chapter, I have used the term "home" in lieu of "settled residence" or some other word or phrase to indicate a sufficiently close connection, short of domicil, between a person and a state to justify bringing that person within that ambit of its concern. In Chapter VI, *supra*, at footnote 21, I called attention to the use of the term in the definition of "domicil" in *Restatement Second*.

there will inevitably be dealings between people in that state and people in the protected categories in other states. One state's policy has to give way. Sometimes the protective law will disclose limitations of purpose or territory that will permit the apparent conflict to be dismissed. Sometimes the factual connection with one state or the other may be so tenuous that its law can be disregarded. Where, however, these escapes are lacking, a general principle or principles of preference seem called for.

The principle here proposed gives preference to the protective law but only under circumstances that would lead to little, if any, interference with ordinary business activity in the nonprotective state. On the other hand, the instances in which this principle would not afford protection to a member of the protected class would be relatively few, even if the nonprotective state's laws were to be applied in all or most of the cases to which this principle did not extend.[3] Evasive tactics to circumvent the protective scheme would also be discouraged.

In the case of protective laws that single out certain types of transactions rather than classes of persons, the place of the home of the person claiming the protection might not be consequential except insofar as it bore upon where the transaction was centered, as might be true in the case of life insurance. Obviously no precise definition can be given to the "center" concept, though a succession of cases could give it greater specificity. It is intended to convey the idea that, in order to justify bringing the protective law into play, it is not enough that it have some contact, or even a substantial contact, with the transaction. The relative strictness of this requirement reflects a bias against pressing protective laws beyond the bounds where justification for their use is clear, a

[3] The fact that a case does not fall within the terms of a given "principle of preference" means only that the court must reach its decision independently of that principle. See p. 136, *supra*; p. 189, *infra*.

bias that I believe would prove to be widely shared and so not to impede mutual acceptance of the principle.

The process of illustration can begin with those casebook favorites: *Milliken v. Pratt*,[4] *University of Chicago v. Dater*,[5] and *Proctor v. Frost*,[6] all of which involve laws limiting the capacity of married women. In two of these cases (*Milliken* and *Dater*), the married woman resided in the state whose protective law was invoked, in the former case, unsuccessfully, in the latter, successfully. In *Proctor*, she did not live in that state, and the court might well have rested its refusal to apply the protective law on that ground, but, perhaps under the first *Restatement*'s influence, it treated the place of contracting as controlling.[7]

In *Milliken* and *Dater*, was the "affected transaction centered" in the same state as the married woman's residence? I think it was not so centered in either case. In each, the wife had aided her husband in obtaining credit in the state denying her protection, signing an instrument needed for this purpose in her home state. In one case, a merchant in the other state was asked to supply merchandise to the husband on credit; in the other case a lender in the other state was asked to lend on the security of a mortgage on land in the lender's own state. It was not clear in either case whether the creditor knew the limitations of the other state's law.

Contrast *Milliken* with a case differing from it in that the Maine merchant had its salesmen regularly soliciting orders in Massachusetts, the state affording protection. Con-

[4] 125 Mass. 374 (1878). A common but erroneous belief is that the court in *Milliken* adopted a jurisdiction-selecting rule, namely, that the law of the place of contracting governs capacity to contract. The court alluded to a case in which the rule "was carried so far" as to apply the *lex loci contractus* to deny capacity to a married woman capable by the law of her domicil. After noting that some authorities had held to the contrary, it then observed, "But that alternative is not here presented." *Id.* at 382.

[5] 277 Mich. 658, 270 N.W. 175 (1936).

[6] 89 N.H. 304, 197 Atl. 813 (1938).

[7] *Id.* at 307, 815, 197 Atl. at 815.

trast *Dater* with a case in which the University of Chicago had lent on the security of property not in Illinois but in Michigan, the protecting state. In either situation, the transaction might well have been found centered in the protecting state, and so, under the proposed principle, their respective laws should apply to protect their married women.

In *Proctor*, the New Hampshire court said of its statute denying married women the power to contract or convey as surety for their husbands that its "primary purpose" was "to protect married women in New Hampshire."[8] There a Massachusetts wife, with full capacity, was allowed to mortgage New Hampshire land as surety for her husband. However, she acted in Massachusetts, borrowing from a lender there. Suppose, in the next case, she executed the notes and mortgage in New Hampshire, mailing them to Boston. I should hope the court would recognize that the mere fact that she acted in New Hampshire did not bring her within the statutory purpose.

Suppose a New Hampshire husband and wife had negotiated a loan in Massachusetts, secured by Massachusetts land, the wife executing the notes in New Hampshire. Even though New Hampshire were the place of contracting according to the first *Restatement*'s rules, I still should consider the transaction centered in Massachusetts. Not so, if she had mortgaged New Hampshire land.

In the field of debtor-creditor relations, most of the questions involve third parties, and this principle does not cover the new factors that consideration of their interests invoke. However, to turn to a case on which I have already published some detailed comment, *Shanahan v. Landers Construction Co.*,[9] the question presented was whether a conditional seller's right of repossession was limited by the law of New Hamp-

[8] *Ibid.* The case scarcely requires resort to the principle.

[9] 266 F.2d 400 (1st Cir. 1959), discussed in Cavers, "The Conditional Seller's Remedies and the Choice-of-Law Process: Some Notes on *Shanahan*," 35 N.Y.U.L. Rev. 1126 (1960).

shire, where the buyer was located and where the repossessed road machinery had been garaged. The seller was a Massachusetts concern; the contract was executed there; the machinery was delivered to the buyer in Vermont, where it was briefly used. The court applied the New Hampshire law and held the seller a converter, thereby protecting the buyer in respect of his possession of the machinery.

Here the protective law was not concerned with the transaction that took place in Massachusetts but with the continuing legal relationships of the parties concerning the machinery in New Hampshire. The conditional seller who deals with a New Hampshire buyer who buys for use in that state ought to resign himself to the protective features of New Hampshire law.[10]

The statute of frauds is a venerable device designed to protect a diverse assortment of people as participants in a variety of transactions. Its purpose is in part to deter heedless transactions; even more to encourage trustworthy, reasonably detailed records of agreements, thereby deterring perjury. We shall probably have to expect decisions for many years in which courts will continue to classify the statute as "proce-

[10] The opinion is noteworthy for its refusal to follow the *Restatement*, § 281, which would have called for application of the law of the chattel's situs at the moment the contract was executed (its whereabouts then being unknown), a position modified by *Restatement Second*, § 281 (Tent. Draft No. 5, 1959), only by calling for inquiry into the *whole* law of the situs, however fleeting the chattel's location there. The court also demonstrated the ability of federal courts to apply with perspicacity the choice-of-law rules of the state in which they sit; it carefully distinguished the superficially similar case of Jewett, Inc. v. Keystone Driller Co., 282 Mass. 469, 185 N.E. 369 (1933).

For a case involving an analogous problem, see Universal C. I. T. Credit Corporation v. Hulett, 151 So. 2d 705 (La. App. 1963), in which the opinion demonstrates the court's familiarity with much of the new literature of choice of law and which is discussed by the opinion's author in Tate, Book Review, "Currie, *Selected Essays on the Conflict of Laws*," 39 TUL. L. REV. 162, 169 (1964). The decision is criticized in Dainow, "Variations on a Theme in Conflict of Laws in Louisiana," 24 LA. L. REV. 157 (1964) and defended in Note, 38 TUL. L. REV. 169 (1963).

dural," but, as this mistaken notion is gradually dissipated, the choice between substantive laws will have to be faced more squarely.

In the statute we have a requirement that relates to types of transactions, not to categories of people;[11] some of the transactions covered are contractual; some are conveyances. Suppose a transaction is centered in State X, which does not require a writing or requires a less exacting one than does the statute of State Y, the parties' home state. Should the promisor be able to claim the protection of the Y statute? The principle we have been considering would not justify an affirmative answer: it would not call for the application of the statute of the home state, Y. State Y, with a statute that is primarily a regulator of transactions, not the protector of a class of people, would not pursue Y citizens with maternal solicitude when they are engaged in out-of-state business.[12]

[11] Statutes of Frauds cover a diversity of transactions. As to certain of these, the protection of domiciliaries may be a primary purpose. Thus, as to contracts to make wills, the requirement of a written contract reinforces the precautionary formalities which a state prescribes for the wills of its domicilaries. The problems posed by state statutes addressed to "testamentary contracts" are discussed in Cavers, "Contracts to Leave by Will and the Choice-of-Law Process: Some Notes on *Bernkrant*," in PERSPECTIVES OF LAW: ESSAYS FOR AUSTIN WAKEMAN SCOTT, 38 (Pound, Griswold & Sutherland, eds. 1964).

[12] *Cf.* Lams v. F. H. Smith Co., 36 Del. 477, 178 Atl. 651 (1935), where the court declared that the Delaware statute "is primarily for the benefit of the citizens of Delaware." *Id.* at 482, 178 Atl. at 653. Of course, most transactions in Delaware involve Delaware citizens, and the citizens of little Delaware would be peculiarly vulnerable to a characterization of the Delaware statute as "procedural," with the risk that as a consequence the statute would be ignored in the courts of neighboring states. These considerations led the court to hold the statute's application dependent on the place where the contract was made, a solution decried by Professor Currie as a manipulation of a mechanical choice-of-law concept which protected some Delawareans while arbitrarily depriving others of its benefit. Currie & Schreter, "Unconstitutional Discrimination in the Conflict of Laws: Privileges and Immunities," 69 YALE L.J. 1323, 1328 (1960), in CURRIE, SELECTED ESSAYS ON THE CONFLICT OF LAWS (hereinafter cited as SELECTED ESSAYS) 445, 451 (1963). This seems to

But, for the same reason, when the Y citizens doing Z business in Z have failed to satisfy the requirements of Z law, the fact that they have met Y's laxer standards would not cure the failure.

For this principle to be defensible, it is necessary that the requirement that the transaction be centered in a given state not simply be given lip service. It would certainly not be enough that the place of contracting be found there (often a finding that could not be made if the terms of the statute were respected). The centering of the relevant parts of the transaction in State X brings the transaction within the purpose of X's transaction-regulating statute. Also X was probably the state toward which the expectations of the parties were directed, insofar as they had any expectation as to the source of law governing their contract. However, if the contract were bad by State X law, the court would probably not defend its application by reference to the expectation of the parties.[13] But what weight ought choice-of-law principles accord to the expectations of the parties? Can the autonomy of the parties—their power to choose the law—coexist with the foregoing principle?

This is a question that will be considered in connection with the principle of preference next suggested. However, the consideration of the principle now under examination cannot be concluded without devoting some attention to the cases which it fails to cover because the transaction is not centered in the state with the protective law but is either centered in a state denying protection or is divided between the two.

---

me a valid objection to the court's use of the place-of-making rule. It would not seem valid if applied to a principle protecting Delawareans (and others) only when they engage in transactions centered in Delaware. I doubt that the court wanted to extend the protection further; however, the only tool it had at hand was the arbitrary place-of-making rule.

[13] Seldom is the expectation of the parties invoked as a ground for choosing a law denying the validity of a contract. See Cavers, *supra* note 11, at 51.

It will be recalled that the failure of a case to come within the scope of a principle of preference does not mean that the proper choice to be made must for that reason be the reverse of the choice indicated by the principle. Instead, the problems presented should be examined with the realization that they are *different* problems from those covered by the principle. On reflection, the reverse result might appear to be the correct one; yet quite possibly a contrary conclusion could reasonably be reached. Study of a number of such cases might soon reveal grounds for the formulation of a distinct principle or principles of preference to cover them, or the question might have to be left to a gradual process of case-by-case solution.

The multistate interest in security of interstate transactions will, of course, exert a pull in favor of the application of the law of the state denying protection and upholding agreements whenever transactions have been centered there. Especially within our closely-knit economy, we expect people to trade and extend credit freely across state lines. When the seller or lender is selling or lending to customers who have sought him out in his own market and wish to engage in transactions that are in accord with the laws prevailing there, the case for allowing him the benefit of those laws would ordinarily be a strong one. Sometimes, however, the size and circumstances of the transactions would render it reasonable to require the local businessman to look into the legal situation of his customer under the laws of the latter's home state and to subject the former to the limitations they impose.

In a recent case which has rejected this view, *Lilienthal v. Kaufman,*[14] the court subjected an out-of-state lender to the protective laws of the forum, the borrower's home state, with-

[14] Lilienthal v. Kaufman, *supra* note 1. Some of the facts are derived from Olshen v. Kaufman, 235 Ore. 423, 385 P.2d 161 (1963), in which the same spendthrift's guardian was allowed to avoid a similar contract with an Oregonian. The periodic accountings filed before and after these transactions showed an increase in the spendthrift's estate from $63,410 to $86,381.

out reference to whether the lender had any knowledge of the borrower's incapacity or whether reasonable inquiry would have revealed it. The borrower, a businessman in Portland, Oregon, engaged in the wholesaling of toys, sporting goods, radios and the like and maintaining an office and bank accounts in Portland, proposed to a San Francisco merchant a joint venture in the sale of binoculars. To finance this the Oregonian secured an advance of about $5,000 from his California associate on a note made and payable in San Francisco. When the venture failed and the maker defaulted on the note, the lender learned that two years or so before his joint venturer had been declared a "spendthrift" in Oregon and placed under guardianship. The Oregon law authorizes the guardian of a spendthrift to avoid his ward's contracts other than for necessaries.[15] The guardian refused to pay the note, and the California merchant sued. California law does not provide for a status of "spendthrift"; its provision for conservatorships seems to be directed to a distinctly different hazard.[16]

A divided Oregon Supreme Court affirmed a judgment for the defendant in a suit on the notes which the guardian had sought to avoid. After examining certain of the foregoing facts, the majority recognized that "all signs have pointed to applying the law of California and holding the contract enforceable," but then asked, "Are choice-of-law principles . . . so superior that they can overcome [the] principle of Oregon law" that spendthrifts' contracts are voidable?[17]

[15] ORE. REV. STAT. §§ 126.006 (6), 126.280.

[16] CAL. PROB. CODE § 1751. This appears to contemplate a person physically incompetent or one "likely to be deceived or imposed upon by artful or designing persons." If, despite its terms, the California law is commonly used to protect persons like the artful Mr. Kaufman, there would be a false conflict and so no reason to protect the California merchant. That the California law might be in accord with Oregon law is suggested in Note 17, STAN. L. REV. 750 n.2 (1965).

[17] Lilienthal v. Kaufman, *supra* note 1, at 546.

With an acknowledgement to Professor Currie, the court embarked on an examination of the conflicting interests of the states and concluded that "the interests of neither jurisdiction are more important than those of the other." In this situation, however, it deemed the Oregon courts "the appropriate instrument" to enforce "the policy chosen by the Oregon legislature."[18] That body had preferred to protect the spendthrift despite the commercial considerations arguing for the honoring of agreements both at home and with citizens of other states. As the court saw its task, it was to carry out this legislative preference. It did so by invoking Oregon's "public policy."

This decision accords with the methodology for choice of law that Professor Currie first advanced.[19] However, he might view the case as affording the Oregon court an appropriate occasion for a "restrained and moderate" construction[20] of the Oregon spendthrift statute, restricting it to Oregon transactions and thereby denying to the Oregon guardian the power to avoid the spendthrift's California notes. The latter solution could scarcely have been sustained by considerations to be found in the statute's own purpose; it would punch a hole, though perhaps not a large one, in the state's scheme of protection. Nonetheless, I submit that there is a marked difference in the fairness of exposing Oregonians to the risk that the Oregonians with whom they deal are under guardianship from that of ex-

[18] *Id.* at 549. A concurring opinion referred to the *Olshen* case, *supra* note 14, applying the statute to an Oregon creditor's detriment and said that to "distinguish [that] case it would be necessary to assume that although the legislature intended to protect the spendthrift, his family and the county when local creditors were harmed, the same protection was not intended where the transaction adversely affected foreign creditors." *Id.* at 550.

[19] It is summarized in Currie, "Notes on Methods and Objectives in the Conflict of Laws," 1959 DUKE L.J. 171, in SELECTED ESSAYS 177 (1963).

[20] See Currie, "Comments on *Babcock v. Jackson*, A Recent Development in the Conflict of Laws," 63 COLUM. L. REV. 1212, 1233, 1242 (1963); Currie, "The Disinterested Third State," 28 LAW & CONTEMP. PROB. 754, 768 (1963).

posing a Californian to the same risk in California. Oregonians have greater reason to be wary and greater opportunities to inform themselves. Moreover, though they may deplore the policies of their legislature, it is their own. Even though the risk that people in other states will not trade with Oregonians may be brushed aside as insubstantial,[21] the denial of recovery to the citizen of a sister state in these circumstances is at least a failure in accommodation. Indeed, if the California lender had acted with reasonable prudence—as to which facts are lacking—the decision would affront one's sense of justice. The court was not compelled to attribute to the Oregon legislature such indifference to the consequences of providing a haven for its spendthrifts who have chosen to find victims to defraud outside their home state.[22]

Most of the cases involving married women who dealt with out-of-state businessmen and later invoked their own protective laws to shield themselves from liability arose at a time when such action would not have violated the reasonable expectations of the other parties to the bargain as grossly as one suspects was true in the Oregon case we have just considered.[23] Knowledge that women might be under certain legal

21 The common preference to rest essentially ethical judgments on "hard," "practical" grounds not infrequently produces imaginary horribles such as this one. The dissent aptly characterized the "majority view . . . as a step backward toward the balkanization of the law of contracts." Lilienthal v. Kaufman, *supra* note 1 at 553.

22 The statute was silent as to extraterritorial application. Courts have often construed statutes not to apply to out-of-state events or transactions even though their literal terms would render them applicable and their purposes, narrowly conceived, would be advanced by their application. In so doing the courts have commonly proceeded "in the light of the applicable principles of the conflict of laws." See Bernkrant v. Fowler, 55 Cal. 2d 588, 594, 360 P.2d 906, 909 (1961), per Traynor, J. The practice now has Professor Currie's approval. See Currie, *supra* note 20.

23 Married women's capacity cases were most common in the nineteenth century and in the early years of the twentieth. However, as the 1936 *Dater* case, *supra* note 5, and the 1938 *Proctor* case, *supra* note 6,

disabilities had long been common enough that, at least for certain types of transactions, a requirement that the banker or merchant check the possible existence of these disabilities in dealing with a married woman from another state would not often have taken him unawares. Today, perhaps, the equality of the sexes before the law has become so endemic that the surviving exceptions to it may constitute a trap for the unwary against which choice-of-law rules should afford a safeguard.

As one examines situations with a view to determining the reasonable expectations of the parties to a transaction and what constitutes fair dealing, it is hard to avoid particularization.[24] A broader line, however, is suggested by the *Dater* case[25] in which, it will be recalled, an effort was being made to subject a Michigan married woman to a deficiency judgment consequent upon the foreclosure of a mortgage on Illinois property.

Naturally, in the process of mortgaging property which is owned jointly or by the entirety or is located in a state where the widow has an immunity against the claims of her late husband's creditors to satisfaction out of his realty,[26] the joinder of the wife in the mortgage would ordinarily be essential to the consummation of the transaction. Apart from the protec-

demonstrate, the problem lingered on and, though I have not surveyed married women's capacity statutes since the publication of 3 VERNIER, AMERICAN FAMILY LAW § 152 (1935), I suspect vestiges are still with us.

[24] Of course, if courts are content to use these criteria simply as labels for broad rules of thumb, such as the nineteenth century presumptions as to the intention of the parties, detailed inquiry can be avoided. Though the opinions of present-day courts do not often reveal the considerations they find controlling, the courts appear to be trying to assess the merits of the individual case more frequently than did their predecessors. The danger is that too often this process will eventuate in two lists of "contacts" with no meaningful indication of why one was more consequential than the other.

[25] University of Chicago v. Dater, *supra* note 5.

[26] For a summary of state laws on the widow's immunity from her husband's creditors, see MARSH, MARITAL PROPERTY IN CONFLICT OF LAWS 31-34, 61-62 (1952).

tion of the mortgagee, there would be a valid concern on the part of the state of the situs that its land be available for capital financing without being subject to limitations imposed by the protective laws of an out-of-state owner's home state. Yet this purpose could be accommodated without subjecting the lady who joins in the mortgage to a personal liability from which her own state's law seeks to shield her. Perhaps it would be appropriate, therefore, to dissociate the two issues, sustaining the validity of the foreclosure while denying enforcement of the claim for the deficiency, a solution that is rendered the more tolerable because the transactions leading to a mortgage on realty are likely to be conducted with such deliberate speed that the lender would have ample opportunity to inform himself of the legal status of the wife in her home state.

These speculations fortify my view that the converse of the situations covered by the above principle of preference is not itself apt for a broad principle or ripe for more specific ones. I shall now turn to a principle that seeks to give a limited scope to the parties' autonomy in choice of law.

7. *If the express (or reasonably inferable) intention of the parties to a transaction involving two or more states is that the law of a particular state which is reasonably related to the transaction should be applied to it, the law of that state should be applied if it allows the transaction to be carried out, even though neither party has a home in the state and the transaction is not centered there. However, this principle does not apply if the transaction runs counter to any protective law that the preceding principle would render applicable or if the transaction includes a conveyance of land and the mode of conveyance or the interests created run counter to applicable mandatory rules of the situs of the land. This principle does not govern the legal effect of the transaction on third parties with independent interests.*

By way of gloss, I should perhaps remark that this principle should be applicable to a separable part of a transaction or to a particular rule of law relating to it, although doubtless such situations would be rare. Similarly rare but unobjectionable would be a situation in which the parties' intention is directed to the whole law of the state chosen by them.

The reference to the intention of the parties invites the question: how about the adhesion contract where one party declares his intention in fine print, and the other is seldom aware of what it is claimed he has agreed to? I believe that, in the ordinary case, the acquiescence of the latter party should suffice to bind him to the declared choice of law, just as it binds him to other clauses in the adhesion contract. However, the forum, aware of the opportunity for trickery or exploitation that the adhesion contract presents, would doubtless be ready to reject such a clause when it was found to result in subjecting the accepting party to oppressive or otherwise unfair conditions or requirements.[27]

The widespread recognition of the autonomy of the parties in choice of law relating to contracts and, to a lesser degree, to other transactions, is an index of the relatively high importance attached to certainty in these areas and the relatively low importance attached to many of the legal restraints

[27] For example, in Siegelman v. Cunard White Star Ltd., 221 F.2d 189 (2d Cir. 1955), the court in upholding the choice of English law by a clause in a passenger ticket, observed, at 195: "And there is no suggestion that English law is oppressive to passengers. We regard the primary purpose of making English law govern here as being . . . to achieve uniformity of result . . . and to simplify administration of the contracts in question." For practical reasons which seldom suggest sinister motives, choice-of-law clauses are to be found most often in adhesion contracts. Professor Ehrenzweig's challenge to their recognition in such contracts, Ehrenzweig, "Contracts in the Conflict of Laws," 59 Colum. L. Rev. 973, 976 (1959), "Adhesion Contracts in the Conflict of Laws," 53 *id.* 1072 (1953), would, if widely heeded, constitute a serious subtraction from the value of the autonomy principle. His position is soundest when applied to an activity in which contracts are subject to close state regulation, e.g. insurance. It is significant that the once common choice-of-law clause is now seldom used by insurers. See Carnahan, Conflict of Laws and Life Insurance Contracts 287 (2d ed. 1958).

and requirements that might defeat the parties' expectations. In this situation, it does not seem unrealistic to anticipate mutual acceptance of the limited role given to autonomy by this principle. It is restricted not only by the reservations expressed in its statement, but also by the fact that the role of a principle of preference is itself limited. Thus, if the forum's law appears applicable and leaves no room for choice of law by the parties, the court presumably would never have occasion to reach this principle. On the other hand, recognition of the principle's existence might make a court slower to find that the forum's rule was restrictive to this degree.

The principle contemplates that the parties' choice will be given effect even though certain of the rules of law in the forum (or in another concerned state) which are overridden are rules that are viewed as "mandatory" in the sense that any of them would invalidate an express provision to the contrary in a wholly domestic transaction. The principle is premised on the assumption that, apart from what I have termed "protective rules" and the special case of land, even the mandatory rules of law may properly be subordinated to the policy that all states share in the furtherance of international and interstate transactions. If the qualifications noted above are respected, a transaction sustained by the law of a state chosen by the parties, to which the transaction is reasonably related, would rarely be such a menace to the forum (or the other concerned state or states) as to require its invalidation. I should add that recognition of this principle should not require a showing that the parties' manifestation of intent is itself embodied in a legally binding agreement; the principle itself is predicated on the manifestation of intent alone. Therefore, it poses no special problem when what is involved is a mandatory rule concerning the formation of contracts.[28]

[28] This seems to me an answer to certain hypothetical cases submitted by J. H. C. Morris in his lively exchange with F. A. Mann. See Morris, "The Proper Law of Contract: A Reply," 3 INT. L. Q. 197, 200 (1950).

If my purpose were more serious than illustration, no doubt I should have refrained from endeavoring to lump both contracts and property transactions in a single principle. However, with respect to personal property, there seems considerable basis for recognizing autonomy with respect to transactions of transfer, notably in the case of trusts.[29] Since the principle does not purport to deal with the effects of a transaction on third parties, the fact that interests in property are involved does not seem a sufficient basis for rejecting autonomy.[30] Where land transactions are involved the importance, from a functional standpoint, of preserving the integrity of the land law is recognized in the principle's exception for mandatory rules concerning modes of conveyance and interests created.[31]

Of course, an expression of intent is vitiated if induced by fraud, and surely courts in self-defense are entitled to deny effect to the choice of a foreign law to govern a transaction which had no other foreign element than that introduced by the choice itself.

[29] See, e.g., Wilmington Trust Co. v. Wilmington Trust Co., 26 Del. Ch. 397, 24 A.2d 309 (1942); Shannon v. Irving Trust Co., 275 N.Y. 95, 9 N.E.2d 792 (1937). Many years ago, I argued for recognition of the intention factor in this field. Cavers, "Trusts *Inter Vivos* and the Conflict of Laws," 44 Harv. L. Rev. 161 (1930).

[30] The Uniform Commercial Code, which allows even wider scope for party autonomy than my suggested principle, covers "property" questions in some of its provisions, but, when the interests of third parties are at stake, it has prescribed special protective choice-of-law rules. The Code's choice-of-law provisions are surveyed in Chapter IX *infra*, pp. 233-40.

[31] If transactions valid by the law chosen by the parties are upheld though invalid by the local law of the situs, doubt as to the validity or effect of the conveyances thus sustained might subsequently arise and cloud titles to land and impair their transferability. If the situs prefers this risk to the disappointment of the parties' expectations, it may give effect to the foreign law. See, e.g., 1910 Uniform Wills Act, Foreign Executed, § 1 (substantially the same as the 1940 Model Execution of Wills Act § 7, 9A U.L.A. 347 (1953)). That the choice of law by the situs should be followed by other jurisdictions if they have a chance to rule on the matter is the theme developed in a number of articles by Professor E. W. Briggs of Montana. See, e.g., Briggs, "Utility of the Jurisdictional Principle in a Policy Centered Conflict of Laws," 6 Vand. L. Rev. 667 (1953).

However, there remain other matters affecting only the parties as to which insistence on applying the law of the situs of land, as against the choice of another source of law, has little justification.[32]

Other Subjects for Principles of Preference

The principles of preference that I have been exposing to critical view are advanced to illustrate a concept that is designed to fill a void in our choice-of-law doctrine. As I have already stated, I am not writing a treatise on the subject or presenting a completed system. Within the limits appropriate to these lectures, I trust I have gone far enough. Instead of presenting more examples, I shall have to be content with listing a few of the subjects for which other principles might be formulated.

To note an obvious example, what principle would be appropriate for a transaction not involving a protective law of the sort covered in the sixth of my principles and for which no intended choice of law has been indicated, expressly or by implication, by the parties? Is this a situation for which an "objective" intent should be fabricated by the court as "the proper law"?[33] Or should the effort be made to locate the state where the transaction is "centered"—where such a state can be found?[34] Or should the law that would permit the

[32] A conspicuous example of a situation in which the local law of the situs may have little claim to application is where the land is subject to a contract of sale or a direction in a will to be sold and the issue in dispute relates to the proceeds. Some cases have employed the situs rule simply because, at the critical date, the property was still "immovable." E.g., In re Berchtold, (1923) 1 Ch. 192; Toledo Society for Crippled Children v. Hickok, 152 Tex. 578, 261 S.W.2d 692 (1953). The latter case is subjected to a detailed critique in Hancock, "In the Parish of *St. Mary le Bow* in the Ward of *Cheap*," 16 STAN. L. REV. 561 (1964).

[33] See, for a statement of the objective view, Morris & Cheshire, "Proper Law of a Contract in the Conflict of Laws," 56 L.Q. REV. 320 (1940).

[34] This concept seems to me useful only where the purposes of the law to be preferred are entitled to preference because the transaction (and

objectives of the transaction to be achieved be applied?[35] If so, should that law be expected to control all issues (including gap-filling), or should the principle recognize the possibility that the choice of a law holding, say, the need for consideration to have been satisfied might be influenced by factors distinct from those to which a court might turn in choosing the most appropriate source of law to provide, say, the measure of substantial performance?[36]

Another principle of preference might serve as an auxiliary to the foregoing, one that could be called the principle of equivalence. Two states concerned in a transaction may have mandatory rules governing the same matter—protective rules, perhaps—which are not the same, yet, in terms of the functions they perform, they do not differ importantly. If so, compliance with the less exacting could be regarded, for choice-of-law purposes, as the equivalent of compliance with the more rigorous.

A difficult problem, but one to which the approach I have been pursuing gives special importance, is the problem of discrimination between people from different states. Suppose a principle is cast in terms of the protection afforded people

---

sometimes also a party to it) are so closely associated with one state that its paramount concern with the matter may justly claim recognition. In situations of the sort we are now considering, the crux of the problem may stem from the fact that there is no such close connection.

[35] Professor Ehrenzweig is the most vigorous champion of this view, CONFLICT OF LAWS 467 (1962), but he is not alone. See Lorenzen, "Validity and Effect of Contracts in the Conflict of Laws," 30 YALE L.J. 655, 673 (1921); STUMBERG, CONFLICT OF LAWS 238 (3d ed. 1963). Both recognize certain exceptions to this principle.

[36] Multiple-issue contract cases are likely to remain infrequent. The risk of having to resort to "an amalgam" of laws from two or more jurisdictions to which I pointed in my discussion of a "personal law" of torts in the preceding chapter, *supra*, p. 154, seems a much less serious hazard in the field of contracts. The possibility that choice of law may proceed on an issue-by-issue basis in contracts cases is recognized, though its implications are not developed, in RESTATEMENT (SECOND), CONFLICT OF LAWS. § 332, Comment *d* (Tent. Draft No. 6, 1960).

in the protected category who have homes in the state with the protective law. A question may then arise whether the claim to protection of a person otherwise in that category who does not have a home in that state should be denied the benefit of the principle. The principle does not purport to answer that question by implication, and I hesitate to suggest how far a principle dealing specifically with the problem should go. However, one rather attractive solution would be to declare that a state giving protection to people whose homes are located there should give the same protection under the same circumstances to people whose homes are in another state if that state had a protective law which was the same as, or substantially similar to, the protective law of the state where the transaction was centered.[37]

There are, of course, many fields of law into which I have not ventured for my illustrations—marriage, for example. Here the *Restatement Second* has already provided the material for such a principle in the designation of a state—the domicil of one party which is also the intended matrimonial domicil—as "the state of paramount interest."[38] Its law may be applied

[37] In the preceding chapter, I proposed this solution in a number of situations. See, e.g., p. 171, *supra*. Since I am proposing principles for general adoption, the extension of the protective law of a given state to a person from another state having a like law seems to me appropriate without regard to whether the state of the forum is either one of those states or a disinterested third state. Professor Currie would have the state with the protective law afford its protection to persons from other states having a like law; indeed he sees it as a matter of "privileges and immunities." Nevertheless, he has viewed this seemingly sensible result as impossible of rational attainment by a court in any state other than the protective state or the state on the law of which the creditor relies. See Currie, "Married Women's Contracts: A Study in Conflict-of-Laws Method," 25 U. CHI. L. REV. 227, 255-57, 262 (1958), in SELECTED ESSAYS 77, 111-13, 120 (1963). For some modification of the latter view, see his articles cited in note 20 *supra*.

[38] Section 132 (Tent. Draft No. 4, 1957). My reference should not be taken to indicate unqualified agreement. The harsh black letter ought to be brought into harmony with Comment *b*. And must a marriage be forever blighted when, at the time of the ceremony, the parties had

to uphold a marriage which is invalid by the law of the place of celebration or to strike down a marriage that would be good by the latter law, provided, at least, this is required by "an overriding public policy" of the state of paramount interest.

This reference to "public policy" suggests another subject on which a principle of preference might be formulated. One might reasonably hope that principles of the sort I have been suggesting would tend to deter the invocation of "public policy" as the basis of a door-closing rule, that is, as a ground for rejecting a claim based on an otherwise applicable law. However, the principles I have ventured to formulate are broad; within their scope or in the interstices between them, occasions could arise, albeit rarely, in which a court that sought to be unwavering in its fidelity to the principles would be confronted by the necessity of enforcing a law like that envisaged by Judge Cardozo in *Loucks v. Standard Oil Co. of N.Y.*, a law violative of "some fundamental principle of justice, some prevalent conception of good morals, some deep-rooted tradition of the common weal."[39]

I see no reason for compelling a court to entertain so obnoxious a claim or, if the forum is an interested state, why it should not pronounce against it by applying its own law.[40]

---

intended to return to the state of "paramount interest" but, being advised that its law would invalidate their match, wisely changed their plans and settled in a state which viewed marriages such as theirs unobjectionable?

[39] 224 N.Y. 99, 111, 120 N.E. 198, 202 (1918). New York, incidentally, has just this year manifested a reluctance to invoke its public policy for door-closing purposes in two important cases: Intercontinental Hotel Corp. (Puerto Rico) v. Golden, 15 N.Y.2d 9, 203 N.E.2d 210 (1964) (gambling debt enforcible in Puerto Rico enforced in New York); Oltarsh v. Aetna Insurance Co., 15 N.Y.2d 111, 204 N.E.2d 622 (1965) (direct action entertained against insurer on Puerto Rican claim).

[40] Professors Paulsen and Sovern conclude from a thorough study of the "public policy" cases that the purported use of the concept as a door-closing device often actually represents a surreptitious choice of its own law by the forum, a tactic which may be resorted to in order to

However, any principle recognizing this authority should note as well the limited function it serves, especially where the claim against which it is invoked may, without question-begging, be termed a "vested right."[41] *Quaere*: Would a principle identifying the special circumstances under which a reference to a "vested right" would not be question-begging do more harm than good?

Some Questions Still to Be Considered

The chief thesis of these lectures, namely, that there is need for principles of preference in the choice-of-law process, is certain to raise many questions in the minds even of those who find themselves responding sympathetically to the idea—and the idea runs sufficiently against the current of forty years of American legal scholarship to make it likely that those whose initial response to it is friendly will be in a minority. These questions are not to be ignored, and I shall endeavor, in the chapters which follow, to anticipate a number of them.

I shall not, however, deal further with the many specific questions that might be posed concerning the content and application of the principles I have suggested. At this juncture in the development of the idea, such questions are not likely to cut to fundamentals. I might be persuaded that every one of my seven samples is deficient in serious respects and still remain convinced that the need for such principles, in improved versions, had not been impugned.

Instead, the questions I shall consider are the following. Is it realistic to expect courts to consider an approach to choice-

---

escape a choice dictated by a mechanical rule. Paulsen & Sovern, " 'Public Policy' in the Conflict of Laws," 56 COLUM. L. REV. 969 (1956); *cf.* Cavers, "A Critique of the Choice-of-Law Problem," 47 HARV. L. REV. 173, 183-84 (1933).

[41] The term seems apt when applied to a claim by one person against another which is recognized as valid by the law of the place where the acts giving rise to the claim were so completely localized that the application of any other law to them would seem a denial of due process.

of-law problems which would entail the use of such principles? Would their employment be consistent with the tradition of the common law? Would not the formulation and application of such principles be a usurpation by the courts of a legislative function? Do we have the prospect of coping more effectively with the choice-of-law problem in the peculiarly difficult environment afforded by the United States by commissioning our federal courts to serve as umpires, relieving them of the necessity of following state choice-of-law rules? And must we not turn ultimately to legislation for genuinely satisfactory solutions of the choice-of-law problem, resorting either to "spatially conditioned internal rules," statutory choice-of-law rules, or to treaties and conventions? Or is federal or uniform legislation to eliminate the need for choice a more promising solution? Finally, if we assume the continuing need for judicially-developed choice-of-law rules and principles, is there any way in which our judicial procedure can be adapted to assure a more satisfactory consideration of choice-of-law problems than is now employed in litigation? And could such an improvement also permit a fairer basis for differentiating, for choice-of-law purposes, between so-called substantive and procedural rules?

It is evident from this catalog of questions that, even though the concluding chapters were protracted, they could do little more than suggest answers or pose new questions for further exploration. A gratifying feature of this subject, for the legal scholar, if for no one else, is that its supply of unanswered questions appears well-nigh inexhaustible.

VIII

PRINCIPLES OF PREFERENCE AND THE COURTS, STATE AND FEDERAL

In the preceding two chapters, I have presented seven examples of principles of preference for use in choice-of-law cases involving true or avoidable conflicts in which a lack of legislative indication, express or implied, as to the applicability of the forum's own law, had left to its courts the question whether that law or the law of another state should be applied. I have suggested that courts could employ these principles in developing patterns of accommodation which, if adhered to, would set reasonable bounds for the application of potentially conflicting laws. Within these bounds, the respective purposes of those laws could be realized without undue interference with the activities and reasonable expectations of the people of the states involved. I have just posed a series of questions to which the propounder of such principles should be ready to respond. The first of these is whether it is realistic to expect courts to consider seriously an approach to choice-of-law problems which would entail the use of such principles. In a word, is the proposal of such principles academic?

A. *Are Principles of Preference Destined to Remain Academic?*

An affirmative answer to the latter question is clearly called for. That is why I address my proposal now to the law schools rather than to the courts, just as in 1933 I addressed my then academic ideas to the law schools rather than to the courts.[1] It is the coexistence of law schools and legal scholars with judges who take academic ideas seriously that gives reality to my hope that principles of the sort I have been advancing here may ultimately become part of the judicial process for choice of law.

The recent ground-breaking decisions have reflected a responsiveness to the academic critics of the received tradition, but they have also left a challenging task of construction for those critics to undertake. Most of those decisions have been what Dr. Nadelmann has called "easy cases,"[2] not easy in terms of doctrine but easy in the sense that, given the law-fact pattern, they seemed clearly "right." Yet each of them is surrounded by a shoal of related cases, almost every one of them more difficult than the decided cases. *Babcock v. Jackson*,[3] the New York guest-passenger case, and *Bernkrant v. Fowler*,[4] the California case of an oral contract to make a will, provide graphic examples of this situation. I have devoted an essay to each of them,[5] and the experience left me with a lively awareness of the difficulties of some of those related cases and an understanding of the courts' wariness to avoid commitments beyond the cases immediately before them.

In the course of one of those essays, I compared these opinions of our venturesome courts to those of the *Cour de Cassation* in which the court compresses its view of the law to the minimum needed to connect it with the relevant Code

[1] Cavers, "A Critique of the Choice-of-Law Problem," 47 HARV. L. REV. 173, 204 (1933).

[2] See Nadelmann, "Marginal Remarks on the New Trends in American Conflicts Law," 28 LAW & CONTEMP. PROB. 860, 864 (1963).

[3] 12 N.Y.2d 473, 191 N.E.2d 279 (1963).

[4] 55 Cal. 2d 588, 360 P.2d 906 (1961).

[5] Cavers, "Comment on *Babcock v. Jackson*, A Recent Development in Conflict of Laws," 63 COLUM. L. REV. 1219 (1963), and Cavers, "Oral Contracts to Provide by Will and the Choice-of-Law Process: Some Notes on *Bernkrant*," in PERSPECTIVES OF LAW: ESSAYS FOR AUSTIN WAKEMAN SCOTT 38 (Pound, Griswold & Sutherland, eds. 1964).

provisions, leaving to the learned writers of comments published in the unofficial reports of the case the burden of placing the case in the stream of doctrine and of projecting its probable impact on future cases.[6] Although our methods of providing such comments are less institutionalized, one might hope that the flow of law review writing which these pioneering choice-of-law cases have been inspiring would serve as a somewhat similar substitute for judicial opinions in providing premises for future decisions.

Unfortunately, until recently the law review commentary has seldom discharged that function. Commonly it has been preoccupied with measuring the extent to which decisions have departed from doctrinal orthodoxy.[7] The penumbra of unsolved cases has been noted, but the cases are left unsolved. On occasion the courts have been treated to counsel of perfection. Professors Cheatham and Reese canvassed the desiderata to be embodied in choice-of-law rules in a much-cited article,[8] desiderata which only lately Professor Reese has stated anew.[9] Thus, he observes, the good choice-of-law rule will be "simple and easy to apply." It will be "designed to make the international and state systems work well" and "seek to achieve certainty, predictability and uniformity of results," applying "the law of the state of dominant interest," if any, and furthering "the fundamental policy underlying the local law field involved." The distinguished German scholar, Dr. Wilhelm Wengler, is devoting much attention to developing the significance of the "principle of equality" in choice of law,

[6] *Id.* at 66 n.

[7] For the report of a survey of law review response to an unorthodox decision (the *Kilberg* case), see Currie, "Conflicts, Crisis and Confusion in New York," 1963 DUKE L.J. 1, in SELECTED ESSAYS ON CONFLICT OF LAWS (hereinafter cited as SELECTED ESSAYS) 690, 696-8 (1963).

[8] Cheatham & Reese, "Choice of the Applicable Law," 52 COLUM. L. REV. 959 (1952).

[9] Reese, "Conflict of Laws and the *Restatement Second*," 28 LAW & CONTEMP. PROB. 678, 682-90 (1963).

urging equal treatment both for the substantive laws of different states and also for the parties.[10]

All these objectives are good, but none of them provides specific guidance to courts having to choose between conflicting laws in hard cases. To be sure, the principle that the legitimate expectations of the parties are to be protected can afford such guidance but only when the expectations are both identifiable and actual and when "legitimate" does not beg the question confronting the court.[11] The "Basic Rule of Validation" which Professor Ehrenzweig would apply to sustain contracts is nothing if not affirmative, but it trails a train of exceptions and extends to only one area of the law, important though that area is.[12]

The *Restatement Second,* endeavoring to escape from the rigidities of its predecessor, has resorted, as we have seen, to a question-begging formula, "the most significant relationship," and then has sought to provide clues to significance

[10] Wengler, "The Significance of the Principle of Equality in the Conflict of Laws," 28 LAW & CONTEMP. PROB. 822 (1963). The pursuit of equality can become too zealous. Concern lest there be inequality in the treatment of multiple and simple contact cases seems to assume that these different situations are to be treated as if they were the same. The author's concern that there be criteria to justify the preference of one law as against the others involved in a multiple contact case, *id.* at 837, accords, of course, with the position I have been advancing in these lectures, but that the "better view" forbids "weighing the interests of the parties" in "shaping choice of law rules," *id.* at 832, is far from self-evident. No doubt Professor Wengler's concern reflects a laudable dissatisfaction with legislation such as some that is to be found in Germany, *id.* at 833-34, which accords German citizens the benefits of their own laws in situations where these are denied to aliens.

[11] In my essay on the *Bernkrant* case, *supra* note 5, at 48, I have discussed some of the problems posed by resort to the "expectations of the parties."

[12] EHRENZWEIG, CONFLICT OF LAWS, 465-90 (1962). Also, see Ehrenzweig, "The Statute of Frauds in the Conflict of Laws: The Basic Rule of Validation," 59 COLUM. L. REV. 874 (1959); Ehrenzweig, "Contracts in the Conflict of Laws, (Pt. 1: Validity)," 59 COLUM. L. REV. 973 (1959).

by listing factors to be taken into consideration by the courts.[13] The fact that this leaves judicial discretion virtually unchanneled—and the lawyer-counselor without guidance—has been inspiring a new round of complaints,[14] but, like the critics of the first *Restatement*, the critics of its successor seldom proffer alternative formulations that would provide more definite answers. The court which is unable to gain a confident sense of "most significant" from *Restatement Second*'s lists of factors or its primer-like Comments and Illustrations may be equally at a loss when it is admonished to apply "the ordinary principles of construction and interpretation" to statutes or common-law rules couched in typically universal terms.[15] I

[13] See, e.g., RESTATEMENT (SECOND), CONFLICT OF LAWS § 332, and § 332b, Comment *b* (Tent. Draft No. 6, 1960) (validity of contracts); *id.* § 379 (Tent. Draft No. 8, 1963) (law governing tort liability). I view the question-begging character of "most significant relationship" as a virtue in so far as it may induce courts to ask the right questions. See Cavers, "Re-restating the Conflict of Laws: The Chapter on Contracts," in XXTH CENTURY COMPARATIVE AND CONFLICTS LAW 349, 354-59 (von Mehren, Nadelmann & Hazard, eds. 1961). Moreover, *Restatement Second* follows its general rules with a series of jurisdiction-selecting rules to cover specific situations, unless some other state than that thereby selected is found to have "a more significant relationship."

[14] Professor Ehrenzweig has characterized the standard in *Restatement Second* as "neo-nihilism," EHRENZWEIG, CONFLICT OF LAWS 351 (1962), and has reinstituted a series of attacks originally aimed at the first *Restatement* under the war cry, "Law and Reason against the Restatement." See, e.g., Ehrenzweig, "The 'Most Significant Relationship' in the Conflicts Law of Torts," 28 LAW & CONTEMP. PROB. 700 (1963). Professor Currie has also been critical of *Restatement Second* on this score. See, e.g., Currie, "Comment on *Babcock v. Jackson*, A Recent Development in Conflict of Laws," 63 COLUM. L. REV. 1212, 1235 (1963).

[15] The difficulty of this feat and its importance in an appraisal of Professor Currie's methodology has been concealed by the fact that, in its original version (as baldly presented in Currie, "Notes on Methods and Objectives in the Conflict of Laws," 1959 DUKE L.J. 171, 177, in SELECTED ESSAYS 175, 183 (1963)) all the court had to do was to determine whether the state of the forum had an interest in the application of its law and, in the case of negative finding, whether the other state or states whose laws were invoked had an interest. Now, however, in the more sophisticated form of his methodology (see, e.g., Currie, "The

submit that a perplexed court might turn with satisfaction to principles of the kind I have suggested, principles with purposes that can be identified and evaluated, principles that can serve as premises from which specific results can be derived in concrete cases.

Despite my belief in the potential usefulness of principles of preference to courts confronting difficult choice-of-law cases, I recognize that the very concept of such principles is sufficiently novel in our law that its acceptance by the courts is unlikely unless it can achieve acceptance among legal scholars, however much the latter may disagree as to the content of particular principles. I was therefore especially pleased, on the eve of these lectures, to encounter an article by a newcomer to conflicts writing, Professor Baxter of Stanford, in which the author made a vigorous plea for the development of "normative principles" in choice of law and advanced a methodology by which he believed specific decisions could be reached through resort to such principles, even in cases of true conflicts.[16] A brief statement of his approach will, I think, reveal its basic resemblance to my own.[17]

In dealing with real as distinguished from false conflicts,

Disinterested Third State," 28 LAW & CONTEMP. PROB. 754, 768 (1963)), the requirement that, even in the case of a true conflict, the court consider whether a restrained and moderate interpretation be given the laws involved, confronts it with an exacting task for which instructions have not been furnished.

[16] Baxter, "Choice of Law and the Federal System," 16 STAN. L. REV. 1 (1963). He would identify, and dispose of, the false conflict cases much as would Professor Currie. *Id.* at 8.

[17] An interesting point of similarity is Professor Baxter's use of an imaginary negotiation between representatives of two states having conflicting laws who were endeavoring to devise a mutually acceptable choice-of-law rule, revealing the negotiators' growing awareness that each side could make certain concessions to the other's objectives without serious impairment of its own. *Id.* at 7. The possibility that a similar recognition might be achieved unilaterally is present in my invocation of Professor Rawls' test for determining the justice of a practice. See Chapter V, *supra*, at p. 130.

Professor Baxter states that "the criterion must be maximum attainment of underlying purpose by all governmental entities."[18] In pursuing this calculus, the "extent to which the purpose underlying a rule will be furthered by application or impaired by nonapplication to cases of a particular category may be regarded as the measure of the rule's application to cases within the category. Normative resolution of real conflicts cases is possible where one of the assertedly applicable rules is more pertinent to the case than the competing rule."[19]

I suspect that, on further investigation, Professor Baxter will find that the "principle of comparative impairment" will not serve to resolve all the cases that he examines. I believe that the test is a useful one but that not uncommonly the invocation of other norms will be necessitated by the fact that the impairment of the purposes of the law of State X which results from its subordination to the law of State Y will seem about the same as the impairment of the State Y law's purpose when it is subordinated to the State X law.[20] Nonetheless, I hope that

[18] Baxter, *supra* note 16, at 12. In elaborating his approach, Professor Baxter distinguishes between "two distinct types of governmental objectives, internal and external. The internal objectives are those underlying each state's resolution of conflicting private interests. These objectives inhere in a case even if the fact situation is wholly localized to a single state. . . . External objectives are introduced when a transaction affects persons identified with different states. They are the objectives of each state to make effective, in all situations involving persons as to whom it has responsibility for legal ordering, that resolution of contending private interests the state has made for local purposes. In each real conflicts case the external objective of one state must be subordinated. The choice problem posed is that of allocating spheres of lawmaking control. . . . The principle is to subordinate, in the particular case, the external objective of the state whose internal objective will be least impaired in general scope and impact by subordination in cases like the one at hand." *Id.* at 17-18.

[19] *Id.* at 9.

[20] His norms will doubtless come to include state objectives which are specific to multistate transactions and are not restricted to "making effective" in external situations "that resolution of contending private interests the state has made for local purposes," as he puts it in the passage quoted in note 18 *supra*.

Professor Baxter will persevere in the development of normative principles and, in so doing, not shrink from making and defending the specific judgments they will call for.

A veteran commentator on choice-of-law cases and problems, Professor E. W. Briggs of Montana, is promising to present "an institutional treatment" of choice-of-law cases which seems likely to lead to the formulation of principles of preference, although undoubtedly bearing a different label and reflecting the author's own distinctive contributions to the subject.[21] As I noted early in Chapter IV,[22] it seems probable that he would join with a number of other scholars (who may some day find themselves tagged as "the American school") in pursuing basically similar lines of attack on cases involving false or readily avoidable conflicts. But he finds that there is a class of cases "in which there is an emerging recognition by all or most states of certain *common* interests. These interests transcend the interests of any one state and are to be 'institutionalized' with the resulting *institutions* becoming the source of the relevant law."[23]

Important in this process, as he sees it, is the "legislative jurisdictional principle," which contemplates the uncoerced recognition by a forum of "a paramount legislative interest" in another state and thereupon calls upon the forum to accept

[21] Professor Briggs, whose writings are now less preoccupied than heretofore with contrasting the role of the choice-of-law rule of a situs with the role of the rule which leads the forum to look to the situs, has developed in outline an as yet unpublished project for a "General Theory for 'Conflicts' based in a Genuine Sociology of Law" cited in Briggs, "An Institutional Approach to Conflict of Laws: 'Law and Reason' versus Professor Ehrenzweig," 12 U.C.L.A.L. Rev. 29, 55n. (1964). His "institutional concept" is also developed in annotations to Briggs, "Jurisdiction by Statute," 24 Ohio St.L.J. 223, (1963). The seeds of Professor Briggs' approach appear to have come from the work of the late Professor Karl N. Llewellyn, that protean scholar whose ideas have left an indelible imprint on American legal thought.

[22] At p. 92, *supra.*

[23] Briggs, "An Institutional Approach," *supra* note 21, at 55. (Italics in original.)

the relevant choice-of-law rules of that state.[24] However, this rather specialized use of the concept appears no longer to be its principal function. Thus, Professor Briggs finds the principle helpful in interpreting a number of cases familiar to the casebooks, e.g., that case of the Minnesota dramshop in which the dramshop was held liable under Minnesota law for an injury caused in Wisconsin by its inebriated customer[25] and the case of the Connecticut auto rental company held liable under Connecticut law for an injury caused in Massachusetts by its negligent bailee.[26] As to these cases Professor Briggs states in a comment which throws some light on his approach[27] that "[their] significance . . . lies in the fact that liability was imposed by the states with which the defendants institutionally were exclusively affiliated, with respect to the precise issues involved. Imposing liability as part of the regulatory procedures

[24] Professor Briggs insists that the "forum's law itself supplies the jurisdictional rule, framed strictly according to the forum's judgment on policy." *Id.* at 56. However, I should suppose that a forum's judgment on policy might well depend on how the other state (State X) had exercised the legislative jurisdiction which the forum was prepared to acknowledge. If, for example, State X had asserted its authority to establish a standard of conduct for the violation of which it was prepared to impose liability, the forum might well accept the X standard with respect to an injury resulting from its violation. But suppose X had been content with a less exacting standard or had referred the matter to the law of Z, a state with a lower standard. Suppose the forum was both a concerned state and possessed of a more exacting standard than X's own or Z's standard. Might the forum not justly insist on applying its own law to a case of conduct violating its own standard though consistent with X's and Z's? A differentiation of this sort is not easily squared with the concepts of exclusive legislative jurisdiction to which the *Restatement* has accustomed us.

[25] Schmidt v. Driscoll Hotel, Inc., 249 Minn. 376, 82 N.W.2d 365 (1957), discussed in Chapter VI at p. 160, *supra*.

[26] Levy v. Daniels' U-Drive Auto Renting Co., 108 Conn. 333, 143 Atl. 163 (1928). I find Professor Briggs and myself in agreement as to certain views of Professor Ehrenzweig suggested by this case. See Cavers, "Some of Ehrenzweig's Choice-of-Law Generalizations," 18 OKLA. L. REV. 238 (1965).

[27] Briggs, "An Institutional Approach," *supra* note 21, at 59.

according to 'situs' is not only reasonable—it expresses a laudable effort on the part of these states to deal with a concern common to all states. On the other hand, institutionally, it would have been indefensible for either Wisconsin or Massachusetts to have imposed such liability, as the places of the injuries, merely by extending established doctrines of legal cause."

If, through the work of such scholars as Professors Baxter and Briggs, the idea and vocabulary of principles of preference or normative or institutional principles achieved currency, one might expect that in time some innovating court would be bold enough to articulate such a principle and to rest a decision upon it. Whether the principle the court thus formulated would come to be "the law of the land" and not merely a guide to future decisions in its own state would, of course, depend on whether the court's preference and the reasons advanced for it commended themselves to other courts. Absent a supercourt or a superlegislature, one cannot ask for more. These principles are value judgments. They do not flow ineluctably from premises laid down in cases sufficiently venerable to conceal the fact that, in their time, those cases too represented value judgments. It is also true that the preferences the principles reflect will seldom be so clearly valid that all reasonable men must find them acceptable. However, these preferences can be compared by reasonable men to opposing preferences and decisions reached on reasonable grounds that other reasonable men can evaluate. Furthermore, like other common-law principles, a principle of preference can be extended or curtailed in response to considerations calling for such treatment.

Without anticipating unanimity either with respect to the basic propositions or their subsequent elaboration, I see greater likelihood that, over time, substantial agreement can be achieved on such principles than I do on a set of jurisdiction-selecting rules, however narrow their scope; or on the proper employment of a variety of "factors" recommended for judicial consideration; or on the significance of a succession of *ad hoc* decisions ascribing to legislatures or courts specific purposes of which no explicit or implicit indications can be found. Yet, even if one could entertain hope of such agreement, would that hope be licit?

B. *Is the Development of Principles of Preference a Proper Judicial Function?*

Would a court having recourse to principles of this sort be recreant to the tradition of the Common Law? In recognizing a principle of preference as the basis of its choice, a court would be adopting a ground of decision materially broader than the particular conflict before it. Given the many variables that choice-of-law cases produce, should a wise court not heed Justice Traynor's admonition to "be prepared to reject unrealistic rules, yet cautious enough not to make formulations that reach too zealously into the future. . ."?[28]

Justice Traynor's prudence is proper enough at the time when, the old premises having been stripped away, no alternatives are in prospect. But courts faithful to the common-law judicial process have on occasion been ready to take a long step forward. From time to time, they have proclaimed principles whose generality permitted both courts and counsel to project the course of decision well beyond the instant case and its closest analogues. Later, perhaps, distinctions have had to be taken, limitations and extensions indicated, but the basic goal and method would have been set.

To be sure, many legal scholars of the present day, having inherited the distrust of generalization from the realist movement of the thirties and recognizing that both judicial law-making and its critical appraisal must entail the making of value judgments, are reluctant to risk affirmative positions that

[28] Traynor, "Is This Conflict Really Necessary?" 37 TEXAS L. REV. 657, 675 (1959). He has been bold in torts. See Escola v. Coca Cola Bottling Co., 24 Cal. 2d 452, 461, 150 P.2d 436, 440 (1944).

are significantly broader than the cases under scrutiny require. Indeed, I suspect we all have some preference for the perspective provided by that rearview mirror which the law reports afford us. Watching it, we can report on the pitfalls encountered and escaped, thereby keeping the courts cautious, if not affording them a long view of the road ahead.

The question I am raising has been posed in stricter than prudential terms. One justification for persevering in a case-by-case approach even when old premises are collapsing is that the judgments entailed in the bolder course of creating new premises are essentially legislative and so the responsibility for making them should be left with the legislatures. Thus Professor Currie has repeatedly questioned the propriety of a court's presuming to establish a preference for the purpose of one state's law as against the purpose of another state's law, especially when the law whose purpose is not preferred is the forum's.[29] When, however, the preference is simply the result of an effort to determine the circumstances in which each kind of law can best be allowed to operate,[30] this does not seem an invasion of a sphere that the legislature has reserved to itself. Indeed, the principles I have advanced suppose, as a prerequisite for their application, the absence of any ascertainable legislative purpose in the forum's law on the issue of application. Moreover, it is well to remember that there is danger in pushing the search for legislative purpose too far. Surely a court should not try to reconstruct what an actual legislature would have done if the particular issue before the court had been presented to that legislature, with all its conflicting interest groups and political alignments. Judges who

[29] See, e.g., Currie, "The Verdict of Quiescent Years," 28 U. CHI. L. REV. 258, 275 (1961), in SELECTED ESSAYS 584, 604 (1963).

[30] A preference of this type is distinguished by Professor Baxter from what he terms "super-value judgments" reflecting the view that the internal law of one state is better than the internal law of another state. See Baxter, *supra* note 16, at 5.

engage in that kind of gaming are substituting a make-believe legislature for a real court.

The fact that legislatures have been so content to leave questions of applicability to the courts is, of course, the most comforting answer to any charge of usurpation by the latter. However, today the consequential problem relates not to the past but to the future. Granted that legislatures heretofore have given the courts a free hand, yet, by all accounts, the courts have not discharged their responsibility with distinction. Instead of urging that the courts release a creativity that has long remained dormant in this field of law, ought one not instead to turn to the legislatures for solutions which the courts have failed to provide?

Before attempting to examine that alternative, I should like to consider still another, although it is one which may be available only in the United States.[31] Is our present predicament due to our failure to utilize the instrumentality of our federal court system? Might it not have achieved a rational scheme of choice of law to effect a just and practical accommodation of conflicting state laws? Moreover, despite the undistinguished record in this respect the federal courts have made in the past, are they not ideally constituted to carry out a kind of reform in the choice-of-law process which has been advocated in these lectures?

C. *Should the Federal Courts Be Free to Choose Law in Diversity Cases?*

Without regard to the historical foundations of *Klaxon*'s[32] requirement that in diversity cases the federal courts must em-

[31] Conceivably in time the European Economic Community will have to establish a court system to handle controversies between parties of diverse nationalities within the Common Market. If so, the alternative I am about to examine would be possible—and under distinctly more auspicious conditions.

[32] Klaxon Co. v. Stentor Electric Mfg. Co., 313 U.S. 487 (1941).

ploy the choice-of-law rules of the state in which they sit, the case for independent choice of law by the federal courts seems a strong one—considerations of a practical nature aside. In the independent federal judiciary we appear to have umpires made to our hand. If they cannot work out a system for the accommodation of conflicting state laws, how can one reasonably expect the state courts to do so? To put a question Professor Baxter of Stanford has recently posed, isn't the latter course rather like transferring "the responsibilities of the umpire" in a baseball game "to the first team member who managed to rule on a disputed event"?[33]

If the task of resolving conflicts of law between states is essentially like a game in which justice in Professor Rawls' sense of fairness is the criterion of valid rules, then the case for the neutral umpire becomes strong, in principle at least. However, this conception of the process places a low estimate on the importance of state autonomy in determining the reach of state law. The Supreme Court has granted ample room for the exercise of that autonomy by imposing constitutional restraint only when a state's assertion of authority goes beyond any reasonable state purpose[34] or is found to impair a national policy.[35] Should a federal district judge be empowered to curtail that state's authority whenever the accident of diver-

[33] Baxter, *supra* note 16, at 23. It was in this article that Professor Baxter advanced the use of what he termed the "comparative-impairment principle," *id.* at 20, which, if effective, might yield principles of choice not unlike the principles of preference I have been urging. Hence his championing the federal courts as arbiters of choice of law is especially pertinent.

[34] Hartford Accident and Indemnity Co. v. Delta Pine Land Co., 292 U.S. 143 (1934); Home Ins. Co. v. Dick, 281 U.S. 397 (1930). In the first of these cases "the activities" on which the application of state law was based "were thought to be too slight and too casual" or, as in the second case, "wholly lacking." Clay v. Sun Insurance Office, Ltd., 377 U.S. 179, 181-82 (1964).

[35] Hughes v. Fetter, 341 U.S. 609 (1951); Order of United Commercial Travelers v. Wolfe, 331 U.S. 586 (1947); *cf.* Broderick v. Rosner, 294 U.S. 629 (1935).

sity litigation brings the state law within his jurisdictional reach? It should be noted that independent federal choice-of-law authority could not be curbed by a state statute expressly specifying the application (or nonapplication?) of state law wherever the statute failed to correspond to the district judge's view of what the appropriate choice of law should be.[36]

In proposing principles of preference for adoption by state courts, I have not failed in respect for the principle of state autonomy. It will be recalled that a principle is not to be invoked where the forum state has asserted either expressly or by implication its purpose to have its law applied. Moreover, the state is left to judge whether any given principle of preference should be proposed by it or accepted by it when proposed by other states. A state can, therefore, be accommodating or not, as its courts think wise; it is to be master of its own house.

But, it may be argued, no state can be completely master as long as other states are free to entertain cases affecting its citizens or their interests. Why should a state not recognize that, on balance, it stands only to benefit by the allocation of authority between it and all other states which the federal courts could achieve by exercising the power to choose between conflicting laws? Doesn't that view accord with the basic considerations that I have advanced in support of the principles of preference?

I must grant, of course, a state cannot compel the applica-

[36] The use of the federal judicial power to curb state legislative autonomy has been questioned by Professor Alfred Hill, now of Columbia, in "The *Erie* Doctrine and the Constitution," 53 NW. U.L. REV. 541, 548 (1958), as well as by myself, Cavers, "The Changing Choice-of-Law Process and the Federal Courts," 28 LAW & CONTEMP. PROB. 732, 735-37 (1963), and by Professor Currie, "Change of Venue and the Conflict of Laws: A Retraction," 27 U. CHI. L. REV. 341, 347 (1960), in SELECTED ESSAYS 431, 437 (1963). Professor Henry M. Hart, Jr., supports the contrary view, Hart, "The Relations Between State and Federal Law," 54 COLUM. L. REV. 489, 513-15 (1954), as does Professor Baxter, *supra* note 16.

tion of its own laws in all cases, and I recognize that it may, on balance, benefit from an impartially conceived and administered set of choice-of-law rules and principles. Even if one assumes such a happy situation, the balance is not easily struck. A state which can determine the applicability of its own laws in cases arising in its own courts can probably enjoy its autonomy with respect to the laws to which it attaches most importance. Those laws, I submit, will most often be laws creating new claims as a part of some new or expanded regulatory scheme. Laws that have long been on the books will have become widely diffused, and important variations among them from state to state will be relatively few. New laws will often reflect state interventions in matters previously left unregulated or governed by common-law rules. A new law likely to create choice-of-law cases will be a law under which the instrument of civil liability is used as one means of achieving the law's objective. The plaintiff as the beneficiary of this intervention by State X can enjoy the advantage of this policy whenever he can sue the defendant in an X court. Therefore, the X rule can be implemented whenever the person against whom it might be asserted can be reached by process. Today this will seldom depend on the defendant's exposure to personal service within X; the mechanism of the long-arm statute is becoming increasingly available to reach out-of-state defendants, especially in the type of case I am envisaging.[37] Accordingly, the plaintiff can neutralize the fact that the other state's courts would reach a different result if they had jurisdiction.

In contrast, if a new law operates by creating new defenses (surely a less common phenomenon), the enacting state's ability to assure its law's use is limited to those cases where the protected person is a citizen of the state and not subject

[37] The long-arm statute now reaches far beyond the motor accident case in which it had its origin. The comprehensive character of the modern statute is exemplified in the UNIFORM INTERSTATE AND INTERNATIONAL PROCEDURE ACT, art. I, 9B U.L.A. 71, 73 (Supp. 1963).

to suit elsewhere. However, the fact that the state cannot assure the application of law is of little consequence in many other cases involving the defense. Thus, where the person whom the state's law could protect if he were a citizen is in fact a citizen of another state, presumably the purposes of the protective state's law would seldom be frustrated by the fact that it was not extended to protect him.

The case for overruling *Klaxon,* at whatever sacrifice of state autonomy, in order to permit the federal courts in diversity cases to develop a suprastate system of choice of law should be appraised, not on the basis of an ideal federal judicial system, but in the light of actualities. It is easy to overlook these in viewing the federal court system as a body of disinterested umpires, able to allocate the legislative competencies of the fifty states wisely in ways which will assure a net benefit to each state. Moreover, for judicially developed principles of preference of the sort I have suggested or Professor Baxter's "normative principles" for choice of law,[38] the federal diversity jurisdiction may seem an ideal instrumentality. Indeed, Professor Baxter urges the overthrow of *Klaxon* on this very ground, reinforced, to be sure, by his belief that the *Klaxon* rule is not historically valid either as a proposition of constitutional law or as an interpretation of the Rules of Decision Act.[39]

Turning to the actualities, one first must note that the federal courts do not constitute a judicial system which is organized

[38] See Baxter, *supra* note 16.

[39] *Ibid.* Professor Baxter argues the constitutional issue at some length on the basis of historical materials. These seem less persuasive than the fact that the Constitution does not require the federal judicial system to respect state lines. If the system were to cease to do so, the command of *Klaxon* would no longer be reasonable. However, the author rests the case for his interpretation of § 34 of the Rules of Decision Act on its concluding phrase which certainly is susceptible of other readings. He disregards the political considerations advanced for the contrary view by Charles Warren in his famous article invoked by Mr. Justice Brandeis in *Erie.* See Warren, "New Light on the History of the Federal Judiciary Act of 1789," 37 Harv. L. Rev. 49, 51-52, 81-88, 108 (1923).

to execute the great responsibility with which it would be entrusted. Such a system requires a supreme court; for the resolution of nonconstitutional choice-of-law cases the federal courts do not have a supreme court, and clearly they should not have one.[40] Hence, the authority to make federal choice-of-law decisions overriding state decisions and statutes would be entrusted to the eleven federal courts of appeals. These courts, while capable only of establishing precedents binding on the district courts in their respective circuits, are sufficiently conscious of their nominal ties so that decisions in one circuit can and do have an impact on the other circuits. Accordingly, when disagreement prevails among the circuits, no one circuit can hope to develop a settled body of decisional law such as a state court system can attain. Finally, the rising flow of diversity cases into the federal courts is creating such problems as to have called forth, at the suggestion of Chief Justice Warren, an American Law Institute study of how the flow might be restrained and rationalized.[41] If progress is made toward these goals, the situations in which a party to a controversy can have recourse to the federal courts will be more restricted than at present, thereby accentuating the paradox of different laws administered within a single state by

[40] Even before *Erie* and *Klaxon* eliminated such diversity cases in the Supreme Court, they had been reduced to a trickle, and federal question cases had been providing very few choice-of-law decisions. In view of the highly selective nature of the Court's exercise of jurisdiction and the great national importance of most of the problems with which it chooses to deal, the Court should not clog its docket with private litigation involving choice-of-law questions. Its wariness of such burdens has just been demonstrated in its recent escheat decision in Texas v. New Jersey, 379 U.S. 674 (1965).

[41] Chief Justice Warren's suggestion was made at the 1959 Annual Meeting of the Institute. See ALI, STUDY OF THE DIVISION OF JURISDICTION BETWEEN STATE AND FEDERAL COURTS v (Tent. Draft No. 1, 1963). The recommendations for revision of the diversity jurisdiction embodied in Tentative Drafts No. 1 and No. 2 would curtail access to it in a number of situations, notably where the plaintiff is a citizen of the forum state.

different courts to which access is not equally available but depends on factors bearing little relation to the laws chosen.

The abolition of *Klaxon* would entail the introduction of this pseudo-system into the difficult transition which the choice-of-law process now seems to be undergoing. The uncertainties of that transition would be multiplied. The possibilities of forum-shopping that now exist would be enlarged since, as in pre-*Erie* days, counsel could shop without sending cases off to other states, often without having the case leave counsel's home town.

The uncertainties that now afflict various choice-of-law rules in many states would be multiplied by the possibility of recourse to the federal courts where either old precedents within the circuit or new precedents in other circuits would threaten whatever stability the state decisions might have been attaining. And, of course, predictability at the planning stage would be impaired, not merely by uncertainties in choice-of-law rules, but also by the uncertainty whether a future controversy would be of such size, and arise under such circumstances, as to permit recourse to the federal courts.

Since the quest for certainty to be implemented by a suprastate system of choice-of-law rules would presumably have been a major factor leading to the rejection of *Klaxon*, the natural response of the federal courts to their restored freedom would not be indulgence in bold doctrinal innovation. Quite the contrary, the pressure would be for a return to the familiar, mechanical formulas which have always been defended on the thesis (however illusory) that they achieve uniformity and certainty. What the new freedom of the federal courts would bring would not be a new set of normative principles or a discriminating effort to narrow the issues in choice-of-law cases but a nostalgic search for a doctrinal lowest common denominator.[42]

42 I have developed this and other criticisms of the contra-*Klaxon* view more fully in Cavers, *supra* note 36, at 737-43.

Though these considerations have persuaded me[43] that the vision of federal courts serving as wise and effective umpires in diversity cases is a mirage, I see a very useful role for them in developing and disseminating a more satisfactory concept of the choice-of-law process than we now have, including the formulation and elaboration of principles of preference, whenever state decisions open the door to such progress. Indeed, the federal courts are exercising a beneficent influence today. Even if on occasion federal choice-of-law decisions should move ahead of state decisions, while respecting their principles, the effect should not be destabilizing. Presumably no federal court would take such action unless the state law were fluid so that the court would not be creating new uncertainties. Moreover, its decision would represent only the law of the state and so would not have repercussions throughout the federal system. Finally, if the federal court had read the state decisions wrongly, the state court would be free in the next pertinent case to correct the misconception.

Though, within the limits set by *Klaxon*, the federal courts seem to me to have a very useful role in ordinary diversity cases, there is reason to endow them with an independent authority in choice of law in special situations where, as in interpleader[44] and in the proposed multistate, multiparty

[43] *Klaxon* has more important supporters, among them the Supreme Court, which reiterated its adherence to the *Klaxon* doctrine as recently as the past term, Van Dusen v. Barrack, 376 U.S. 612 (1964), and the American Law Institute, which has approved the recommendations of its Reporter, Professor R. H. Field, and his associate, Professor Paul Mishkin, whose proposed revision of jurisdictional provisions governing diversity cases, *supra* note 41, assumed a retention of *Klaxon* save in special situations. Their recommendations are discussed in Cavers, *supra* note 36, at 743-52.

[44] The proposals of the American Law Institute Study would do away with the application of the *Klaxon* rule to cases under the Federal Interpleader Act, established in Griffin v. McCoach, 313 U.S. 498 (1941). See ALI, *op. cit. supra* note 41, at 35.

cases,[45] they can exercise an authority which jurisdictional rules preclude state courts from exercising. In this limited body of cases, they can contribute to the development of doctrine from a national viewpoint without introducing new elements of uncertainty into the state law or curtailing the exercise of substantive state power.[46]

45 This is recommended by the Institute Study, *id.* § 2344 (c) at 98, for cases in which federal power is used to join a party beyond the reach of state process when inclusion in a litigation is "necessary for a just adjudication." The departure from *Klaxon* is intended to extend only to issues involving the third party. *Id.*, Commentary, at 98-101.

46 The dangers noted above, which the Institute proposal would avoid, seem to me invited by the recent adoption of Rule 4f permitting a federal court in a diversity case to reach a third party in another state if served within 100 miles of the federal courthouse. For a criticism of this rule, see Cavers, *supra* note 36, at 750-52.

IX

LEGISLATION AS A MEANS OF SOLVING CHOICE-OF-LAW PROBLEMS

Given the long history of frustration in the solution of choice-of-law problems by judicial decision, despite a vast outpouring of scholarly writings, one might wonder why the answer to the difficulty should not have long since been found in legislation. In fact, a considerable amount of legislation has been enacted, especially outside the common-law jurisdictions, but experience in its employment has not been so encouraging as to induce widespread recourse to this method of dealing with choice of law. Yet certainly there is room for legislation in this field. Its actual use, its potentialities, and its limitations have not been adequately explored for the Anglo-American states, and the task is too large to be essayed in these lectures.[1] However, I should like to call attention to the diverse uses of legislation in choice of law and comment on a few of the problems that legislation in this field presents.

The legislatures have intervened in choice-of-law problems in several ways, not infrequently combining more than one in a single statute. Most common, perhaps, is the enactment of what Professor Nussbaum has called "spatially conditioned internal rules,"[2] which I shall call "legislatively localized laws"—or

[1] One of the leading protagonists of legislative solutions for choice-of-law problems, especially those involving international conflicts, is Dr. K. H. Nadelmann. See Nadelmann, "The United States and Plans for a Uniform (World) Law on International Sales of Goods," 112 U. Pa. L. Rev. 697 (1964), and the author's articles cited therein.

[2] Nussbaum, Private International Law 71 (1943).

"localized laws" for short. Such localized laws are substantive laws of the enacting state which are limited by their terms either (1) to certain events or transactions within the enacting state or (2) to certain persons connected with that state in a specified way, even though the acts or events involving them occur outside the state (a characteristic that renders me somewhat dissatisfied with my terminology).

An example of the first type of localized law is afforded by Section 155 of the New York Insurance Law forbidding certain clauses in life insurance policies "delivered or issued for delivery in this state."[3] An example of the second type is afforded by the Massachusetts Workmen's Compensation Act which is "localized" to employees insured under the Act but extends to injuries received in the course of employment "whether within or without the commonwealth."[4] Provisions of the latter sort, sometimes called "unilateral rules," are not uncommon in European codes where nationality is frequently the "localizing" tie.

Professor Nussbaum contends that these localizing conditions on the application of the forum's law are not to be considered choice-of-law rules, a distinction that can be significant when an uncritical attempt is made to use the same criteria that limit the forum's law in determining the application of foreign law.[5] He also notes that the inhibition which might deter another forum from looking at a state's choice-of-law rules should not restrain it from examining the conditions localizing that state's internal rules, even, I take it, when the condition results in the application of the internal rule to acts or events in another state.[6] These propositions do not trouble me, but, as I shall indicate shortly, the localizing of an internal

[3] N.Y. Insurance Law § 155.1.
[4] Mass. Gen. Laws Ann. c. 152, § 26.
[5] Nussbaum, *op. cit. supra* note 2, at 72.
[6] *Id.* at 71.

rule can produce unanticipated gaps and anomalies in choice-of-law situations.

A second type of statute prescribes a choice-of-law rule. Thus, to determine the validity of a will not conforming to the law of the testator's last domicil, the Model Execution of Wills Act prescribes, by way of alternate reference, the law of the place of execution or the law of the testator's domicil at the time of execution, provided either law would uphold a written will subscribed by the testator.[7] A variant of this type is a statute ruling out a choice of law that, but for the statute, would ordinarily have been made, as where the Uniform Marriage Evasion Act denies the application of the law of the place of celebration to uphold the marriage of a domiciliary that would have been unlawful by the law of the domicil to which the would-be spouses intend to return.[8]

In addition to statutes, bilateral treaties and multilateral conventions can provide vehicles for choice-of-law rules, though the former are seldom used for this purpose. Some conventions may have no other function than to prescribe such rules. The utilization of various forms of international agreements will be considered in the next chapter.

So much for the categories; now for certain problems which, though not insuperable, suggest some reasons why recourse to localizing statutes has not provided an easy way out.

A. *Some Difficulties in the Application of Localized Laws*

Probably the main motivation leading to the enactment of localized statutes is the simple desire to be sure that the substantive rule will be applied in the most obviously appropriate circumstances. I suspect that seldom is the specification of the localizing conditions the product of a nice calculation

[7] Sec. 7, 9A U.L.A. 341, 347 (1957).

[8] 9 U.L.A. 479 (1942). This act was withdrawn in 1943 after adoption by five states. See HANDBOOK OF THE NATIONAL CONFERENCE OF COMMISSIONERS ON UNIFORM STATE LAWS 64 (1943).

that excludes all other situations or that reflects a determination to subject every case falling within the condition to the substantive rule. Consider, for example, the provision noted earlier in which New York provided for certain clauses in every life insurance policy "delivered or issued for delivery" in New York State.

The Court of Appeals for the Second Circuit had to decide a case under that provision a few years ago, *Zogg v. Penn Mutual Life Insurance Co.*[9] A naval officer, domiciled in New York, while stationed in Boston entered into a binder for a policy with the defendant company, a Pennsylvania corporation doing business in both New York and Massachusetts. The policy itself, the jury found, was later mailed to the officer's New York address. Subsequently he committed suicide while insane. Under New York law, this was not a defense to the insurer; under Massachusetts law, it was. The insurer contended that the contract had been made in Massachusetts, where the binder had been entered into, and that delivery of the policy could not be used to bring a Massachusetts contract under New York law. The Second Circuit, applying New York choice-of-law rules, found that the most significant contacts of the transaction were with New York,[10] and held that the place of delivery represented a valid legislative determination calling for the application of New York law in an interstate situation, even though in this case the policy's delivery came after the contract had been "made." Accordingly, the court applied New York law and enforced the policy.

If this case were to arise in Massachusetts today, the likelihood is considerable that the Massachusetts law would be applied as the law of the place of contracting. If, however, a like case were to arise in the future after courts had become accustomed to utilizing principles of preference, the Massa-

[9] 276 F.2d 861 (2d Cir. 1960).

[10] Apparently the court considered this step necessary to defeat the defendant's contention that "delivered or issued for delivery" should be construed to embody the place-of-contracting rule.

chusetts court might well consider the case an appropriate one for the application of a principle like my sixth example.[11] It would see in the New York substantive law, reinforced by its localizing provision, a purpose to protect New York residents who were entering into insurance transactions centered in New York and would find no countervailing need to protect the defendant insurer which had dealt with a New Yorker temporarily in Massachusetts in the manner noted.[12] For a court taking this approach, the delivery provision in the New York statute would be helpful, perhaps decisive.

Consider, however, two variations on the Zogg case. In one the sailor is a Bostonian. After the binder has been issued to him in Boston, he receives an order to report for cruise duty in New York and arranges to have the policy sent to his aunt's home in Brooklyn before he sails from that port. Here surely the New York law ought not to apply; by the New York choice-of-law test,[13] Massachusetts is plainly the

[11] If at least the parties have not indicated an intention to choose another law, the prevailing Massachusetts rule appears today to call for the *lex loci contractus.* West Side Motor Express, Inc. v. Finance Discount Corp., 340 Mass. 669, 165 N.E.2d 903 (1960); Fine, "Massachusetts Contract Cases and Problems in Choice of Law," 43 MASS. L.Q., No. 3, p. 46 (1958). The principle stated in my sixth example, see p. 181 *supra*, calls for the application of a protective law restricting freedom where the protected person had a home in the state and the affected transaction was centered there. Presumably it would apply to a domiciliary having no settled residence elsewhere.

[12] The conflict is not a false one; the application of the New York law undermines the security of a Massachusetts transaction. Massachusetts, however, has no statute or legal policy committing it to the application of its own law. If it is to make a reasonable choice, it can scarcely avoid expressing a preference as between security of transactions and the effectuation of protective legislation in the circumstances noted above.

[13] ". . . the most significant contacts with the matter in dispute." Rubin v. Irving Trust Co., 305 N.Y. 288, 305, 113 N.E.2d 424, 431 (1953), quoted and applied in Auten v. Auten, 308 N.Y. 155, 160, 124 N.E.2d 99, 102 (1954). The *Zogg* case and the hypotheticals are discussed in Danson, "Territorially Limited Statutes and the Choice-of-Law Process," 1 HARV. J. LEGIS. 115, 122-23 (1964), an article based on a paper originally submitted in a conflict-of-laws seminar of mine.

state whose law has the most significant relationship to the issue presented by these facts. New York's statutory condition of "delivery" ought to be interpreted to require delivery in a more meaningful sense than the mere physical tradition of the instrument within New York territory. Indeed, the application of New York law in these circumstances might give rise to constitutional doubts.[14] However, it is easier to conclude that the New York law should be held inapplicable than to draft an amendment that would cover this case.

In the second variant, the sailor who has obtained the binder in Boston is a New Yorker, as in the *Zogg* case. He has been ordered to report for duty outside Massachusetts but has been granted two weeks' leave which he is to spend on Cape Cod. He arranges to have the policy mailed to him there. The rest of the case follows the original pattern.

Here it seems clear that, but for the statute, the New York insurance law would have been applied by a New York court. Has the statute prevented that result? I submit that it should not be allowed to do so, yet the statute has made the plaintiff's case a difficult one. So, by the way, do the terminologies Professor Nussbaum and I have used: if the internal insurance law has been spatially conditioned or localized, then it would seem that there is no New York rule to protect the plaintiff from the serious consequences of an otherwise inconsequential change of address. The solution that I would find most satisfactory would be a holding that no negative inference is to be drawn from the specification of "delivery or issued for delivery," that the legislature was concerned to assure the coverage of those cases but not to preclude the use of choice-of-law principles to deal with cases that failed to satisfy the statutory conditions. In other words, the internal rule is not

[14] However, delivery has been used so long and often as a connecting factor in insurance legislation, see CARNAHAN, CONFLICT-OF-LAWS AND LIFE INSURANCE CONTRACTS ch. 3 (2d ed. 1958), that the mere fact of delivery might be accorded sufficient weight to sustain the use of New York law.

spatially conditioned, but its application is subject to a statutory directive.

If not treated in this fashion, "spatial" or "localizing" conditions on internal rules can produce absurd results. Consider the following case, based on an actual one.[15] A railroad operating in Quebec starts a fire in New Hampshire by casting sparks across the boundary. The plaintiff's ability to prove negligence is doubtful. Both New Hampshire and Canada have statutes imposing strict liability on railroads setting fires. However, the New Hampshire statute originated in an 1840 provision limited in application to railroad corporations "established" in New Hampshire, a reflection, no doubt, of the situation prevailing in 1840 when probably no other railroads could have caused such fires. The court assumed without discussion that only the New Hampshire law could apply to the New Hampshire injury. Hence, if negligence could not be proved, the absurd result would be achieved of allowing this railroad to escape liability despite the fact that both the concerned states had adopted the standard of strict liability for railroad-caused fires.

Yet what route should the New Hampshire court have followed to impose strict liability? One route to that end would be to hold the Canadian law applicable by invoking a principle of preference like my third,[16] a decision eased by the identity of the two states' rules, demonstrating the absence

[15] Connecticut Valley Lumber Co. v. Maine Central R.R., 78 N.H. 553, 103 Atl. 263 (1918).

[16] This principle would prefer the application of a liability-creating "special control" to an actor who was engaged in the controlled conduct in the state imposing the control, despite the fact that the plaintiff sustained the injury complained of in his own state which imposed no such control. See p. 159 *supra*. This route might be taken by a New Hampshire court even though Canadian courts had held, or the Canadian legislature had declared, that the Canadian law did not "want" to be applied to out-of-Canada injuries. See p. 105 *supra*. If that spatial limitation had been asserted, it would render difficult disposing of the case as a false conflict. The states would have the same substantive policies but there would be a potential conflict as to their reach.

of any conflict in substantive policy. Another route would be to reinterpret the common law of New Hampshire to extend the same standard of liability to out-of-state railroads as the statute provided for in-state railroads. A third route would be to consider the statutory rule applicable to all railroads setting fires in the state, the New Hampshire railroads having been specified to assure their coverage but no negative inference being drawn as to other railroads.

For a court habituated to the place-of-injury rule and to a more literal reading of statutes, all of these routes would be difficult. The New Hampshire court's requirement of proof of negligence for the New Hampshire injury was the unintended consequence of the localizing condition in the 1840 statute. Of course, the removal of that condition for the future presents no technical difficulty, but this is just the kind of defect in statutory law that a legislature will always be too busy to correct.[17]

B. *The Treatment of Problems of Application in Two Major Uniform Laws*

Legislative approaches to the problems of determining under what circumstances a new law should be applied and when recourse should be had to another law are many and diverse. They result in posing many alternatives for the draftsmen of

[17] The difficulties created by localizing statutes have led the distinguished general editor of *Dicey*, John H. C. Morris of Oxford University, to advocate recourse instead to the enactment of choice-of-law rules by a legislature which is not content to leave the choice-of-law process to the courts. If it is assumed that renvoi will not be practiced, a court, confronted by the choice-of-law rule that another state has enacted, can simply ignore it and apply that state's internal law. If that law had been spatially limited, this opportunity might be thought not to be available. See Morris, "The Choice of Law Clause in Statutes," 62 L.Q. Rev. 170 (1946). A recent commentator has suggested that the preference for putting rules in a form in which they can be ignored indicates that the rules themselves are "arbitrary and mechanical." Danson, *supra* note 13, at 137.

any uniform legislation that covers a substantial range of activities extending into other states. The fact that the draftsman's goal is complete uniformity within the nation does not dispel for him the need to cope with this problem. Few uniform laws are uniformly adopted, and the process of adoption is often protracted. Deviations from the model by legislatures and differences in interpretation by courts add other sources of conflict. Moreover, dealings with nations outside the federation or national community for which the uniform laws have been drawn promise a perpetual need for choices of law. Consequently, the draftsmen of the Uniform Commercial Code[18] and the Uniform Securities Act[19] have had to wrestle with problems of application and choice. However, the two laws differ materially in nature. As a consequence, there have been marked differences in the solutions reached so that their examination together should be rewarding.

(1) *The Uniform Commercial Code.* The Code contains both statutory rules for choice of law and conditions localizing its provisions, though not restricting their application solely to transactions or property within the enacting state. As originally drafted, the Code contained rules for its application that stretched beyond the pale of reasonableness. They soon came under attack, one of the most powerful assaults being a philippic by Professor Rheinstein.[20] A drastic revision was undertaken. The basic choice-of-law rule is now contained in

[18] The Code had been adopted in 29 states and the District of Columbia by July 1964.

[19] The Act had been adopted, sometimes with modifications, in 18 states and Puerto Rico by July 1, 1964. The states are Alabama, Alaska, Arkansas, Colorado, Hawaii, Indiana, Kansas, Kentucky, Maryland, Michigan, Montana, Nevada, New Jersey (in part), Oklahoma, South Carolina, Utah, Virginia, and Washington.

[20] "Conflict of Laws in the Uniform Commercial Code," 16 LAW & CONTEMP. PROB. 114 (1951). The author was skeptical that a satisfactory substitute could be prepared, but he advocated retention of a provision permitting party autonomy if properly qualified, "a difficult and delicate task" for the draftsman. *Id.* at 137.

a single sentence in subsection (1) of Section 1-105, to which the succeeding subsection lists exceptions contained in six other sections of the Code.

Subsection (1) provides the following choice-of-law rule: the parties are authorized to agree that either the Code or the law of another state shall apply if their transaction "bears a reasonable relation" to both states. Presumably, it is a matter of no consequence that the choice-of-law rules of the other state would select the local law of the Code state or of a third state to govern the transaction. Similarly, if the parties were to choose the Code state by an agreement entered into in a jurisdiction denying party autonomy and holding its own or a third state's law applicable, the Code would nonetheless provide for its own application. In both these contingencies, the choice of forum would appear decisive.

The parties may choose not to exercise their option to choose the law. In that event a liberal localizing condition applies: Section 1-105(1) renders the Code applicable to "transactions bearing an appropriate relation to this state." Plainly one need not fear difficulties of the sort discussed in connection with Zogg or the New Hampshire fire case. One cannot conceive a situation where this rule would compel the enacting state or another forum to apply the Code where it should not be applied or to deny its application where it should be applied.

Opinions, of course, may differ as to what is "an appropriate relation." The Comment argues that policy considerations reflecting the nature of the Code should encourage courts to depart from past choice-of-law rules in order to permit the Code's application, and, in particular, to prevent its application piecemeal (although it should be noted, the Code does not purport to codify all the enacting state's laws that may bear upon the transactions it covers). There is, incidentally, at least a suggestion of a choice-of-law rule here: if the relation to the forum is not found to be appropriate, should not the court use the "appropriate" test to determine the law to be chosen?

Despite the Comment's admonition against piecemeal application, I should hope that the courts would be ready on occasion to resolve questions of appropriateness in relation to the specific rules in conflict, rather than always seeking to find appropriateness in relation to the transaction as a whole. The recognition that certain problems call for reference to specific sources of law, embodied in the mandatory references discussed below, suggests strongly that other issues may sometimes call for equally discriminating treatment. Indeed, one would expect that a similar power of differentiation should be enjoyed by the parties in exercising the autonomy that the first sentence of Section 1-105(1) accords them. In the light of Section 1-102(5)(a), the fact that that sentence refers to "law" in the singular is not restraining; the context does not forbid the singular from including the plural.

Having given the parties and the courts such a free hand, the Code's draftsmen tightened its requirements by the exceptions to Section 1-105(1) listed by section number in subsection (2). Each of the listed provisions specifies what law is to be applied in certain situations, and agreements to the contrary are permitted only where the law thus specified (including its conflict-of-laws rules) allows this to be done. The first two of the listed exceptions provide rules that operate either as localizing or choice-of-law rules, depending on whether the controlling contact is within or outside the enacting state. The first exception (Section 2-402) applies the law of the situs (which, of course, may be the enacting state) to determine the effect of retention of goods by their seller as against a creditor of the seller.[21]

[21] The adoption of the law of the situs is subject under § 2-402 (2) to an exception: "retention of possession in good faith and current course of trade by a merchant-seller for a commercially reasonable time after a sale or identification is not fraudulent." Suppose the situs, a non-Code

The next exception (Section 4-102(2)) adopts a tort theory to characterize a bank's liability for "action or nonaction" in handling collection items and refers the liability issue to the law of the place where the bank or its branch is located.[22] A third excepted section (Section 6-102) simply subjects "all bulk transfers of goods located within this state" to the bulk transfer article, a localizing provision plainly designed to protect third parties at the situs.

The listed section drawn from the Article on Investment Securities (Section 8-106) prescribes another localizing or choice-of-law rule so as to govern the validity of a "security" (e.g., a share of stock or a corporate bond) by the law, including the conflicts rules, "of the jurisdiction of organization of the issuer." As a choice-of-law rule, that is commonplace (renvoi apart) as regards shares of stock but not necessarily as to bonds other than municipals.[23] If a Code state is the prescribed jurisdiction, its conflict-of-laws rule offers no opportunity to escape by an agreement to govern a bond issue's validity by another law, however substantial are the issue's connections with that other law and however formal is its connection with "the jurisdiction of organization."

The most complex of the excepted sections are those relating to secured transactions. Section 9-102(1) asserts the

---

state, does not make such an exception and has no choice-of-law rule pointing elsewhere. If the seller's creditor asserted his right, the buyer could not take advantage of the exception. The exception is useful only as it may modify the local law of a Code state when it is the situs.

22 Here it would seem likely that "a contrary agreement" by the parties to the collection transaction would be permitted by the law of the place specified in § 4-102 (2) and so come within the privilege accorded by § 1-105 (2) to agreements contrary to any choice of law it specifies "to the extent permitted by the law (including the conflict of laws rules) so specified."

23 Except where the question to be decided is the capacity of the issuer, there seems little basis in pre-Code authority for dealing with the validity of corporate bonds as constituting a question distinct from the validity of other contracts to lend money.

application of the Article "so far as concerns any personal property and fixtures within the jurisdiction of this state," subject to Section 9-103. Subsection (1) of the latter section (to which a complex exception has now been introduced)[24] makes the application of the Code turn on record-keeping within the state by the assignor of accounts receivable; if the records are kept in another state, then the subsection has a choice-of-law rule prescribing the latter state's law. Subsection (2) deals with security interests in "general intangibles" and mobile equipment, using the debtor's "chief place of business" as the decisive contact for localizing or choice-of-law purposes (a recent amendment adding a special rule for foreign airplanes).[25]

The validity of a security interest in other personalty is required by subsection (3) to be determined by the whole law of its situs at the time the security interest attached, subject to a localized exception for property intended to be kept in the enacting state and brought to it within thirty days after the security interest attached. When property already subject to a perfected security interest elsewhere is brought into the state, the Code's own filing requirement may be met as of the date of entry by filing in the state within four months from that date. A later filing is effective from the date of filing. These seem reasonable rules of thumb, rendering unnecessary the proof of knowledge of, or consent to, the change of situs.

This completes virtually the entire scheme for determining

[24] U.L.A., U.C.C. § 9-103 (5) (1964 Supp.). It provides that if the office where the assignor of accounts or contract rights keeps his records concerning them is not in a jurisdiction of the United States and the accounts or contract rights are within the jurisdiction of an enacting state or the transaction bears an appropriate relation to that state, the article governs the validity and perfection of the security interest.

[25] *Id.* § 9-103 (2). For the purpose of determining the validity and perfection of a security interest in an airplane, the chief place of business of a debtor who is a foreign air carrier under the Federal Aviation Act is the designated office of the agent upon whom service of process may be made on behalf of the debtor.

the applicability of the rules to be found in the most elaborate body of statutory law as yet developed in the United States to govern private transactions. Its key concepts of "reasonable relation" and "appropriate" in Section 1-105(1) will defy automatic application and leave opportunity for flexibility outside the areas covered by the listed exceptions. Neither party autonomy nor the standard of appropriateness should lead to a jurisdiction-selecting approach. The parties in choosing the state whose law is to govern their contract will ordinarily consider its rules at points of consequence to their transaction. Similarly the court in determining the appropriate law to govern an issue will, it is to be hoped, consider the content of the rules between which choice is to be made. In their evaluation, reference could aptly be made to principles of the sort I have suggested, but the desideratum of uniformity would also have to be given weight.

The exceptions to Section 1-105(1) do select jurisdictions without reference to the content of the laws thereby chosen, but the problems are such that a strong case can be made for each jurisdiction selected, whatever its law.[26] The need for predictability in the handling of those problems is also relatively strong. Of course, as long as there remain many non-Code states, the scheme cannot fully assure uniformity and predictability as to the governing law where the choice-of-law rules of non-Code states differ and claims may be asserted in those states. For the courts of the Code states, however, these rules provide surer guidance than the decisional law they supplanted could ever have afforded. Moreover, where a precise line was needed, as for the secured transactions just noted, this could only have been done by statute; no court could have created the four months' or the thirty-days' rule.

[26] As I have already pointed out, my position does not stigmatize jurisdiction-selecting rules as bad *per se*; a good jurisdiction-selecting rule may emerge from a process of evaluating the claims of the competing rules in contrasting law-fact patterns. See p. 9, note 24, *supra*.

As the Code comes to cover more and more of the commercial centers of the country, its pronouncements on choice of law may exert an attractive force, bringing courts in non-Code states into line with them. And certainly its numerous references to "the conflict of law rules" of other states should be influential in breaking down a reluctance to consider such rules. Yet the silence of its Comment on the consequences of a reference by another state's conflict-of-laws rules to the Code state's own law suggests either that the draftsmen are subscribing to the jurisdictional principles of Professor Briggs of Montana[27] or they have brushed the complications of renvoi under the rug. Perhaps adoption of the relaxed approach to those problems that I confessed to in an earlier chapter[28] would enable the courts to keep them there.

If the Code should sweep the country, as it appears to be doing, the foregoing provisions would steadily lose their significance as the nation's commercial law grew more nearly uniform. However, with respect to dealings with other countries, its principal contribution would be its recognition of party autonomy. As to this, the Code seems, if anything, too liberal; nothing is excepted from the parties' power save the listed sections and those provisions, concerned chiefly with protection of third parties, do not include those portions of the

[27] Professor E. W. Briggs in a series of articles, e.g., "The Jurisdictional-Choice-of-Law Relation in Conflicts Rules," 61 HARV. L. REV. 1165 (1948), has called for a distinction to be taken between the forum's rule "which recognizes exclusive legislative jurisdiction in the other state" (termed a "jurisdictional rule") and a rule of the state having such jurisdiction which calls for the application of another state's law (termed a "choice-of-law rule"). *Id.* at 1167. Since he views the "choice-of-law rule" as pointing only to the internal law of that other state, the author notes that a reference by the forum to the whole law of the state having legislative jurisdiction would not give rise to the logical difficulties of renvoi. The rules embraced by the Code's list of exceptions would doubtless be viewed as jurisdictional rules, and any differing conflict-of-laws rules in the states to which those jurisdictional rules refer would be considered "choice-of-law rules" in Professor Briggs's sense.

[28] See pp. 106-7 *supra*.

enacting state's law which the Code itself does not cover and which the Code (Section 1-103) declares include "the law relative to capacity to contract, principal and agent, estoppel, fraud, misrepresentation, duress, coercion, mistake, bankruptcy or other validating or invalidating cause." Since the power to choose another law is not confined to the matters covered by the Code, the legal safeguards under the enumerated headings in the Code state could be contracted away by the choice of another state's law—unless perhaps they could be invoked to defeat the efficacy of that choice.[29]

The Uniform Commercial Code provides a comprehensive body of rules for the facilitation of business transactions: buying and selling and the extension of credit. The rules it employs differ in various respects from those in use in other states for the same purposes. These differences are significant chiefly in terms of the relative efficiency with which they perform their functions. Therefore, a statutory scheme for determining the applicability of these rules has as one of its most important criteria the need to avoid interferences which will impair efficiency. Judged from this standpoint, the general provisions in Section 1-105(1) for choice of law and the application of the Code are excellently devised; they do about all that unilateral action can to achieve certainty and minimize conflict. Perhaps, for the reason I have just noted, they may go rather too far in removing safeguards for the parties to transactions, even though the exceptions seem to provide adequate protection for third parties.

29 A choice of law prescribed in a contract presumably could be set aside if induced by fraud, misrepresentation, coercion, or mistake. See RESTATEMENT (SECOND), CONFLICT OF LAWS, § 332a, which would set aside a choice "obtained by unfair means" or as "the result of mistake." Professor Rheinstein has suggested that advantage might, in a proper case, be taken of the Code provision (§ 2-302) permitting a court to "refuse to enforce or strike any unconscionable clauses in a sales contract." See Rheinstein, *supra* note 20, at 137. He suggests that this section be moved to Article 1 and so made applicable to the entire code. *Ibid.*

(2) *The Uniform Securities Act.* When one turns from the Code to the Uniform Securities Act, one shifts to a very different legal operation. The Securities Act is concerned primarily with regulation, with subjecting the free flow of commerce in securities to restraints imposed by the enacting states to assure the protection of the investing public. It is concerned with efficiency only to the extent that it seeks to avoid, to the extent possible, interferences with commerce in securities which are unnecessary for the achievement of the Act's regulatory objectives.

One of the sanctions of the regulatory scheme as well as one of the modes of providing financial protection to the public is the imposition on regulated dealers of civil liability to securities purchasers, typically for rescission of the sale and recovery of the purchase price by the investor, although Section 410 of the Act allows damages to an investor who has already sold. This liability can be very heavy for the seller since suit is likely to be brought only after a severe fall in price. It is a liability, moreover, which does not depend on fraud and misrepresentation (though they can give rise to it) but can be incurred by failure of a broker-dealer to register, by his offering an unregistered, nonexempt security, by his failing to file a prospectus where this is required by rule, etc. The law-abiding broker-dealer may have complied fully with the law in the state where his office is located but find himself violating the law of a neighboring state by transactions which cross its boundary. On the other hand, the unscrupulous operator may look for a base in a state with a loose law from which to ensnare customers in another state with a strict law. The draftsman confronting these contrasting types of business must therefore find a way to protect the former while not giving a free hand to the latter. For the draftsman to have used a provision such as the "appropriate relation" rule of Section 1-105(1) of the Commercial Code would have been disastrous.

The solutions adopted in the Uniform Securities Act were

developed painstakingly through more than a score of drafts by Professor Louis Loss, the chief draftsman of the Act, aided by a group of conflicts scholars, principally his colleague, Professor von Mehren, with the counsel of advisers from the securities bar, the industry, and the state blue sky law administrators.[30] The result is a set of provisions of unusual specificity, most of which are confined to a single section, Section 414, entitled "Scope of the Act and Service of Process." The section uses no choice-of-law rules but operates exclusively through localizing provisions.

Subsection (a) of Section 414 applies to sellers; subsection (b) to buyers. Subsection (a) lists certain sections of the Act applicable to persons who sell or offer to sell when either an offer to sell is made, or an offer to buy is made *and accepted*, "in this state." Subsection (b) does the same with respect to persons who buy or offer to buy when either an offer to buy is made, or an offer to sell is made *and accepted*, "in this state."

Then, in subsections (c) and (d) respectively, the concepts of "offer in this state" and "acceptance in this state" are elaborated. These do not depend on the presence of the parties in the state when the acts are done. An offer to be covered must either have originated in the state or have been directed by the offeror to the state and received where directed (thereby eliminating the risk of putting the offeror in jeopardy by having his offering letter forwarded to another state). An offer is accepted when the acceptance is communicated to the offeror in the state, if it has not previously been communicated to him outside the state. The communication must be directed to the offeror in the state and received where directed. These provisions not only protect against forwarding

30 Loss & Cowett, Blue Sky Law, v-vii, 180n. (1958). This volume includes the text of the Uniform Act with the Official Comment and the Draftsmen's Commentary. Chapter V is devoted to the choice-of-law problem.

but also allow the confirmation of prior acceptances outside the state.

It should be noted that while this scheme indicates the coverage of the Uniform Act with some precision, it does not assure the broker-dealer who complies with the Act of freedom from liability. He must also be sure that he is not violating the law of the other state involved in the transaction. As the Official Comment to Section 414(c) points out, "an offer which originates in State S and is directed to State B is made in both states."

The Act has provisions for consent to service of process on a designated official (Section 414(g)) and for substituted service in the absence of consent (Section 414(h)) which enable an injured party to bring suit in State X, an enacting state, for a cause of action arising under the X Act, irrespective of the whereabouts of the defendant. However, if a case were to be brought under the X Act in another state, say, Y, which had not adopted the Act, the Y court would have difficulty in choosing the X Act as the governing law if the circumstances of the case were such that Y's usual choice-of-law rule would point to its own or a third state's law. Perhaps the concern expressed by X's unilateral effort to extend its Act to such a case as a part of its regulatory scheme would induce the Y court to apply the X law. Rather than hazard that risk, the plaintiff would be well advised to sue in X and take his judgment to Y for enforcement.

Another, more likely problem case would be presented by a suit in X for a cause of action arising in Z, a state not having adopted the Act, under circumstances in which the applicability of the X Act would be excluded by its terms. Rather than resort to its pre-Act choice-of-law rule for such a case, the X court might well apply a liability-creating rule in the Z law if the connections with Z were such that Z law would have been applicable if the Uniform Act had been in force there. Suppose, however, Z cases indicated that the Z law did not "want" to be applied. Z's unilateral preference might be respected in X but, for reasons I have noted earlier,[31] I do not believe this should be decisive.

A variation of that case should be considered. Suppose this time the Z law did want to be applied but the transaction's connections with State Y would equally have brought the case under the Uniform Act if Y had adopted it. Assume that Y's law denied liability. Without more facts, one could not decide whether the conflict between Y's and Z's rules could be labeled "false." If the conflict were true or not readily avoidable, the case might be an apt one for the application of Z law on the basis of my third principle.

Even more than the Code, the Uniform Securities Act has had to cope with problems that could not be handled by resort simply to legal concepts. Suppose, for example, a security is advertised in a metropolitan newspaper circulating in several states, in a national magazine, and on the radio. Is an offer made wherever one of these communications reaches a potential buyer's eye or ear? The Act in Section 414 (e) (1) disposes of the bona fide newspaper and magazine of "general, regular and paid circulation" by considering it as the vehicle of an offer to sell or buy only in the state of its publication and then only if one-third of its circulation has been in the state during the past twelve months. Section 414(e) (2) provides that a radio or television program is covered only if it originates in the state.

Where a broker-dealer has most of his business activities outside the enacting state, how much business in the state should subject him to its registration requirements? The answer, to be found in the Act's definition of "broker-dealer" (Section 401 (c)), is to allow the out-of-state broker-dealer freedom from its requirements if "during any period of twelve consecutive months he does not direct more than fifteen offers to sell or buy into this state in any manner," other than to

[31] See pp. 105-7 *supra*.

certain excepted classes of persons. This provision must operate mainly as a deterrent to gross violation; complete policing of telephoned transactions seems impracticable.

Obviously, even over a protracted period, no courts could hope to work out a body of case law as comprehensive as the Act's provisions governing offers to buy or sell, and such specific provisions as those prescribed in the Act concerning the circulation of periodicals or offers to buy and sell by out-of-state broker-dealers could never emanate from judicial decisions. But the simplicity of exact rules is purchased at a price: the out-of-state newspaper or broadcaster is free from the enacting state's control. On balance, however, the rules governing the scope of the Uniform Act seem well calculated to enable the securities industry to remain subject to regulation without exposing its honest members to unexpected liabilities. Yet a curious phenomenon must be reported. Section 414 of the Act delimiting its scope has been adopted by only nine of the eighteen states which have thus far adopted the Uniform Act in whole or in part.[32] In the states that have omitted Section 414, presumably the interest groups which shape legislation in fields such as this preferred the uncertainties of existing law to clearly defined statutory boundaries dividing the lawful from the unlawful. Such clarity can cut in two directions. Moreover, statutory localizing rules of such precision are a novelty, and novelty is seldom popular in legislation. Yet it should be noted that the more recent adoptions have included Section 414; its novelty appears to be wearing off.

C. *The Use of Federal Legislation*

The grant in the Full Faith and Credit Clause of the Constitution to the Congress of power "by general laws" to "pre-

[32] The states enacting § 414, sometimes with modification, are Alaska, Arkansas, Colorado, Maryland, Michigan, New Jersey, Oklahoma, South Carolina, and Utah. Puerto Rico has also adopted this section.

scribe the manner in which such [public] Acts, Records and [judicial] Proceedings shall be proved, and the Effect thereof" has dangled a tantalizing alternative before scholars who have brooded over the difficulties of developing a satisfactory system of judge-made rules to govern choice of law by the states of the Union. Yet such promise as the Clause holds has been all but completely ignored by the Congress. It has made only minimal provision for the proof of legislative acts, records, and judicial proceedings of the sister states and territories; it has echoed the Clause in requiring that full faith and credit be given to them, but, as to "the Effect thereof," the statute states only that they "shall have the same full faith and credit . . . as they have by law or usage in the courts of the [jurisdiction] from which they are taken."[33]

The resulting century and three quarters of inaction has evoked few complaints. The task of providing a set of statutory rules that would do less harm than good has seemed increasingly infeasible as the years have gone on, and the scale and complexity of the job have grown with the nation and with the volume of state laws. Moreover, national policy in this field is difficult to identify save in broad terms that can more readily be articulated and applied by courts than by legislators. The Supreme Court has proceeded with caution and, of late at least, on a basis which preserves a high degree of autonomy for the individual state to assert its legislative authority.[34]

If the Congress were to embark on an active legislative

[33] 28 U.S.C.A. § 1738 (1948).

[34] The Court's liberality in this respect dates from Alaska Packers Ass'n v. Industrial Accident Comm'n, 294 U.S. 532 (1935). Professor Currie concluded, after a detailed analysis of the precedents, that they supported the thesis that "a state court's choice of law will be upset" under the Full Faith or Due Process Clause "only when the state whose law is applied has no legitimate interest in its application." Currie, "The Constitution and the Choice of Law: Governmental Interests and the Judicial Function," 26 U. Chi. L. Rev. 9, 75 (1958), in Selected Essays 188, 271 (1963).

program under the Clause, it would find itself confronting a legislative problem much more difficult than that which has preoccupied the French jurists who, for nearly twenty years, have been engaged in developing a new set of choice-of-law provisions for inclusion in a revised French Civil Code.[35] A recent French commentator views this effort as having been premature in view of "the new problems which put in question points that one had believed settled" and of the risk that codification might "retard, perhaps compromise" the evolution of private international law that is now in progress.[36] Yet the task of the French draftsmen had been only to provide a body of choice-of-law rules and principles that is satisfactory to French interests, not to work out a scheme for the mutual accommodation of the laws of fifty states. A more nearly comparable assignment would be the drafting of a choice-of-law code for the member states in the Common Market.

The pessimism which I share with many others in viewing the prospects for a federal code of choice-of-law rules does

[35] After World War II, the French Government appointed a commission to revise the Civil Code of 1804, which contains very few rules on conflict of laws. The commission in 1953 presented a draft for the first part, with a Preliminary Book including provisions on choice of law and on jurisdiction. COMMISSION DE REFORME DU CODE CIVIL, AVANT-PROJET DE CODE CIVIL, art. 34-146, pp. 215-32 (1955). The late Professor J. P. Niboyet was draftsman. For an English translation, see Nadelmann & von Mehren, "Codification of French Conflicts Law: Draft Law on Private International Law," 1 AM. J. COMP. L. 416 (1952). The French conflicts specialists subjected the draft to severe criticism. COMITÉ FRANÇAIS DE DROIT INTERNATIONAL PRIVÉ, LA CODIFICATION DU DROIT INTERNATIONAL PRIVÉ (1956). After reactions had been obtained from the courts, the draft was withdrawn. A substitute draft, containing only 31 articles (as compared to 112 in the Niboyet draft) and eliminating some of the criticized nationalistic features, has not yet been made available generally. The entire project for the revision of the Code appears moribund.

[36] SIMON-DEPITRE, DROIT INTERNATIONAL PRIVÉ 44 (1964). The author sees in the fact that the Code revision project is at "le point mort" a favorable circumstance from the standpoint of private international law "puisqu'elle laisse le temps de la réflexion." *Ibid.*

not extend to the possibility of enacting useful federal legislation now and then which would prescribe choice-of-law rules for certain specific situations, perhaps statutory principles of preference. Yet I suspect that opportunities for such action that would be consequential enough to attract the attention of our over-burdened Congress are also likely to fall within the ambit of federal power to legislate on matters of substance. Accordingly, instead of rules to govern choice of law with respect to damages caused by airline crashes, I should think a federal law governing such claims to be more likely. And the uncertainties left by the Supreme Court's application of the First Amendment to protect interstate news media from the threat of huge retaliatory verdicts in politically inspired defamation cases may give rise to new federal legislation preempting that corner of tort law.[37] Only last winter, I urged in a law review article the creation of a federal cause of action to impose strict liability on the operators of federally licensed nuclear reactors, already the beneficiaries of a half-billion-dollar federal indemnity against public liability.[38] (I should add that I have proposed this federal law as a result of pessimism concerning the legislative prospects of the excellent Model Nuclear Facilities Liability Act which Professor Pierce of Michigan drafted for the Commissioners on Uniform State Laws.)[39]

[37] The recent case of The New York Times Co. v. Sullivan, 376 U.S. 254 (1964), leaves open to the plaintiff the recovery of damages upon proof of "actual malice," i.e., the making of the statement complained of with knowledge of its falsity or with "reckless disregard of whether it was false or not." *Id.* at 280, Justices concurring in the result pointed to the danger of "allowing the imposition of liability to depend upon a jury's evaluation of the speaker's state of mind." *Id.* at 300.

[38] See Cavers, "Improving Financial Protection of the Public Against the Hazards of Nuclear Power," 77 HARV. L. REV. 644, 672 (1964).

[39] See HANDBOOK OF THE NATIONAL CONFERENCE OF COMMISSIONERS ON UNIFORM STATE LAWS 228 (1961). As yet the Model Act has not been adopted by any state; reasons for opposition to it are discussed in Cavers, *supra* note 38, at 649. The Model Act, § 3, provides rules governing its territorial application.

I hope that what I have written on the subject of legislation, state, as well as federal, as a source of solutions to choice-of-law problems does not make me seem a foe of statutory development in this field. As I have tried to indicate, I see for it a limited, but by no means unimportant, opportunity. The legislative process may offer prospects of greater fruitfulness in the international area, which I shall consider briefly in the succeeding chapter. However, I also see little hazard of technological unemployment for conflict of laws scholars as a result of having to share our field with legislative counsel, commissions, committees, and conferences. We shall not soon go the way of the alchemists.

X

TREATIES AS A MEANS OF SOLVING CHOICE-OF-LAW PROBLEMS

Since, save in the United States and a few other federal states, choice-of-law problems are almost entirely international,[1] the role with respect to choice-of-law problems which has been played by legislation within the United States has generally been played elsewhere by treaties. The treaty has been used both to establish choice-of-law rules and to make uniform the domestic laws of the nations subject to it, an objective which can also create choice-of-law problems, as our examination of two American uniform acts has demonstrated.

The vehicle to which the nations of the world have most commonly resorted has been the multilateral convention. The United States for reasons discussed below, which spring from its federal character, has not been party to as many of these conventions as have other nations. Indeed, it was only late in 1963 that the Congress authorized active participation by United States delegations in such a venerable source of these conventions as the Hague Conference on Private International

[1] In some federal states, the federal government is the sole source of private law, thereby eliminating conflicts of law among the states. In some unitary countries, such as pre-war Poland, the existence of legal systems inherited from previous sovereigns led to conflicts of law. In many countries, of course, systems of personal law coexist with territorially organized law, and conflicts can arise between persons adhering to different personal laws.

Law and the somewhat younger Rome Institute for the Unification of Private Law.[2]

Typically bilateral treaties, such as treaties of friendship, commerce, and navigation, have been used to establish machinery for judicial assistance and in particular to afford the nationals of the contracting parties access to courts and assurance against discrimination.[3] The antidiscrimination provisions have not often been invoked in American litigation, but it is conceivable that they may become entangled in future choice-of-law developments since they reflect the use of contacts characteristic of conventional conflicts doctrine, e.g., the place of injury for tort cases.

To render this hazard more specific, let us suppose a case brought in the United States by a national of a "High Contracting Party" who is domiciled and resides in the country of which she is a citizen, against her spouse for personal injuries sustained in the United States. Suppose the plaintiff's national law grants one spouse immunity to claims by the other spouse for personal injuries whereas the law of the American state where the injury took place and suit is brought does not. The *Restatement Second* reflects the new view that the place of the injury should look to the law of the dimicil in a case involving a claim of inter-spousal immunity.[4] This reference

[2] Pub. L. No. 244, 88th Cong., 1st Sess. (Dec. 30, 1963), 77 Stat. 775. This step had been recommended by leading organizations, including the American Bar Association, the Association of American Law Schools, the National Conference of Commissioners on Uniform State Laws, and the American Association for the Comparative Study of Law. See *Hearings on H. J. Res. 732 Before the Subcommittee on International Organizations and Movements of the House Committee on Foreign Affairs*, 88th Cong., 1st Sess. (1963).

[3] The treatment of conflict-of-laws problems in United States treaties, both bilateral and multilateral, has been surveyed in Bayitch, "Conflict Law in United States Treaties," 8 U. MIAMI L. REV. 501 (1954), 9 *id.* 9 (1954), 125 (1955).

[4] RESTATEMENT (SECOND), CONFLICT OF LAWS § 390g (Tent. Draft No. 8, 1963).

would defeat the claim, whereas a claim brought by a citizen of the forum state against her husband would have resulted on otherwise identical facts in a judgment for the plaintiff. Would such a decision violate a treaty providing: "The nationals of either . . . Party, regardless of alienage or *place of residence*, shall be accorded rights and privileges no less favorable than those accorded to the nationals of the other . . . Party, under laws and regulations within the territories of such other . . . Party that (a) establish a civil liability for injury or death, and give a right of action to an injured person. . . ."[5] Probably an American court would adhere to its choice of the domiciliary rule on the ground that it would similarly have applied the law of the domicil to a plaintiff who was a national of the United States.

One of the relatively few choice-of-law provisions to be found in our bilateral treaties appears in the 1850/1855 Treaty of Friendship, Commerce, and Extradition with Switzerland.[6] This specifies in Article VI that any "controversy that may arise among the claimants to the same succession, as to whom the property shall belong, shall be decided according to the laws and by the judges of the country in which the property is situated."

In the first of the Bilateral Studies in Private International Law which he edited, *American-Swiss Private International Law*, Professor Arthur Nussbaum, who was also the author of this study, devoted a number of pages to questions arising under this article.[7] As the reader may recall, this article was relevant to the much-discussed decision of a New York surro-

[5] The provision quoted, with emphasis supplied, is from the Treaty of Friendship, Commerce, and Navigation between the United States and Italy, T.I.A.S. 1965 (1948/49), art. XII, 1.

[6] 11 Stat. 587.

[7] NUSSBAUM, AMERICAN-SWISS PRIVATE INTERNATIONAL LAW 23-32 (2d ed. 1958).

gate, In re *Schneider's Estate*,[8] a decision of which Professor Nussbaum heartily disapproved.[9] Other American courts have been guilty of errors of omission; Professor Nussbaum observes, "Quite frequently the treaty has been overlooked by American courts."[10]

With this demonstration that the treaty path is not free from pitfalls for choice of law, let us turn to a brief survey of multilateral conventions relevant to our subject. Some of these, it should be added, are self-executing; others have required the enactment of legislation pursuant to their terms.

A. *The Use of Multilateral Conventions in the Conflict of Laws*

The most comprehensive conflict-of-laws conventions are those to be found among Latin American nations. The Montevideo Conventions date back to 1889, and the Bustamante Code, to 1928. They have not been put to use often, and today they appear to be in an advanced stage of obsolescence, although the revision of the latter may be undertaken in the near future.[11]

[8] 96 N.Y.S.2d 652 (1950). An American citizen, born in Switzerland and domiciled in New York, died leaving realty in Switzerland, which was sold, and the proceeds were transmitted to New York. New York law was applied on a renvoi theory, depriving the widow and next of kin of the *légitime* under Swiss law.

[9] He views the treaty's reference to "laws" as meaning internal laws and also considers the surrogate to have misinterpreted Swiss decisions. See NUSSBAUM, *op. cit. supra* note 7, at 26-27.

[10] *Id.* at 28.

[11] For the Montevideo Treaties of 1889, revised in 1940, see 37 AM. J. INT'L L. SUPP. 95 (1943); for the Bustamante Code of 1928, see 4 HUDSON, INTERNATIONAL LEGISLATION 2279 (1932). The 1940 revision of the Montevideo Treaties was technical. Efforts to revise the Bustamante Code and to make the law uniform for Latin America have had no success so far. See Nadelmann, "The Question of Revision of the Bustamante Code," 57 AM. J. INT'L L. 384 (1963). However, the Inter-American Council of Jurists decided recently to recommend to the Council of the Organization of American States that it call a specialized

Early in the century, a series of conventions on personal status by the Hague Conference on Private International Law stimulated hopes for the device, but subsequent experience with their rules based on nationality has led to their abandonment.[12] One of the most successful of the Hague conventions has been the 1905 Convention on International Civil Procedure (judicial assistance).[13] A convention making minor improvements in the 1905 Convention was adopted in 1951 and has been ratified by sixteen Continental European nations.[14]

Family obligations have given rise to several post-war conventions, and, unlike most conventions sponsored by the Conference, these have been securing ratifications. Thus, the forward-looking 1956 Convention on the Law Applicable to Obligations to Support Minor Children has been ratified by six countries,[15] and the Convention of 1958 concerning the Recognition and Enforcement of Decisions Involving Obligations to Support Minor Children, by five countries.[16] Both conventions are now in effect.

The Uniform Reciprocal Enforcement of Support Act,

---

conference on private international law in 1967 to undertake a revision of the Bustamante Code (parts: General Rules, Civil Law, and Commercial Law), "taking into account the advances in legal science and the Montevideo Treaties of 1889 and 1940 on private international law." Inter-American Council of Jurists, Fifth Meeting, San Salvador, Jan. 25–Feb. 5, 1965, Final Act, Res. No. II.

12 For a discussion of the Hague conventions antedating World War I, see 1 Rabel, Conflict of Laws: A Comparative Study 33-36 (2d ed. 1958).

13 See *id.* at 35.

14 For the text of the 1951 Convention, see 1 Am. J. Comp. L. 282 (1952). Thirteen of the 19 member nations have ratified, and 2 non-member nations have acceded to, the Convention. (The Hague Conference members at present are confined to the European Continent, plus the United Arab Republic, Japan, and now the United States.)

15 Austria, France, West Germany, Italy, Luxembourg, The Netherlands. For the text, see 5 Am. J. Comp. L. 656 (1956).

16 Austria, Belgium, West Germany, Italy, The Netherlands. For the text, see 5 Am. J. Comp. L. 658 (1956).

adopted with minor deviations by all fifty of the United States,[17] has provided a pattern for the United Nations Convention of 1956 on the Recovery Abroad of Maintenance,[18] which had been ratified, as of December 1962, by twenty-four nations, large and small. The reception accorded this act bespeaks a widely recognized social need. It contrasts in this respect with a convention dealing with property law but of consequence to the family, the 1961 Convention on the Conflict of Laws Relating to the Form of Testamentary Dispositions. Its failure to have acquired more than four ratifications (one by the United Kingdom)[19] may reflect doubt as to the appropriateness of this subject for convention treatment.

Commercial law has been somewhat more fertile as a field for international agreements. Among the most successful have been the 1930 and 1931 Geneva Conventions for the Settlement of Certain Conflicts of Laws in connection with Bills of Exchange and Promissory Notes and with Checks.[20] The United Nations Convention of 1958 on the Recognition and Enforcement of Foreign Arbitral Awards, designed to take the place of the Geneva Conventions of 1923 and 1928, has

[17] For its text, see 9C U.L.A. 1. Similarly, the Canadian Reciprocal Enforcement of Maintenance Orders Act is in force in all Provinces. For its text, see CONFERENCE OF COMMISSIONERS ON UNIFORMITY OF LEGISLATION IN CANADA, MODEL ACTS RECOMMENDED FROM 1918 TO 1961 INCLUSIVE 260 (1962).

[18] For the text of the Convention of June 20, 1956, see 268 U.N.T.S. 3 *et seq.* It is discussed in Contini, "United Nations Convention on the Recovery Abroad of Maintenance," 31 ST. JOHN'S L. REV. 1 (1956).

[19] Austria, The United Kingdom, Yugoslavia, and Japan. For the text, see 9 AM. J. COMP. L. 705 (1960). The Convention is now in effect. Its application is not limited to the contracting parties nor does it depend on reciprocity (Art. 6).

[20] For their texts, see 143 L.N.T.S. 317, 325; 5 HUDSON, INTERNATIONAL LEGISLATION 550, 915 (1936). They are discussed in 4 RABEL, *op. cit. supra* note 12, at 129; Hudson & Feller, "The International Unification of Laws Concerning Bills of Exchange," 44 HARV. L. REV. 333, 370 (1931); and Feller, "The International Unification of Laws Concerning Checks," 45 HARV. L. REV. 668, 692 (1932).

been widely ratified,[21] though not by the United States.[22] The 1951 Convention on the Law Applicable to International Sales of Goods had marked time for want of five ratifiers to render it effective until Belgium, France, and Italy, the only ratifiers before the past year, were joined by the Scandinavian states.[23] It has acquired new significance as a consequence of a recent development discussed below: the signing of a convention for a Uniform Law on the International Sale of Goods.

The Hague Conference on Private International Law is still very much alive. Its tenth session was held in October 1964, with the United States represented by an official delegation for the first time. On its agenda were proposed conventions on the following subjects: Adoption; Recognition of Foreign Judgments; Choice of Forum Clauses; and Service of Documents Abroad (designed to replace the first part of the 1951 Convention on International Civil Procedure (Judicial Assistance)).[24] Of these, the Conference completed work on all but the draft convention on Judgments. Work on it will be continued at a special session to be held within two years. Work has started on Recognition of Foreign Divorces.

Efforts at regional conventions in conflict of laws have been pursued unsuccessfully by the Benelux countries, only Luxembourg having ratified their 1951 Convention,[25] and success-

21 Ratified by 26 nations, as of Dec. 1962. For the text, see 330 U.N.T.S. 38 and 53 AM. J. INT'L L. 420 (1959).

22 See Quigley, "Accession by the United States to the United Nations Convention on the Recognition and Enforcement of Foreign Arbitral Awards," 70 YALE L.J. 1049 (1961).

23 For the text of this convention, see 1 AM. J. COMP. L. 275 (1952). Certain difficulties in it are noted in Nadelmann, "Uniform Legislation vs. International Conventions" in INTERNATIONAL TRADE ARBITRATION 167, 172 (Domke ed. 1958). And see note 37, *infra*.

24 For the texts of the new conventions, see 13 AM. J. COMP. L. No. 4 (1964). For the Report to the Secretary of State of the U.S. Delegation to the session, see 52 DEP'T STATE BULL. 265 (1965).

25 For the text of the Benelux Convention of 1951 on Uniform Rules of Private International Law, see 1 INT'L & COMP. L. Q. 426 (1951). The Convention is discussed by one of its draftsmen, a leading Dutch

fully by the Scandinavian countries which have adopted five conventions in this field.[26] Their resort to conventions departs from the practice followed by them in substantive areas where agreement is reached on the principles of uniform legislation, a process that does not entail a striving for verbatim identity in the acts passed by the national legislatures.[27]

Efforts to avoid conflicts by the unification of substantive law have been pursued in both maritime and commercial law. Under the sponsorship of the *Comité Maritime International*, a series of conventions has been negotiated, among which perhaps the most relevant is the Brussels Convention of 1924,[28] which was designed to unify the law relating to bills of lading involving carriage of hull cargo, in particular, the problem of clauses limiting the carriers' liability for negligence. The outstanding achievements in the commercial field are the Geneva Conventions of 1930 and 1931 unifying the law of negotiable instruments and of checks in Continental Europe.[29] More recently under the sponsorship of the International Institute for the Unification of Private Law in Rome, the Convention Relating to a Uniform Law on the International Sale of Goods

---

scholar, in Meijers, "The Benelux Convention of Private International Law," 2 Am. J. Comp. L. 1 (1953). Ratifications by Belgium and The Netherlands seem no longer to be expected.

[26] The conventions deal with marriage, adoption, and guardianship (1931); maintenance (1931); recognition and enforcement of judgments (1933); inheritance and succession (1934); bankruptcy (1935). See Philip, "The Scandinavian Conventions on Private International Law," 96 [Hague] Académie de Droit International, Recueil des Cours 245 (1959).

[27] See Von Eyben, "Inter-Nordic Legislative Cooperation," in 1962 Scandinavian Studies in Law 63.

[28] For the text, see International Convention for the Unification of Certain Rules Relating to (Ocean) Bills of Lading, 120 L.N.T.S. 155, U.S.T.S., No. 931, 6 Benedict on Admiralty 483 (7th ed. Knauth 1958). See Yiannopoulos, Negligence Clauses in Ocean Bills of Lading (1962).

[29] For their texts, see 5 Hudson, International Legislation 516, 889 (1936). They are discussed in Hudson & Feller, *supra* note 20; Feller, *supra* note 20.

was prepared at The Hague in April 1964, the product of labors extending, with protracted interruptions, over some thirty years.[30]

B. *The Convention Relating to a Uniform Law on the International Sale of Goods*

The Convention represents a different and radical attack upon the choice-of-law problem. It seeks in effect to abolish the problem by establishing, through the medium of the Convention, a supra-state law to cover all international sales coming before the courts of the countries ratifying it—or, at least, of those countries who do so without reservations. The Uniform Law (which is an appendix to the Convention) rides roughshod over choice-of-law rules, expressly excluding them in Article 6. Instead, it determines its application by reference to its concept of the international sale, broadly defined in Article 7. Only the parties to such a sales transaction can elude the Law's grasp; they can take the precaution (permitted by Article 3) of agreeing that it shall not apply to their contract.

So important is this proposal that a brief report seems indicated with respect to its background and the association of the United States in its conception, since an official delegation from this country was present at the Conference held in April 1964. This was a sequel to a conference held at The Hague in November 1951.[31] At that conference, which considered a draft prepared by the Rome Institute before the war, the United States was not represented (except by an observer who took

[30] For the text, see 13 Am. J. Comp. L. 453 (1964). See Honnold, "A Uniform Law for International Sales," 107 U. Pa. L. Rev. 299 (1959); Nadelmann, "The United States and Plans for a Uniform (World) Law on International Sales of Goods," 112 U. Pa. L. Rev. 697 (1964). A separate convention was signed at the same time relating to a Uniform Law on the Formation of Contracts for the International Sale of Goods. For its text, see 13 Am. J. Comp. L. 474 (1964).

[31] On this conference, see Rabel, "The Hague Conference on the Unification of Sales Law," 1 Am. J. Comp. L. 58 (1952).

no part in the work) and no United States representative was put on the Special Committee created to revise the draft.[32] At the conference in April 1964 the delegation thus was confronted with a draft on which it had not collaborated. More than hundred provisions of the draft Uniform Law on the International Sale of Goods had to be considered at the Conference called to sit for three weeks. No time existed for a substantial revision if it had been found desirable. The head of the United States delegation at the closing session took the position that the draft of the Uniform Law was still defective in certain respects (which he identified) and that the Convention with the Uniform Law appended was not ready for final action at the meeting.[33] The objections did not prevail. The Convention was approved and formally signed July 1, 1964.

The failure of the objections to prevail is rendered the more consequential by the fact that the path to early ratification of the Convention had been smoothed by provisions in the Convention allowing nations to ratify with reservations of various kinds specified in the Convention. Most striking is Article V, sponsored by the United Kingdom, authorizing a nation to ratify with the reservation that the Uniform Law shall apply only when it has been chosen by the parties to a contract. This privilege may well entice ratifications on the part of nations which would shrink from incorporating the Uniform Law in their legislation on a mandatory basis.

The other authorized reservations point up the fact that, despite its aspirations, there is a choice-of-law problem created by the Uniform Law in its rejection of choice-of-law limitations on its application. A hypothetical case will bring the problem into focus. If the Uniform Law becomes effective but

[32] The history of the draft up to the 1964 Conference is given in Nadelmann, *supra* note 30. For an American comment on the draft, see Honnold, *supra* note 30.

[33] The objecting statement is quoted in Nadelmann, "The Uniform Law on the International Sale of Goods: A Conflict of Laws Imbroglio," 74 YALE L.J. 449 (1965).

the United States and Canada refrain from ratifying, a sales contract lacking a clause excluding the Law's application which calls for delivery of goods by a seller in either of those countries to a buyer in the other country will be governed by the Uniform Law in a case arising in any nation that had become a party to the Convention without reservations. Moreover, in the foreign forum,[34] the disadvantaged party, confronted by a law which had no contact whatever with his transaction, would not, of course, have the protection of a due process clause to shield him from injustice.[35]

The other optional reservations include two that, if resorted to, would diminish this hazard. Article III of the Convention permits a reservation restricting the Uniform Law to contracts

[34] Of course, to be exposed to the risk I have noted, the defendant must be subject to suit abroad, but, in this connection, it should be observed that, in Germany, Austria, Denmark, Sweden, and possibly other nations, the mere presence of assets (including receivables) is sufficient to found jurisdiction *in personam* and to sustain a judgment which is not limited to those assets. See Nadelmann, "Jurisdictionally Improper Fora," in XXTH CENTURY COMPARATIVE AND CONFLICTS LAW 321 (von Mehren, Nadelmann & Hazard, eds. 1961). Such a judgment might be recognized and enforced in other countries in which the defendant was doing business or had additional assets.

[35] Even if the United States criteria of personal jurisdiction were satisfied, the application of the Uniform Law to an international sale occurring in noncontracting nations between parties there who did not choose the Law's application would doubtless be viewed as a denial of due process of law by an American court if the effect were to confer on the plaintiff a right denied him by the laws of both interested states or deny to the defendant a defense conferred on him by both. Home Insurance Co. v. Dick, 281 U.S. 397 (1930). If the plaintiff in such a case secured a judgment in a foreign forum which was based on the Uniform Law and thereafter sought to enforce it in the United States, the defendant would have an opportunity to plead "public policy" since the impediment to that plea to the judgment of a sister state in Fauntleroy v. Lum, 210 U.S. 230 (1908), does not extend to judgments of other countries. The defense is left open by the Uniform Foreign Money-Judgments Recognition Act § 4 (b) (3), which permits nonrecognition if the claim "on which the judgment is based is repugnant to the public policy of" the enacting state. The use of the *Dick* analogy as a basis for invoking public policy would be novel but seems sound.

entered into by parties having their respective places of business (or habitual residences) in different states, both of which have ratified the Uniform Law. Article IV permits states which have already ratified the Hague Convention on the Law Applicable to International Sales of Goods[36] to ratify the Convention Relating to a Uniform Law with the reservation that the latter's application will be determined by the choice-of-law rules prescribed in the Hague Convention. These rules, although the target of criticism that was largely responsible for the long delay in securing five ratifying nations,[37] at least do not have the cavalier grasp of the Uniform Law.

In a trenchant article[38] on the conflicts problems created by the Convention Relating to a Uniform Law on the International Sale of Goods, Dr. Kurt H. Nadelmann calls attention to the parallel between the jurisdictional reach of that Convention and the provisions governing the applicability of the Uniform Commercial Code in the form in which the Code was first presented to the states for enactment. Though the latter, unlike the Uniform Law, would have required some contact with the enacting state, they would have stretched its power to apply

[36] For a translation of its text, see 1 AM. J. COMP. L. 275 (1952). An error in art. 3 is corrected in Nadelmann, *supra* note 33, at 463.

[37] The West Germans were the principal critics, complaining that the provision for party autonomy did not cover choice of law by implication and that the law of the buyer's state was made operative merely because the buyer's order was received there. The latter provision was sharply criticized in 3 RABEL, CONFLICT OF LAWS: A COMPARATIVE STUDY 58-60 (2d ed. 1964). See Nadelmann, *supra* note 33, at 452. Though the point made by Dr. Rabel seems well taken, the requirement of the further contact of delivery in the buyer's state which he proposed still preserves a jurisdiction-selecting rule. Such a rule would result in the application of the law of the buyer's state to afford the seller a claim or defense which the seller's own law would deny him. With respect to some claims or defenses, this might be justified, but the desirability of a rule that does not leave these circumstances open to inquiry seems to me at best doubtful.

[38] Nadelmann, *supra* note 33. Dr. Nadelmann has been a member of the United States delegations to the Hague Conferences in Private International Law.

the Code to or beyond constitutional bounds.[39] As I noted in the preceding chapter, the outcry which these sweeping provisions precipitated[40] led to their withdrawal and the substitution of Section 1-105 of the Code discussed in the previous chapter. The substitute should meet all reasonable needs, and it is winning general acceptance. It appears to have dissipated the demand for the federal version of the Code which would have eliminated most conventional choice-of-law problems within the jurisdiction of the United States[41] in the way the Uniform Law would do if it could be a mandatory legislative

39 Section 1-105 of the Code in the version proposed for state enactment would have rendered the Code applicable (to quote only a few of the points of contact listed in the subsection relating to Art. 2 on Sales) to any contract "made, offered, or accepted" or to any "transaction" which "occurs within this state," or a contract "to be performed or completed wholly or in part within this state" or "involves" a document "sent or received within this state" or a credit of which "confirmation or advice" is "received within this state." Although one can readily conceive situations in which these contacts would be virtually meaningless, they do at least provide some connection with the enacting state. For the text of § 1-105 as it then was, see UNIFORM COMMERCIAL CODE, Text and Comments Edition (Official Draft, 1952). For an excellent comment on both the 1952 version of § 1-105 and its successor, see Burton, "The Uniform Commercial Code and Conflict of Laws," 9 AM. J. COMP. L. 458 (1960).

40 The provisions were subjected to devastating criticism in Rheinstein, "Conflict of Laws in the Uniform Commercial Code," 16 LAW & CONTEMP. PROB. 114 (1951). For a fuller account of the critical response, see Burton, *supra* note 39.

41 The sponsors of the Code provided a version for enactment by the Congress which would be applicable "whenever the contract is in or affects interstate or foreign commerce." This would have substituted the question whether a contract fell within that vague but extensive range for the usual choice-of-law questions. Plainly it would have reached many foreign transactions that by choice-of-law rules would have been left to the laws of other countries. Its arrogation of this authority to the United States, though less universal than the parties to the Convention would claim for themselves, was defended, Dr. Nadelmann points out, on the same ground: the intrinsic superiority of the proposed law. See Nadelmann, *supra* note 33, at 458 citing Goodrich, "Conflicts Niceties and Commercial Necessities," 1952 WIS. L. REV. 199.

emanation of the United Nations. The sponsors of the Convention might take a leaf out of our book.

C. *The Special Problems of a Federal State*

From the standpoint of the United States, the use of conventions has been a source of some embarrassment. The federal nature of our government has made it hard for us to adopt conventions dealing with matters ordinarily left to the domain of the state law. Even though, as to many of these, the exercise of the treaty power might sustain the federal government's authority, the vigilance of supporters of states' rights in the Senate, especially since the crusading days of Senator Bricker of Ohio,[42] has meant that any intrusion into the traditional realm of the states would almost certainly be denied ratification. Indeed, the spirit of Senator Bricker has long outlived his tenure in the Senate, as witness the belated acceptance by the United States Government of membership in the Hague Conference and the Rome Institute.[43]

There are certain subjects as to which federal participation creates no problems. Thus, the Brussels Convention was implemented by the Carriage of Goods by Sea Act which was

[42] In 1951 Senator Bricker of Ohio championed the adoption of an amendment to the Constitution to substitute a new paragraph for the second paragraph of Article VI. This amendment would have imposed restrictions on the treaty-making power (some declaratory) and have drastically curtailed the use of executive agreements. For a discussion of this and other amendments proposed in the same period and for like purposes, see Sutherland, "Restricting the Treaty Power," 65 HARV. L. REV. 1305 (1952). For comment on a later version of the amendment, see Sutherland, "The Bricker Amendment, Executive Agreements, and Imported Potatoes," 67 HARV. L. REV. 281 (1953). A vigorous opposition to the Bricker Amendment was organized by a group of lawyers in which law teachers played an important part. The opposition in time prevailed.

[43] See note 2, *supra*. We sent observers to the 1956 and 1960 Sessions of the Conferences. See 5 AM. J. COMP. L. 611 (1956); 9 *id.* 583 (1960). Our nonparticipation had been sharply criticized in Nadelmann, "Ignored State Interests: The Federal Government and International Efforts to Unify Rules of Private Law," 102 U. PA. L. REV. 323 (1954).

adopted, in the exercise of the admiralty power, even before the Convention was ratified.[44] We joined in the Warsaw Convention of 1928 setting limits to liability for injury and death to passengers in civil aircraft, but this is restricted to international flights.[45]

Lately, the possibility of our joining in the International Atomic Energy Agency's convention on civil liability for nuclear damage has been considered, a subject that could be justified by whatever powers the federal government invokes to sustain its regulatory authority over the peaceful uses of atomic energy.[46]

However, in the case of a convention like that providing for the validation of wills by prescribing choice-of-law rules of alternate reference or, arguably, of a convention for the recognition and enforcement of foreign judgments, the possible invasion of state domains creates difficulties even where the substance of the conventions is otherwise acceptable. In this situation, the United States observers to the 1956 session of the Hague Conference argued persuasively for the use of the technique of the uniform law instead of the convention.[47] They pointed out that for many subjects the binding effect of a convention is no special value; it may indeed be a hindrance if it

[44] Carriage of Goods by Sea Act, 49 Stat. 1207 (1936), 46 U.S.C. § 1300 (1958). See GILMORE & BLACK, THE LAW OF ADMIRALTY 87 (1957); YIANNOPOULOS, *op. cit. supra* note 28, at 47.

[45] Warsaw Convention of 1929 for the Unification of Certain Rules Relating to International Carriage by Air, 49 Stat. 3000 (1934); "Hague Protocol of 1955," 5 AM. J. COMP. L. 90 (1956).

[46] For the text of the convention (which is not as yet in force and has few signers), see IAEA Document CN-12/46 (May 20, 1963), in 2 AMERICAN SOC'Y OF INTERNATIONAL LAW, INTERNATIONAL LEGAL MATERIALS, CURRENT DOCUMENTS 727 (1963); also in IAEA, CIVIL LIABILITY FOR NUCLEAR DAMAGE, Legal Series No. 2, p. 501 (1964). For a brief consideration of some of the problems which the question of our joining would raise, see Cavers, "Improving Financial Protection of the Public Against the Hazards of Nuclear Power," 77 HARV. L. REV. 644, 677 (1964).

[47] See Nadelmann & Reese, "The American Proposals at The Hague to Use the Method of Uniform Laws," 7 AM. J. COMP. L. 239 (1958). (The authors were both United States observers.)

freezes terms that later developments render obsolete.[48] The main objective of international action should be agreement on the substance of the rules, as in the Scandinavian practice noted above. To be sure, in the course of the enactment of a uniform law proposed by an international conference, some minor deviations from the agreed-upon version may be introduced. But seldom will this be serious. Moreover, the process of amendment can be greatly facilitated. These considerations led the Hague Conference to adopt a resolution in 1960, on the basis of the report of a special committee, in which the Conference, while adhering "primarily" to its practice of preparing conventions in order to retain its own diplomatic character, recognized the desirability of drafting those conventions in such form as to facilitate the adoption of their substantive provisions as statutes by nations having difficulties in adopting them as conventions.[49]

There are two alternatives to the usual convention which, if used, could enable the products of The Hague and Rome to be offered so that participation by the United States would pose no difficulty for the states of the Union, even where the subject matter was peculiarly within their jurisdiction. One way would be to allow the United States Government (or any other federal state with a like division of legislative power) to sign a convention providing that a constituent state which enacted a law in accordance with the convention's terms would be entitled to the benefits of reciprocity vis à vis other nations signing the convention, a method sometimes used by the United Kingdom on behalf of other members of the Commonwealth.[50] The other

[48] A multilateral convention, once in force, can be varied only pursuant to such provisions as it specifies though, to be sure, a state can always denounce it.

[49] For the resolution's text, see 9 AM. J. COMP. L. 592 (1960).

[50] See STEWART, TREATY RELATIONS OF THE BRITISH COMMONWEALTH OF NATIONS 247 (1939). An example of an accession clause for this purpose is to be found in Article 11 of the Convention of 1934 on recognition and enforcement of judgments concluded by the United Kingdom with France. 171 L.N.T.S. 183.

way would be for a proposal to be offered, alternatively, as a convention and as a uniform law. The states of the United States could view the law proposed thereby much as they now view the proposals of the National Conference of Commissioners on Uniform State Laws. In cases where Congressional action on an international uniform act did not seem appropriate, the National Conference could examine the possibility of harmonizing amendments to their uniform act in the domestic field.

Even if advantage is taken of either of these possibilities[51] and if the United States Government frees itself still further from the spell of Brickerism, it seems likely that the utilization of multilateral conventions will remain a rather specialized, albeit useful, technique, adapted for handling specialized situations in which uniformity of rule or cooperation among nations is important and the need to preserve state and national laws intact is relatively small. Sometimes a compromise solution or effective collaboration may even require state and national laws to be subordinated to the need to provide a common basis for international activities involving nations with widely disparate economic standards or differing legal techniques, as appears to have been true in the case of the Warsaw Convention with its much-criticized limitation on liability,[52] and may also be the case with the IAEA Convention on Civil Liability for Nuclear Damage.[53]

51 The alternatives have been discussed in Nadelmann, "Ways to Unify Conflicts Rules," DE CONFLICTU LEGUM—ESSAYS PRESENTED TO R. D. KOLLEWIJN AND J. OFFERHAUS 349 (1962), also printed in 9 TIJDSCHRIFT VOOR INTERNATIONAAL RECHT (Oct. 1962). Dr. Nadelmann finds the source of the latter alternative in an 1869 proposal by "the intellectual father and first president of the Hague Conference, T. M. C. Asser." *Id.* at 358.

52 See note 45 *supra*. See Lissitzyn, "The Warsaw Convention Today," 1962 PROC. AM. SOC'Y INT'L L. 115; Sand, "Limitation of Liability and Passengers' Accident Compensation Under the Warsaw Convention," 11 AM. J. COMP. L. 21 (1962).

53 See note 46 *supra*.

It should not be assumed that even the widespread acceptance of a multilateral convention is an assurance of uniformity. Experience under the Brussels Convention of 1924 has fallen well short of the reasonable hopes of its sponsors, for neither national legislatures nor national courts have gone as far as they should to assure its uniform application. Nevertheless, Professor Yiannopoulos, who has pointed out their many shortcomings, is able to conclude that "the Brussels Convention has not been in vain. Before its adoption the situation was untenable and uncertainty reigned in all cases; today, while there is still uncertainty in a number of cases, in the vast majority of bills of lading exoneration clauses will be given the same effect one way or another in all contracting states."[54]

[54] YIANNOPOULOS, *op. cit. supra* note 28, at 182. Moreover, in the course of time, revisions may eliminate a number of the defects the author has scored. A number of proposals for amendments, including one directed at Article 10 governing applicability, have been approved at meetings of the Comité Maritime International at Rijeka in 1959 and at Stockholm in 1963. For the English text of the draft amendatory convention, including the article to replace Article 10, see 187 LE DROIT MARITIME FRANÇAIS 402 (1964).

XI

PROCEDURE FOR—AND IN—THE CHOICE-OF-LAW PROCESS

A. *Procedure for Choice of Law: An Emergent Problem*

Of the divers criticisms inspired by that 1933 article of mine, the complaint which I felt least able to answer convincingly made the point that, whatever the academic virtues of the approach to choice of law I was advocating, it was well beyond the power of the average trial judge to pursue under combat conditions. The trial judge, it was argued, needed plain, easy-to-apply, jurisdiction-selecting rules. Moreover, he had to be able in many instances to make his decision at the start of the trial; he could not wait to take account of the considerations that my conception of choice of law would have him weigh.

It is, of course, true that an approach to choice of law which requires the evaluation of the conflicting laws' purposes in the light of facts extending beyond such relatively distinct touchstones as place of injury, place of making, situs, and domicil is an approach that can be prescribed with much more confidence for an appellate court than for a trial court. The former has the benefit of a record, briefs, argument, and time for research and reflection. However, now that even *Restatement Second* is calling for such determinations as "the most significant relationship" in tort and contract cases and inviting inquiry into the whole law of foreign states in property and marriage cases, I need no longer look upon myself as an isolated, would-be trouble-maker whose views, if they were taken seriously, would make unreasonable demands on the trial courts. Now I believe that all protagonists of change in choice of law should recognize the serious procedural barriers that stand in the way of the realization of their respective proposals.

There seems to have been little investigation directed to the question whether anything could be done to improve the opportunity for an informed and deliberated choice by the judge of first instance when confronted by conflicting laws. In contrast, a great deal of attention has been devoted to the process whereby that judge decides what is the content of the law he has chosen. Preoccupation with this problem has produced provisions in two uniform acts[1] and in a model code and uniform rules of evidence.[2] It has recently inspired a proposed Federal Rule (Rule 44.1).[3] But betterment of the underlying process of choice remains to be considered.

That this should be the case is not surprising. The received common law treated the law of another state (including a sister state)[4] as a fact to be pleaded and proved by evidence to the jury. This obviously cumbersome and inapt procedure, alleviated only by presumptions, had to be eliminated. Judicial notice was first seized upon as a handy means of giving to the judge the task of resolving questions of foreign law, and the 1936 Uniform Judicial Notice of Foreign Law Act was widely adopted.[5] Though giving the judge power to determine

[1] UNIFORM JUDICIAL NOTICE OF FOREIGN LAW ACT, 9A U.L.A. 318 (1957); UNIFORM INTERSTATE AND INTERNATIONAL PROCEDURE ACT, art. IV, 9B U.L.A. 71, 89 (Supp. 1963).

[2] ALI MODEL CODE OF EVIDENCE (1942); UNIFORM RULES OF EVIDENCE ACT, Rule 9, 9A U.L.A. 188, 194 (Supp. 1963).

[3] Preliminary Draft of Proposed Amendments to Rules of Civil Procedure, May 5, 1964, U.S. CODE CONGRESSIONAL AND ADMINISTRATIVE NEWS, 88th Cong. 2d Sess., No. 7, at 1034.

[4] RESTATEMENT, CONFLICT OF LAWS § 621 (1934).

[5] Twenty-seven states have adopted the Act. 9A U.L.A., 182 (Supp. 1963). The official comment notes that thirteen states have enacted

all questions of foreign law, the Act confined the use of judicial notice to the laws of sister states,[6] and today only seven states have extended the notice device to the laws of foreign countries.[7] In the transition to judicial notice, the requirement of pleading the law that was noticed came to be viewed as not essential and an alternative requirement of a "reasonable notice" was added by the Uniform Act.[8] This did not exclude the possibility that the judge—or even an appellate court—might take judicial notice of a foreign law on his—or its—own motion.[9] The 1962 Uniform Interstate and

---

similar judicial notice of foreign law statutes, and of these, five states have since adopted the Uniform Act. 9A U.L.A. 318-19. And see CAL. CODE CIV. P. § 1875; N.Y. CIV. PRAC. L. & R. § 4511; TEXAS R. CIV. P. § 184a; UTAH R. CIV. P. 44(f); VT. STAT. ANN. tit. 12, §1699. Though judicial notice has been substituted for evidentiary proof by statute, at least one court has held without statutory authority that foreign law is to be proved to the court rather than the jury. Saloshin v. Houle, 85 N.H. 126, 155 Atl. 47 (1931).

6 Section 5 provides that the laws of a foreign country are to be proved to the judge, but § 1, in providing for judicial notice, does not include them. The new UNIFORM INTERSTATE AND INTERNATIONAL PROCEDURE ACT, *supra* note 1, in providing for "the determination" of foreign laws by the judge, does not distinguish between the laws of sister states and those of foreign countries. It does not invoke judicial notice.

7 The states permitting judicial notice of the laws of foreign countries are: CAL. CODE CIV. P. § 1875; MASS. ANN. LAWS ch. 233, § 70 (1956); MISS. CODE ANN. § 1761 (1956); N.Y. CIV. PRAC. L. & R. § 4511 (1962); N.C. GEN. STAT. §§ 8-4 (1953); VA. CODE ANN. § 8-273 (1957); W. VA. CODE ANN. § 5711 (1955). The UNIFORM RULES OF EVIDENCE ACT, *supra* note 2, sponsored by American Law Institute and the National Conference of Commissioners on Uniform State Laws now provides in Rule 9(2) for judicial notice of the law of foreign countries.

8 UNIFORM JUDICIAL NOTICE OF FOREIGN LAW ACT, *supra* note 1, § 4. Two enacting states, New Jersey and South Carolina, require laws to be pleaded as a condition to their being noticed. See *id.* at 382. The Act has been held not to change the requirement of pleading the law of foreign nations. Abramson v. Abramson, 161 Neb. 782, 74 N.W.2d 919 (1956).

9 A Massachusetts court did so in 1936. Walker v. Lloyd, 295 Mass. 507, 4 N.E.2d 306 (1936). However, as pointed out in Currie, "On the Displacement of the Law of the Forum," 58 COLUM. L. REV. 964, 992

International Procedure Act, Article IV, and, for foreign law, the proposed new Federal Rule[10] (but not the newly revised New York Civil Practice Law[11]) drop the judicial notice concept (which had been subject to criticism in application by Professor Nussbaum[12] and in principle by Professor Currie[13]). The alternative is a judicial hybrid: an issue of law on which a judge may require evidence if he is not prepared to inform himself.[14] Brief mention of some questions raised by this solution may be useful by way of background for the procedural problem to be considered.

The texts of the two uniform acts are silent on the authority of the judge to take the initiative if neither party chooses to "raise an issue concerning" foreign law "in his pleadings or other reasonable written notice."[15] The Advisory Committee note to the proposed Federal Rule indicates that the judge may do so.[16] The New York law requires the judge to take notice to sister state law "without request." However, it gives him discretion as to noticing laws of governmental agencies, political subdivisions, and other countries, unless a request to do so is made by a party, accompanied by "sufficient information" concerning the law and notice to the other party

n.83 (1958), reprinted in SELECTED ESSAYS ON THE CONFLICT OF LAWS (hereinafter cited as SELECTED ESSAYS) 36 n.83 (1963), the practice has been criticized in Massachusetts.

[10] Rule 44.1, *supra* note 3.

[11] N.Y. CIV. PRAC. L. & R. § 4511 (1962).

[12] Nussbaum, "The Problem of Proving Foreign Law," 50 YALE L. J. 1018, 1019-23 (1941).

[13] Currie, *supra* note 9, at 981-1001, reprinted in SELECTED ESSAYS at 23-46.

[14] UNIFORM JUDICIAL NOTICE OF FOREIGN LAW ACT, *supra* note 1, § 2.

[15] UNIFORM INTERSTATE AND INTERNATIONAL PROCEDURE ACT, *supra* note 1, § 4.01; UNIFORM JUDICIAL NOTICE OF FOREIGN LAW ACT, *supra* note 1. In one case the judge interpreted § 1 of the latter act to permit judicial notice without requiring a prior request. Strout v. Burgess, 144 Me. 263, 68 A.2d 241 (1949).

[16] Rule 44.1, *supra* note 3, Advisory Committee's Note at 1035.

of his intent to make a request "in the pleadings or prior to the presentation of any evidence at the trial," though the court "may require or permit other notice."[17] All sources leave uncertain the question whether a party who does not himself undertake to offer proof can raise an issue concerning his adversary's failure to prove a foreign law which, on the basis of existing choice-of-law rules, the facts show to be applicable to the adversary's claim (or defense).[18] They also do not attempt to prescribe the effect of the failure of *both* parties to satisfy the court as to the content of another law once an issue concerning it has been raised,[19] a matter that *Erie* might render beyond reach of a federal rule as to a foreign nation's law.

If the only problem posed by the possible relevance in a case of the rules of decision of a sister state or foreign country were the difficulty of ascertaining what those rules were, the procedure which has been evolving might well be clarified by decision and prove satisfactory. However, in a not inconsequential proportion of those cases, there will be a question whether the forum, the sister state or foreign country, or even a third state or country is to be the source of the law. Sometimes the case will present two or more distinct issues for which choices must be made. And surely these lectures will have been in vain if they have not established the proposition that, for many years to come, there will continue to be many difficult choice-of-law questions lacking plain, clear-cut answers.

17 *Supra* note 11, 4511 (a) and (b).

18 In the much-discussed case of Walton v. Arabian-American Oil Co., 233 F.2d 541 (2d Cir. 1956), *cert. denied*, 352 U.S. 872, 77 S. Ct. 97 (1956), the trial judge had dismissed the case because the plaintiff had failed to establish Saudi-Arabian law which the judge held essential to a claim arising out of a Saudi-Arabian accident. The plaintiff "had abundant opportunity to supply the missing element and chose not to avail himself of it." 233 F.2d at 546. The decision is criticized at length in Currie, *supra* note 9.

19 Professor Currie in this situation would apply the forum's relevant "rules of decision" (as distinguished from its "rules of conduct"). See Currie, *supra* note 9, at 1017-22, 1026-28, in SELECTED ESSAYS 64-69, 75-76. *Cf.* Walton v. Arabian-American Oil Co., *supra* note 18.

Sometimes a choice of law will obviously be decisive in a case: if State X's law is applied, the plaintiff will win; if State Y's law, he is certain to lose. In other cases, the application of Y's law may simply make the plaintiff's case more difficult or allow the defendant a chance to establish a defense. Sometimes only the measure of damages will be at stake. In certain situations, the basic theory of the case will depend on which state's law is applied; the evidence that is relevant and the tactics of counsel will vary with the applicable law. How is the difficult question of choice to be posed and determined?

In the first place, the plaintiff, though alleging some foreign facts, may think it best not to commit himself at the start to a choice of law and so does not plead any other law. The defendant may be convinced that the forum's law should be applied, but what he can do to assure its application is limited as long as the plaintiff keeps silent. He cannot plead the forum's law as he would foreign law in the event he wished to invoke it. Of course, the case may be such that the forum's law, if applicable, would sustain a motion to dismiss for failure to state a claim on which relief can be granted or a motion for summary judgment. Either motion would smoke out the plaintiff's position as to the applicable law and also provide a good basis for a deliberated decision of the question. However, the availability of either motion may be a matter of luck: the difference in laws may not have a decisive influence at that stage in the proceeding, although in this connection the opportunity that Rule 56 of the Federal Rules and its state counterparts afford for the use of the "partial summary judgment" should be kept in mind.

If the plaintiff has pleaded a foreign law or has given timely notice, what can the defendant do if he believes the forum's law or the law of a third state should be applied? Presumably, in the latter event, he too can plead or give notice. However, if the application or nonapplication of one of the laws pleaded or noticed is not decisive of the whole case or a separable issue in it, neither the motions noted above nor a motion for judgment on the pleadings would be available. And, incidentally, if the case is in the federal court and a choice between the laws of sister states is involved, apparently neither pleading nor written notice will be required to apprise either party of the other's choice-of-law objective. The federal court will take judicial notice of whichever law will at some point in the litigation be held applicable.[20]

It has been suggested that the pretrial conference is the place to iron the matter out, to get agreement on the applicable law. But the cases I am concerned with are those as to which the choice is too important and too difficult to render agreement by the parties likely. However, the functions of the pretrial conference are not limited to recording agreements.[21] Once a

20 The federal courts have long taken judicial notice of the laws of the several states. The doctrine was set forth in Owings v. Hull, 9 Pet. 607, 625 (1835), by Story, J.:

> We are of opinion, that the circuit court was bound to take judicial notice of the laws of Louisiana. The circuit courts . . . are created by Congress, not for the purpose of administering the local law of a single state alone, but to administer the laws of all the states in the union, in cases to which they respectively apply. The judicial power conferred on the general government, by the constitution, extends to many cases arising under the laws of the different states. And this court is called upon, in the exercise of its appellate jurisdiction, constantly to take notice of and administer the jurisprudence of all the states. That jurisprudence is then, in no just sense, a foreign jurisprudence, to be proved, in the courts of the United States, by the ordinary modes of proof by which the laws of a foreign country are to be established; but it is to be judicially taken notice of in the same manner, as the laws of the United States are taken notice of by these courts.

Despite Erie R.R. Co. v. Tompkins, 304 U.S. 64 (1938), the rule in Owings continues to be applied to all cases in the federal courts. See 1A Moore, Federal Practice, ¶ 0.316 (4) at 3523-28 (2d ed. 1961), suggesting that most of the post-*Erie* cases have not applied state rules of judicial notice because the question relates to pleading and evidence rather than to substantive law and is not necessarily outcome-determinative.

21 While the reports do not show that pretrial conferences have been used to decide contested choice-of-law issues, such a use should advance the purpose of the conference to expedite litigation. Under Rule 16 of the Federal Rules, courts have ruled on questions of law and admissibility of evidence. See 3 Moore, Federal Practice, ¶ 16.16 at 1122, (2d ed.

difficult choice-of-law issue has been identified, the judge could, if he thought it wise, require the issue to be briefed and include a ruling on it in his pretrial order. Unfortunately, in many states and federal districts, pretrial conferences are not customary or are perfunctory. Moreover, if the conference is held as the time of trial approaches, an effort to resolve the choice-of-law question then could easily result in the necessity of a considerable postponement.[22]

These difficulties, of course, are not inherent in the pretrial conference as a device for solving the choice-of-law procedural problem. However, their existence in some jurisdictions, together with the possibility that the need to determine the

---

1963) and 1962 Supplement at 133. Cases have also been adjudicated at pretrial conferences in the federal courts by summary judgment and dismissal. See NIMS, PRE-TRIAL, 130-32, 140 (1950); 3 MOORE, *op. cit. supra*, ¶ 16.04 at 1105-6.

The Michigan pretrial rules give the court authority to rule on specified defenses and would seem to grant the court power to determine the governing law in the process of clarifying the pleadings or simplifying the issues. See MICH. STAT. ANN., Gen. Ct. Rules, Rule 301.1 (1), (2), (12) (1964).

In the *Walton* case, *supra* note 18, the applicability of Saudi-Arabian law was discussed at several pretrial hearings. The judge intimated his view that that law was applicable, but no pretrial order was entered, plaintiff's counsel having absented himself from the last two conferences. Argument of counsel for defendant, as reported in Walton v. Arabian American Oil Co., Civ. Action No. 50-170, U.S. Ct. of Appeals, 2d Cir., Appendix to Appellant's Brief, 17 (1956).

[22] See 3 MOORE, *op. cit. supra* note 21, ¶ 16.08 at 1110, contending that experience has shown that pretrial conferences are most successful when held shortly before the trial, chances for settlement then being brightest. Moore quotes, at page 1111, the Recommendations of the Judicial Conference of the United States with Respect to Pre-Trial (Sept. 1944): "The Committee approves of the practice of the great majority of the judges using pre-trial procedure regularly, of holding the pre-trial conference shortly before the actual trial is had, the preferable interval before the trial being not less than one week or more than three weeks. In exceptional cases it may also be advantageous to call a pre-trial conference immediately after issue is joined." Also quoted in NIMS, *op. cit. supra* note 21, at 307. The view reported above is substantially in accord with the views of the New Jersey judges reported in ROSENBERG, THE PRETRIAL CONFERENCE AND EFFECTIVE JUSTICE 89 (1964).

applicable law might present itself when, as to other matters, a pretrial conference would be untimely, suggests that exclusive reliance should not be placed on the conference as a procedural instrumentality for choice of law. Independently of the pretrial conference, therefore, either party should have an option to raise a choice-of-law issue by motion in advance of trial if the case is not one in which the problem can be disposed of by a motion directed to the pleadings or for summary judgment.[23] The motion might be filed by the party relying on the foreign law if he wished to make his right to rely on it more nearly certain, or it might be filed by his adversary. The motion ought also to serve another function: the ascertainment of just what the foreign law provides, to be embodied in a ruling by the court which, unless withdrawn or modified by the trial court or reversed on appeal, would serve as the law of the case.[24]

The disposition of a motion for the identification and ascertainment of the applicable foreign law might entail a greater knowledge of the facts of the case than had been revealed by the pleadings. In that event, a sufficient clarification might be achieved by the filing of affidavits.[25] It should be kept in mind

[23] There seems no such procedure for the federal courts at this time. That the absence of specific authority for a particular type of motion need not, however, be a barrier to its employment in a proper case is demonstrated by Grant v. Kellogg Co., 3 F.R.D. 229 (S.D.N.Y. 1943) (motion for order permitting special appearance; the motion's aptness was not questioned).

[24] I have found no evidence that such a motion is employed. Where the choice-of-law issue, though not such as to sustain a motion to dismiss or for summary judgment, nevertheless could be viewed as involving "a controlling question of law as to which there is substantial ground for difference of opinion" and where an immediate appeal from an order determining "may materially advance the ultimate termination of the litigation," an interlocutory appeal may be permitted by the Court of Appeals in its discretion. 28 U.S.C. § 1292(b).

[25] The federal rules now provide for filing of supporting and opposing affidavits on motions for summary judgment. FED. R. CIV. P. 56. However, the foreign law question might not always sustain such a motion.

that even the most fact-oriented rule for choice-of-law will ordinarily be concerned only with facts important to the process of choice. These may be clear and undisputed. They may have merely a tangential role in resolving the issues in dispute once the governing law is chosen. Often the difficult choice-of-law question before the court would turn on the proper construction of the conflicting laws in the light of applicable choice-of-law principles.

Sometimes, no doubt, the opposing party could satisfy the court that a choice of law in response to the motion would be premature, that his position on the issue would have to await the procurement of further facts by discovery. If so, a decision on the motion could be postponed. Sometimes factual uncertainties would make it plain that a final decision on the proper law would have to await the full development of the relevant circumstances at the trial. However, before a decision to that effect had been reached in the proceeding, evidence might have been taken concerning the pertinent provisions of the law or laws of the states other than the forum which might be chosen at the trial. An early finding (or conclusion of law) as to the rules of foreign law might be made, although the determination of their applicability might have to be postponed till later.[26]

In any event, the fact that a ruling on the applicable law had been made before trial would not preclude its withdrawal or modification at or after the trial if facts not available at the time of the motion were to convince the court that the original ruling was erroneous.[27] It seems reasonable to suppose that such changes in position would be infrequent. Also infrequent but not inconceivable would be a case in which a choice of

[26] The chief value advanced by this is convenience; proving the content of a foreign law could be an expensive business. It should not have to be repeated.

[27] A similar procedure prevails as to pretrial orders. They can be amended at the discretion of the trial judge "to prevent manifest injustice." FED. R. CIV. P. 16; NIMS, *op. cit. supra* note 21, at 158-63.

law emerged, to the surprise of both parties, during the trial itself.

In all probability, the federal courts and the courts of a number of states already have the power to entertain such motions as I have suggested under existing rules[28] and from time to time, such motions are in fact made, argued, and ruled on. However, this does not seem an adequate reason for such a procedure to have to depend on the insight and initiative of counsel, without the explicit guidance and support of any statutory authority or rule of court. As the determination of foreign law has changed from a fact issue to an issue of law, the procedural implications of the change for choice of law have been obscured. Accordingly, a tendency to let the matter slide over to, or till the eve of, the trial would be a natural one.

It may be contended that all this is much ado about very little, that the litigants and courts have managed reasonably well without the intrusion of such burdensome procedures. To this a number of answers may be made. In the first place, the procedure would not be compulsory; if both parties wished to leave the issue to be resolved by a judicial impromptu at the trial, this would be their privilege (though a party's failure to utilize the pretrial machinery would have a bearing on the reasonableness of his notice where notice was required). Second, the lack of a procedure to assure an adequate opportunity for informed deliberation may help to explain why trial judges have tended to persevere in mechanical dispositions of choice-of-law issues—not to mention mechanical determi-

[28] The problems of protracted litigation have led to resort to successive pretrial conferences in connection with big cases in which motions disposing of preliminary issues appear to have been extensively used. See Proceedings of the Seminar on Protracted Cases for United States Circuit and District Judges, N.Y. Univ. Law Center, 21 F.R.D. 395 (1957), especially App. A, Preliminary Draft of Checklist of Procedural Devices for Handling the Big Case (Civil), *id.* at 523. For a summary of state provisions for pretrial conference procedures, see ROSENBERG, *op. cit. supra* note 22, App. E, at 210. Pretrial conferences are mandatory in only four of the 44 states having such provisions.

nations as to the content of foreign law.[29] Finally, and most important, the problem to which this proposal is addressed is essentially a new one. It is posed by the whole trend of development in choice of law. For that development to thrive, the trial courts should be able to make rulings that require more time for discriminating thought than trial judges have customarily been free to devote to choice of law in the past. The suggested procedure should provide that time when it is most needed.

B. *Choosing "Procedural" Rules in Choice-of-Law Cases*

The procedural improvement suggested above might, if put into effect, have as a by-product a marked reduction in the area of controversy over the application of the procedural rules of the forum. Before I explain this further benefit that might be derived from resolving choice-of-law questions on motion before trial, I must consider the difficulty which it would serve at least to mitigate.

In every case in which a court is called upon to employ a rule drawn from the law of another state, there is the risk that differences in judicial procedure between the forum and the other state will defeat the objective which the court has

[29] Compare the observations of Judge Charles Wyzanski, "A Trial Judge's Freedom and Responsibility," 65 HARV. L. REV. 1281, 1300-1: "The impression that I gather from the cases is that a federal judge sitting in a diversity jurisdiction case is less willing to depart from obsolete doctrines than when he sits in a purely federal case. And this reluctance is not apt to be modified by the action of his superiors in the federal courts. On questions of state law federal appellate courts repeatedly state their reliance on the knowledge possessed by federal trial judges sitting in the locality. Thus the total tendency of the Erie Railroad doctrine has a strong reactionary direction which it is hard to believe its proponents and expansionists appreciated. Perhaps, indeed, this is part of a larger problem of the twentieth century judicial emphasis on conflict of laws. *Every time judges are called upon to apply the law of a foreign jurisdiction, are they not inclined to give undue weight to the recorded landmarks and to underestimate the mobile qualities and the thrusts of principle we discern in our domestic law?*" (Italics supplied.)

sought to attain in turning to the latter state for the rule of law. Where the forum has had no prior connection with the event or transaction giving rise to the litigation, the court may properly be viewed as sitting only because the forum is convenient. It should therefore seek, so far as practicable, to resolve the controversy as would a court in the concerned state. To this end, it should be prepared to draw all the rules required for the litigation from the law of that state, subject only to the limitation imposed by the need to preserve the integrity of its own judicial procedure both as an operating mechanism and as a reflection of certain important values.

This is not a necessary view of the forum's function in such a case. The concept of the transitory action can be viewed as a means of enabling the forum to treat a claim from another state or country exactly as it would one of its own, save for the use of the substantive rules of the other jurisdiction. The forum's procedure reflects its view of a fair method of dispute settlement through litigation. Therefore, one might contend, the forum should not be expected to give up or modify that procedure in any respect simply because its use might have a different effect on the outcome of the case from that which would be caused by the use of the other state's procedure.

Up to recent years, this latter conception of the forum's function was clearly the prevalent one in common law jurisdictions.[30] There were a few areas of controversy over classification, relating mainly to the statute of frauds, the statute of limitations, and the survival of actions. Courts confronting the problem tended to analyze each state's rule to determine whether it could be classified as "remedial" or "procedural." If the forum's rule were such, it was applied; if the other state's rule were procedural, it was not applied. Gaps could and did develop[31] when the forum's law was held

[30] See Ailes, "Substance and Procedure in the Conflict of Laws," 39 Mich. L. Rev. 392, 392-93 (1941).

[31] Among American cases, the classic example is provided by Marie v. Garrison, 13 Abb. N. Cas. 210 (N.Y. Super. Ct. 1883), in which, as an

"substantive" and the other state's law, "procedural." Domestic precedents were often relied upon to aid in the process of analysis.

The validity of this process was sharply challenged by Professor Walter Wheeler Cook in an article in 1933 which became one of the gospels of the realist movement, " 'Substance' and 'Procedure' in the Conflict of Laws."[32] In it he warned that "The tendency to assume that a word which appears in two or more legal rules, and so in connection with more than one purpose, has and should have precisely the same scope in all of them runs all through legal discussions. It has all the tenacity of original sin and must constantly be guarded against."[33]

Professor Cook listed eight categories of cases in which the substance-procedure dichotomy appeared and, looking back at them, added, "We see at once that a person asking where the line *ought* to be drawn might well conclude that this ought to be at one place for one purpose and at a somewhat different place for another purpose." (Italics in original.)[34]

Cook rejected the view that the forum ought to use all its own "procedural" rules in a case based on an out-of-state event or transaction. For him the proper question to put was: "How far can the court of the forum go in applying the rules taken from the foreign system of law without unduly hindering or inconveniencing itself?"[35] This plainly accords with the first statement above of the forum's objective.

The transition to Professor Cook's approach, which has

---

alternative ground of decision, the forum's statute of frauds was held inapplicable to a Missouri-formed contract because it was considered substantive, while the Missouri statute was not applied because it was held to be procedural.

[32] 42 YALE L.J. 333 (1933), reprinted in COOK, THE LOGICAL AND LEGAL BASES OF THE CONFLICT OF LAWS 154 (1942). The Cook thesis was vigorously challenged in Ailes, *supra* note 30.

[33] Cook, *supra* note 32, at 337, in THE LOGICAL AND LEGAL BASES at 159.

[34] *Id.* at 343, reprinted at 165.

[35] *Id.* at 344, reprinted at 166.

been steadily gaining support, was materially advanced by *Erie R.R. v. Tompkins*[36] and its sequelae, notably *Guaranty Trust Co. v. York*,[37] decided in 1945, seven years later. The determination in the former case that, in a diversity case, a federal court had to apply substantive rules of state law, as declared by state courts as well as legislatures, rather than "general law" of its own making, was also seen as a way to make plain, to quote Mr. Justice Frankfurter's opinion in *Guaranty Trust*, that "for the same transaction the accident of a suit by a non-resident in a federal court instead of in a State court a block away should not lead to a substantially different result."[38]

The *Erie* rule gave constitutional importance to the distinction between "substance" and "procedure"; the *Guaranty Trust* case gave to outcome determination a critical role in the drawing of the distinction. It no longer sufficed to justify the use of the federal forum's distinctive rule by saying that it pertained to the remedy if the consequence of its application was a different result from that obtainable in the state court. Moreover, this development is relevant to cases in which a state court's task is to apply the law of another, concerned state. Once this task is seen as an endeavor to decide the case much as would a court in the concerned state, then a state case applying another state's law becomes very much like a federal diversity case applying the forum state's law. In both, outcome determination ought therefore to be an important criterion in deciding what parts of the other state's law the forum should apply.

That criterion, however, is not always an easy one to apply. Some rules labeled "procedural" are decisive whenever applied; others will be important only when the available proof renders them crucial. Some "procedural" rules are designed to effectuate a substantive policy of the enacting state, as where a change is made in the burden of proof with respect to contributory negligence; others appear to be neutral. The

[36] 304 U.S. 64 (1938). [37] 326 U.S. 99 (1945).
[38] 326 U.S. 99, 109 (1945).

applicability of some "procedural" rules would have to be decided only once in a litigation, often before trial; in the case of others, the question might pop up repeatedly and often unpredictably during the trial. The relevance of considerations of this type was pressed by Professor Cook and others of like mind, notably Professor Edmund M. Morgan. Professor Morgan, however, thought it easier to preserve the familiar domestic category of "procedural" and change the choice-of-law rule that the forum always applies to its own procedural law.[39]

Rather surprisingly, the original *Restatement*, against which Professor Cook directed many of his critical shafts in this area as in others, explained the adoption of the forum's procedural law, not by defending the propriety of a forum's always employing its own procedural system, but, rather apologetically, in terms of the inconvenience and impracticability of an "all-inclusive reference to the foreign law."[40] Because of the "heavy burden" that "would be thrown upon the courts of the forum and the orderly administration of justice," the Introductory Note to Chapter 12, "Procedure," explained that a "limitation upon the scope of the reference to the foreign law is thus necessary." However, inspection of the black letter rules and comments of Chapter 12 reveals little reference to the convenience criterion; a remedial classification is given to most rules, an exception being made for those found to have been intended by the enacting state "to condition the right" and therefore to be substantive.[41] Unfortunately, clues are lacking to enable one to tell whether a given statute simply regulates actions in the local courts or instead "conditions a right."[42]

[39] See Morgan, "Choice of Law Governing Proof," 58 HARV. L. REV. 153, 157-58 (1944).

[40] RESTATEMENT, CONFLICT OF LAWS ch. 12, "Procedure," Introductory Note at 699-701.

[41] *Id.*, Topic 3. See especially Scope Note at 717-18, and § 601.

[42] Apart from the difficulty of interpretation conceded by the *Restatement*, *id.* Scope Note at 718, its rationale of the distinction was assailed as the product of faulty analysis in Morgan, *supra* note 39, at 182.

Use of the outcome-determinative test can yield results that collide with those produced by a convenience test. Thus, rules as to admissibility of evidence may on occasion be decisive of a plaintiff's ability to prove his case or a defendant's to establish his defense,[43] but they may recur frequently in the course of a trial. If the court had to be instructed as to the terms of the foreign evidentiary law each time a new point involving it were to arise, the trial could be slowed down intolerably. Probably, if one party were accorded this privilege, the other would claim it too. Moreover the court would often find it hard to decide whether in fact the rule was likely to be outcome-determinative. Rules as to presumptions, *res ipsa loquitur*, the competency of witnesses and the safeguarding of privileged communications,[44] though often important and sometimes crucial to a case's outcome, all might give difficulty in application.

The coexistence of three tests: outcome determination, procedural convenience, and conceptual analyses, has not made for a coherent body of decisional law. However, that it is susceptible of being reduced to order was shown last year by Professor Robert A. Sedler of St. Louis University who surveyed the entire procedural field in an article entitled "The *Erie* Outcome Test as a Guide to Substance and Procedure in

[43] *Cf.* Bernkrant v. Fowler, 55 Cal. 2d 588, 360 P.2d 906 (1961); see Cavers, "Oral Contracts to Provide by Will and the Choice-of-Law Process: Some Notes on *Bernkrant*," in PERSPECTIVES OF LAW: ESSAYS FOR AUSTIN WAKEMAN SCOTT 38 (Pound, Griswold & Sutherland, eds. 1964). See also Sedler, "The *Erie* Outcome Test as a Guide to Substance and Procedure in the Conflict of Laws," 37 N.Y.U.L. REV. 813, 865-71 (1962).

[44] It has been pointed out that logically decisions as to privilege may call for a recognition of the interest of the state where the communication was made even though neither the forum nor the place with which the cause had its most significant relationship accords the privilege in question. See Sedler, *supra* note 43, at 870-71. But see Weinstein, "Recognition in the United States of the Privileges of Another Jurisdiction," 56 COLUM. L. REV. 535, 537-39 (1956).

the Conflict of Laws."[45] Adopting outcome determination as the principal criterion, he subjected it to qualifications which led to the formulation of the following principle:[46] "*To the extent that the matter in question materially affects the outcome of the case, the forum should use the* lex loci *as a model except where to do so would interfere with the efficient operation of the forum's judicial system or violate a strong procedural policy of the forum.*" (Italics in original.)

Professor Sedler followed this test with an extensive review of decisions involving substance-procedure issues. It disclosed some instances where, though the outcome-determinative test would have allowed the application of the *lex loci,* the label of "procedural" or "remedial" had been applied to require recourse to the forum's law. But even if outcome determination had been accepted as the basic criterion, Professor Sedler's qualification, interference with "the efficient operation of the forum's judicial system," would have denied the application of the *lex loci* in a number of cases. In certain of these situations, the convenience factor was controlling. But suppose it could have been clearly determined at the start of the trial, that one or more specified rules, drawn from the *lex loci* and relating to such matters as the admission of evidence, presumptions and *res ipsa loquitur,* might be employed in its course. Such a pre-arranged and limited departure from the forum's customary procedure would not have embarrassed the conduct of the proceedings.

The desideratum of being able in this way to reduce the convenience factor as an obstacle to the use of the *lex loci,* reveals another advantage of the procedure I have suggested in the preceding section as a means of resolving choice-of-law questions before trial. Should not each party be afforded an opportunity to move the court that some rule or rules of the kind ordinarily deemed procedural be brought from the law of

[45] *Supra* note 43.
[46] *Id.* at 824.

State X (the source of the substantive law of the case) and applied in the pending trial? The court, in considering the motion, could decide not only whether it should be granted but also what, precisely, was the content of the X rule. Hence, if the motion were granted, the X rule could be applied without precipitating argument as to its terms during the trial.

This plan seemed to me open to the objection that, if the materiality of a given rule's impact on the outcome of the particular case were to be the test, a demonstration that that specification could be met might often prove time consuming and difficult in advance of trial. Consideration of this problem has suggested a solution that may at first blush seem drastic: discard the outcome-determinative test in cases where one or more other states are involved.

This is not nearly as radical as it may seem. A lawyer with a case to try in State F is not going to burden the F court with a request to use a procedural rule or rules of State X unless he has a pretty good reason for doing so. Perhaps, now and then by doing so he would obtain the use of a rule that the outcome-determinative test would bar, but the time and trouble saved in being able to eliminate that issue from controversy would more than compensate for any burden caused by requests by counsel to import inconsequential rules for use in the forum.

I would, of course, preserve the qualifications on the privilege noted by Professor Sedler (subject to minor disagreements as to their application which I shall not discuss). The power to invoke these limitations of efficiency and policy would prevent the practice from putting the forum's courts or its policies in jeopardy. It should be noted, moreover, that the possibility of obtaining rulings on procedural points before trial would sharply diminish the threat to efficiency that their use might otherwise pose. The further fact that each party might be seeking a favorable ruling on a point it proposed to draw from State X's law would make for a live-and-let-live spirit, facilitating the resolution of these questions at the pretrial conference.

I have, to be sure, simplified the problem by assuming, as is often done in its discussion, that the case posing it involved no real choice-of-law question concerning substantive law. Whenever such a question did exist, then often the importation of certain parts of State X procedure could be agreed upon at the same time that the court decided that State X was the proper source of substantive law.

There is, of course, the chance that, in a given case, there would be more than one choice-of-law issue. The forum might choose to apply substantive law as follows: its own law on issue A; State X law on issue B; and State Y law on issue C. How, after reaching these conclusions, should the court rule on the plaintiff's motion to apply a procedural rule of State X and on the defendant's motion to apply the Y law on the same point and the X law on another point?

This question may seem more difficult in the abstract than it would appear in actuality. In a number of such situations, each of the procedural rules would have its impact on a matter covered as to substance by the law of a particular state. Suppose, for example, the plaintiff moved to apply the law of X to a question of procedure relating to the very same phase of the case to which the court had determined to apply the substantive law of X. In such a situation, the plaintiff's motion would in all probability be granted. To be sure, some procedural motions might not have that convenient correspondence but might instead go to the whole case. I doubt, however, that this would render a reasonable solution impossible; I am also certain that this problem (which might, of course, arise under existing law) could be resolved more wisely if the court had been given the opportunity to deliberate it which the proposed motion practice would permit.

The review of the rulings of the trial judge presents a problem calling for consideration in connection with my suggestion that the outcome-determinative test be abandoned if the proposed procedure were to be adopted. The test might still have significance with respect to an appeal. If the use of a rule of State X's law would determine the outcome of a case, I should suppose that a refusal by the trial court to allow the X rule to be applied in a proper case for its application would constitute reversible error. Suppose, however, that whether the use of X law would affect the result of the case importantly would be uncertain in advance of trial. Suppose, moreover, that the use of the X law in the trial of the case would be attended by some difficulties. In that event, the trial judge would have to exercise discretion in deciding whether the importance of the employment of the X rule would justify the burden that it would impose. Surely that decision should be set aside on appeal only for abuse of discretion. Incidentally, in the exercise of that discretion, the closer the relation of the X procedural rules to the X substantive rules being employed in the case, the stronger the justification for enduring some inconvenience in the use of the former—and *e converso*.

The fact that the scheme I have been outlining may be put in operation in cases involving two or more states would not require a federal court to go to the same length in diversity cases with respect to the forum state's procedural rules. Indeed, there are good reasons for retaining the same outcome-determinative test that has been developed in diversity cases and perhaps also for preserving somewhat stricter standards to protect the federal court's efficiency and procedural policy than I should hope would be used in state courts if they were to adopt the practice I have proposed. In the first place, in the diversity case the temptation would be great to gamble by resorting to the forum state's procedural rules in lieu of the federal rules. Counsel would be at least as familiar with them as with the federal; hence the inhibiting effect of the unfamiliar would not serve to render counsel selective in their requests. Second, instead of being a matter arising only now and then in the occasional case presenting a choice of law, the possibility of resort to the forum state's procedure would be present in every diversity case. The burden could be considerable. Finally, it must be remembered that the federal law still permits recourse to state rules of evidence[47] and, so long as this rule is preserved (its elimination has been proposed[48]), the existing law in diversity cases is considerably less restrictive than the rule now existing with respect to cases involving the choice of another state's law.

To summarize the proposal I have advanced: Before trial each party could move, by preliminary motion or at pretrial conference, for the use of one or more specifically identified procedural rules, to be drawn from the law of the state supplying the substantive law of the case relevant to the issue or issues to which the procedural rules related and to be used for specified purposes in the trial or other proceedings in the case. If the motions were granted, the rules thereby allowed to be used would take the place of the rules of the forum that would otherwise be applied for the same purposes. The motion would be denied as to any rule which the court found would, to quote Professor Sedler, "interfere with the efficient operation of the forum's judicial system or violate a strong procedural policy of the forum."[49] This proposal would not apply to permit the use of the forum state's procedural rule in a diversity case in lieu of a federal rule; in such cases, the outcome-determinative test would continue to be applied.

[47] FED. R. CIV. P. 43 (a).

[48] Judicial Conference of the U.S., COMM. ON RULES OF PRAC. AND PROC., RULES OF EVIDENCE ix, 23-26 (1962).

[49] *Supra* note 43, at 824.

XII

A WORD IN CONCLUSION

An apt valedictory for these lectures can be found in that first American work on the conflict of laws to which I referred in my opening lecture. One hundred thirty-five years ago, at the end of *Dissertation I*, Samuel Livermore wrote:

"If I do not mistake the matter, it is particularly important in this country, to have established some fixed and correct principles for the determination of the questions, which may be expected to arise from the various opposing laws of the several states . . . there should be some settled principles and . . . these should be uniformly observed. No such uniformity exists at present; and unless I am greatly deceived we have no cases decided by our various courts, in which we find so much error and confusion, as in those which involve the conflicting laws of different states."

As I have endeavored to persuade you, there continues to be need for "principles for the determination of the questions, which may be expected to arise from the various opposing laws of the several states." And while I would not join Mr. Livermore in insisting that the principles needed to provide guidance in these cases be "fixed" and "uniformly observed," I am not convinced that courts and scholars should now rest content with *ad hoc* decisions, however policy-oriented their grounds may be. I am therefore able to repeat for myself—and without reservation—Mr. Livermore's closing apologia:

"It has therefore occurred to me, that my time would not be uselessly employed in . . . stating such considerations, as my own reflections, in the course of a study of these principles, have suggested to me. I may fail in the attempt to establish true and certain principles, for the decision of the various difficult questions growing out of the contrariety of laws; and yet my labour may not have been in vain, as it may tend to excite a spirit of inquiry into a subject but little understood in this country, and may lead to discussions, by others more capable of accomplishing the object desired."

APPENDIX

DYM V. GORDON IN THE NEW YORK COURT OF APPEALS

The New York case of *Dym v. Gordon* was discussed in Chapter VI of these lectures on the basis of the decision in the Appellate Division.[1] The case was argued in the Court of Appeals on February 11, 1965, but the Court's decision was not announced until the last day of the term, July 8th. The three opinions presented many points of consequence for the developing methodology of choice of law. Indeed, I think it fair to say that in none of the decisions which have reflected this methodology has there been as penetrating an attack upon a choice-of-law problem. Hard questions were asked, and the answers given command respect even though, of course, they cannot all induce agreement. As one reads the three opinions, it becomes easy to understand the lapse of five months between argument and decision day.

Given the importance of the case to the changing choice-of-law process, I was fortunate that this decision had come down before my deadlines had been crossed. However, the opinions reached me when the lectures were already in galley proof and page proofing was in process. The solution was to provide this appendix devoted to a comment on the case.

First, a restatement of the stipulated facts.[2] The plaintiff sued for personal injuries which she sustained in an automobile accident in Colorado. The defendant was driving her to a golfing lesson at Longmont, Colorado, ten miles or so from the University of Colorado campus at Boulder. Both were enrolled

[1] 22 A.D. 2d 702, 253 N.Y.S.2d 802 (1964), *rev'g* 41 Misc. 2d 657, 245 N.Y.S.2d 656 (Sup. Ct. 1964), discussed at p. 173, *supra*.

[2] These are derived from the opinions of the three courts and the briefs of the parties in the Court of Appeals.

as students in the University's six weeks' summer school course. About a month before, they had come separately from their homes (and domicils) in New York, the plaintiff by bus, the defendant by the car involved in the accident. It was registered and insured in New York.

The accident was caused by ordinary negligence. The defendant had driven through a stop light, colliding with a Kansas car driven by a Kansan. The parties both returned to New York shortly after the accident.

The plaintiff moved for judgment that the Colorado guest statute[3] was not applicable.[4] The act denies recovery by a guest passenger from his host except where the latter has acted with "a willful and wanton disregard of the rights of others" or has caused the injury intentionally or while intoxicated. New York permits recovery upon proof of ordinary negligence. The defendant moved for summary judgment on the basis of the Colorado law.

The trial court granted the plaintiff's motion, holding the New York law applicable and, after trial, awarding the plaintiff $20,000 in damages. A sophisticated opinion by Judge Meyer drew heavily upon *Babcock v. Jackson.*[5] He held that the distinguishing Colorado contact—the temporary residence there of the parties—did not "alter the center of gravity sufficiently to warrant application" of Colorado's guest statute. Since the state of injury, Colorado, had "opted for the lesser standard" of care, it would have no cause for complaint if New York's higher standard were applied to the New York driver. His liability would not affect insurance rates in Colorado, and his insurer had bargained to assume risks under New York law. The guest was not shown to have relied on Colorado law. The court saw its decision as in accord with *Restatement Second.*

[3] Colo. Rev. Stat. § 13-9-1 (1963).

[4] This use of the motion for a judgment disposing of a defense is pertinent to a suggestion advanced in Ch. XI, "Procedure for—and in—Choice of Law," at pp. 273-78, *supra.*

[5] 12 N.Y.2d 473, 191 N.E.2d 279 (1963). (New York common law and not Ontario guest statute applied in action between New York guest and host for negligent injury in Ontario in short motor trip from New York and back.)

The Appellate Division, Second Department, contented itself with a memorandum opinion. After noting that, under "the Colorado Guest Statute, the manner of the defendant's operation of his vehicle was an important issue,"[6] the court concluded unanimously that Colorado, "the place where the parties resided, albeit temporarily, where their guest-host relationship arose and where the trip began and was to end . . . had the dominant contacts and the superior claims to the application of its law," citing *Babcock*.

At this juncture, I hoped that the Court of Appeals would not follow the Appellate Division's tactic of simply cataloging contacts without an illuminating evaluation of their significance. A more likely alternative was that it would follow *Babcock* in concluding that the case presented a false conflict and that New York's interest in the application of its law could be advanced without prejudice to Colorado's interest in protecting Colorado drivers and insurers from Colorado claims. This would have laid the basis for the "personal law of torts," with the problems incident to the concept that I have noted.[7]

The Competing Rationales

The dissent by Judge Fuld does follow the latter course, though he does not pursue its implications. He finds "no material distinction between the factual situation here presented and that in the *Babcock* case. . . . Nothing turns on the circumstance that in this case the guest-host relationship was formed in the foreign jurisdiction. It seems indisputably clear that a jurisdiction may be said to be 'concerned' with a specific issue, if that term is to have a meaningful content, only when its governmental interests and policies enter into the making of a particular decision. Accordingly, the decisive consideration, in the present case, is that Colorado's guest statute, paralleling Ontario's, has as its prime objective the protection of Colorado

[6] The relevance of this circumstance is questionable in view of note 14 to the opinion in Babcock v. Jackson, *supra* note 5, where the court says, ". . . the result would be the same . . . where the foreign guest statute requires a showing of gross negligence."

[7] See p. 150, *supra*.

driver-defendants and their insurance carriers against fraudulent claims and lawsuits. . . . New York, on the other hand, just as in *Babcock*, as the permanent residence of the plaintiff and the defendant and the place to which they returned to live shortly after the accident, has a predominant interest in vindicating its own policy of requiring negligent driving hosts to compensate their injured guests. It is apparent that the consequences resulting from an uncompensated injury generally affect the community in which the injured party resides, in this case New York."

Judge Burke's opinion for the majority meets this evaluation head on. It describes the method to be followed in terms of *Babcock:* isolation of the issue, identification of the policies of the laws in conflict, and examination of "the contacts of the respective jurisdictions to ascertain which has a superior connection with the occurrence" and therefore "a superior interest in having its policy or law applied."[8] However, when Judge Burke comes to identify Colorado policies, he does not restrict them to the one policy which Judge Fuld attributed to the Ontario law in *Babcock* and to the Colorado law in *Dym:* protection against false claims.

The majority see two other policies also reflected in the Colorado law. The additional policies are (1) the prevention of suits by "ungrateful guests" and (2) "the priority of injured parties in other cars in the assets of the negligent defendant." To establish a Colorado interest in the application of the former policy, the court points to the fact that "the parties were dwelling in Colorado when the relationship was formed and the accident arose out of Colorado based activity," thereby giving Colorado

[8] Judge Burke's formulation, which derives a state's "superior interest in having its policy or law applied" from its "superior connection with the occurrence," is probably intended to mean the same as Judge Fuld's formulation which seeks the state having " 'the greatest concern' with the matter in issue." The latter formulation more explicitly recognizes that the state's connection must be evaluated in terms of the specific issue raised in the litigation, a point that the new formulation in the *Restatement* unfortunately masks. See Restatement (Second) Conflict of Laws § 379(1) (Tent. Draft No. 8, 1963). (The need to compose this appendix before the *Dym* decision was in print has precluded reference to the pages in the opinions from which quotations are drawn.)

"such significant contacts with the *relationship itself* and the *basis of its formation* that the application of its law and underlying policy are clearly warranted." (Italics in original.) The court saw the latter policy as giving rise to a Colorado interest in its application because, unlike the accident in *Babcock*,[9] the accident in *Dym* involved another car, the driver of which might have competed with Mrs. Dym for the defendant's insurance and other assets.

Of these two policies, only the former had been noted in a Colorado case.[10] When the wave of guest legislation swept the country, tales of ungrateful guests who had sued their hosts vied with stories of collusion between guest and host in bringing legislatures to enact, and courts to uphold, guest statutes. The public's sense of the injustice of the guest's suit against a host who had been guilty of no more than ordinary negligence doubtless dates from the days when liability insurance was less common or less adequate than it is today. In Massachusetts, it goes back to the milkman's horse and wagon and the neighborhood kids.[11] In some instances, indignation inspired by ingratitude was reinforced as a motivation by less convincing rationalizations, such as the guest act's tendency to render pas-

[9] Judge Fuld notes in his opinion in *Dym* that the driver in *Babcock* lost control of his car which went off the highway and into a stone wall.

[10] See Dobbs v. Sugioka, 117 Colo. 218, 220, 185 P.2d 784, 785 (1947). This theme is frequently encountered. See *e.g.*, Hasbrook v. Wingate, 152 Ohio St. 50, 53, 87 N.E. 2d 87, 89 (1949): "The Ohio Guest Act and similar acts in other states were undoubtedly enacted to carry out a policy of social equity to the effect that the owner or operator of an automobile should not be made liable to a guest riding therein to whom the owner or operator is doing a favor or is extending a courtesy, except for wilful or wanton misconduct on his part and that a guest should assume the risk of ordinary negligence."

[11] Massachusetts, one of the minority of states which, as a matter of common law, did not hold a driver liable to a guest for ordinary negligence, refused in an automobile case to abandon its rule which dated from West v. Poor, 196 Mass. 183, 81 N.E. 960 (1907), involving a horse-drawn milkwagon. See Massaletti v. Fitzroy, 228 Mass. 487, 510, 118 N.E. 168, 177 (1917), in which the court declared, "Justice requires that the one who undertakes to perform a duty gratuitously should not be under the same measure of obligation as one who enters upon the same undertaking for pay."

sengers more careful in accepting rides and, at the same time, inducing drivers to be more generous in tendering them. In justifying these laws, general allusions to their character as regulation of the state's highways are also to be found.

The second additional policy appears, as Judge Fuld claims, to be original with the majority, yet the problem with which it is concerned is not fanciful. The blameless driver of the other car and his injured passengers would be forced to share with the out-of-state plaintiff who, as the defendant's guest, would have no claim under the law of the place of injury.[12] If the other driver had been held liable in a suit by the guest, he might also be entitled to pursue the host with a claim for contribution under the law of the guest's and host's domicil, a good fortune which he would be denied under the law of the state of accident and perhaps the law of his home state as well.[13]

When note is taken of these policies, it seems evident that we have accepted too easily the explanation of *Babcock* in terms of an Ontario guest law that pursued a single goal. One may still credit the deterrence of collusion against insurers as the factor most likely to have motivated successful lobbies in the states enacting guest statutes without being ready to dismiss the other policies as illusory and the interests based on them as unreal. Moreover, the idea that Colorado, in enacting a guest statute, is concerned with the protection of drivers and insurers only when they are Coloradan is an over-simplification. The Colorado legislature can, to be sure, protect Colorado drivers and insurers more effectively than drivers and their insurers from other states who injure guest passengers in Colorado, and its law will impinge chiefly upon Colorado people. However, if a conflicts scholar in the Colorado legislature had offered an amendment reading, "provided, however, that this statute shall not apply to persons domiciled in other states who operate

12 To be sure, the defendant driver's insurance policy—if he had one—would ordinarily provide greater coverage for an accident in which there was more than one claimant. However, the policy as thus enlarged might still be inadequate.

13 *Cf.* LaChance v. Service Trucking Co., 215 F. Supp. 162 (D. Md. 1963), noted, *supra*, at p. 179; Goulding v. Sands, 237 F. Supp 577 (W.D. Pa. 1965).

motor vehicles in this state with respect to injuries inflicted in this state on guest passengers domiciled in other states," would this have truly reflected the legislative purpose?[14]

What has emerged is a true conflict instead of the false conflict which has been associated with *Babcock*. But since neither the majority nor the dissenters share Professor Currie's inhibition against "weighing" interests, each opinion devotes not a little attention to deflating the interests discerned by the other. Thus, the dissent sees in these "alleged policies" a valid concern on the part of Colorado only when they relate to "matters within its legislative competence, such as the burdens of the Colorado courts, the regulation of the affairs of Colorado citizens or the protection of Colorado claimants or insurers." The New York lawsuit between New Yorkers is of no consequence to Colorado courts or citizens; even the majority's emphasis on the plight of the driver of the other car is "misplaced" since he was from Kansas.

Here we see the logic of the "statute personal": Colorado enacts its laws to govern its citizens and those out-of-staters whose conduct may adversely affect its citizens. It is not concerned with the justice or injustice of claims based on conduct within its bounds if that conduct does not jeopardize its citizens and the claims are between outsiders, at least if those claims can be pressed in another state's courts. The fact that a Kansan may be denied full recovery for a Colorado injury because his claim runs against outsiders is of no concern to Colorado: he is a Kansan.[15]

[14] If that bill were ever studied in committee, I should hope that someone would offer an amendment confining its effect to persons from states not having guest statutes. One of the uncertainties left in the opinions of Judge Fuld and Chief Judge Desmond is whether they (1) would extend the benefit of their position to a citizen of another state which held drivers to the common-law standard and (2) would impose its burden on a driver from a third state with a like law. Surely an affirmative answer ought to be given to both questions; perhaps it would be constitutionally required. The basic problem is considered briefly in Ch. VI. See, especially, p. 144, n. 8, 171, and p. 175, *supra*.

[15] Kansas has a guest statute. KANS. GEN. STAT. § 8-122b (Corrick, 1949). This attribution to Colorado of indifference to the plight of citizens in other states undermines the hope I expressed in note 14, *supra*.

On the other hand, New York's concern follows New Yorkers wherever they go, at least if they return to New York. To the majority, this solicitude seems "reminiscent of the days when British citizens travelled to the four corners of the world secure in the belief that their conduct would be governed solely by the law of England."[16] The risk that the plaintiff's injuries would, if uncompensated, cause her to become a public charge is "an argument" that is "hardly legal." For that matter, Judge Burke notes, a defendant, mulcted in damages in excess of his insurance, might become a public charge himself.

A Place for a Principle of Preference

At this point of conflicting purposes and values, I see the need for a principle of preference that would allocate the authority of the concerned states fairly as between them and as between the parties. Such a principle could guide the court that must decide when to apply to parties who come from outside the state of injury a standard higher than that existing in the latter state's law. In Chapter VI I have submitted a principle[17] that seems to me basically in harmony with the majority's view: where the matter at issue is the application of a standard of conduct or of financial protection incident to a relationship which is higher than that prevailing in the state of injury, the court should apply the higher standard when it exists in the state where the relationship has its seat.

A relationship need not be complex, nor must the incident be "special" in the sense of a rule applicable only to parties to the relationship in question.[18] In states having guest statutes,

[16] I am sure that the English indulged this illusion in their travels, and with considerable—but not complete—justification. Thus, a Briton who sued in England for a tort alleged to have been done him abroad could recover only if the act complained of were "actionable as a tort, according to English law, . . . and not justifiable, according to the law of the foreign country where it was done." DICEY, CONFLICT OF LAWS 940 (7th ed. 1958).

[17] The relevant principle is the fourth of those presented in Chapter VI. See p. 166, *supra*.

[18] For example, in Kilberg v. Northeast Airlines, Inc., 9 N.Y.2d 34, 172 N.E.2d 526 (1961), the relationship involved was that of carrier

one may say that the incident of the standard of care owed by the host to the guest is "special," but elsewhere it may be the same as the standard of care owed by drivers to nonpassengers. If the majority rationale is accepted, the justification in *Babcock* for preferring New York's general incident to Ontario's special incident is the fact that there the relationship had its seat in New York.

In justifying such a principle, one must confront Judge Fuld's objection which I have already quoted: "Nothing turns on the circumstance that in this case the guest-host relationship was formed in the foreign jurisdiction." Is there any more reason for a New York court to apply New York law to a guest-host relationship formed by New Yorkers in New York than to a like relationship formed by New Yorkers in a state in which the incidents of the relationship differ from those in New York?

I believe that an affirmative answer can be given to this question, but it requires us to go back to another proposition and to a series of other questions. Every state provides rules for the regulation of its highways, including provision for financial protection against injuries caused in their use. A state may—and Colorado does—limit the protection accorded persons who have entered into the guest-host relationship as guests. In so doing, it limits the host's exposure to the claims of guests and so the exposure of the host's insurer. Why should that state's law not apply to guests and hosts who come from other states and who are injured on that state's highways?

The best reason for not applying the restrictive law of the state of injury would be a determination that its purposes would not be advanced by its application to the out-of-state driver and his out-of-state passenger. This is what Judge Fuld assumes —and assumed in *Babcock*. If, as the majority and I believe, for reasons already noted, that assumption is not valid, does it follow that the Colorado law must be applied to *every* injury involving a guest-host relationship that occurs within its

---

and passenger, created by the sale of a ticket and embarkation from New York. The incident, however, was the passenger's right to full protection accorded by the New York Wrongful Death Act, a right not limited to carrier-passenger cases.

bounds? Is it not proper to recognize that the laws of states from which drivers and their guests have come also have purposes and that these may conflict with the purposes of the Colorado law and yet deserve concern? If so, then a question of how best to accommodate the conflicting purposes is posed, and this leads to a further question: Does Colorado have the same degree of concern in every case of a claim by a New York guest against a New York host for a negligent injury in Colorado?[19] Does New York?

It is at this point that the connections of the relationship with the respective states become relevant: they suggest a basis of accommodation. Where New Yorkers have formed a guest-host relationship in New York for a motor trip to Ontario or to Colorado, New York law determines the incidents of that relationship in New York. Let its concern be recognized as continuing after the border is crossed and even after an injury has occurred.[20] Therefore, let the incidents that New York law specifies remain in effect. When, however, any guest-host relationship is more closely associated with Ontario or Colorado, let each of those jurisdictions be free to limit the host's duty of care to his guest. As Judge Burke said, "Since the relationship itself is the reason for the special treatment, we concluded that the jurisdiction where the relationship was seated had the primary interest in having its laws applied."

Is this basis of accommodation unfair to the parties? Few speculations are more slippery than assessing the expectations of parties as to the laws applicable to their activities, and especially is this true when the expectations relate to the law of torts. However, the party of New Yorkers who sally forth from

[19] In referring to Colorado's "concern," I am uncomfortably conscious of the anthropomorphism in which I am indulging. I hope the reader will accept this and like expressions as verbal short-cuts for a statement that the purpose of the Colorado law may fairly be advanced by its application in the situation with respect to which Colorado is said to be "concerned."

[20] I suppose that a guest-passenger relationship can be said to have its seat in New York most often in those cases in which the relationship had its beginning there. Nevertheless, as I point out at p. 303, *infra*, I do not believe the majority intend the "seat" concept to be limited to such cases, nor do I think that reason requires such a limitation.

New York for a week-end in Ontario may reasonably expect that their claims against their host would be referred to New York law. On the other hand, if a group of Mrs. Dym's fellow students had piled into Mr. Gordon's car for the jaunt with her to the Longmont golf course, it seems improbable that each would expect that his or her claim against Mr. Gordon would be determined by whether his or her home state's law happened to coincide with that of New York[21]—and this even if each had noticed the New York license plate.

However, expectations of the parties surely are not the only test of fairness to them. In this territorially divided world, I believe we have come to accept as fair the application of territorial law except in some unusual situation as where the parties, the event, or the transaction central to a controversy are closely linked to the law of another state that is relevant to the matter in dispute. Where the dispute concerns an incident of a relationship, the fact that the relationship was closely associated with the other state provides a fair basis for proposing the application of the higher standards of that state's law.

How close must the connection be? This is a question that I refused to pursue in Chapter VI, deliberately obscuring its difficulties by using the convenient label "seat of the relationship" to epitomize the connection between the relationship and the state recognized as having the most significant contact with it.[22] I was interested to note that Judge Burke had turned to the same term for the same purpose. In wrestling with the question when a guest-host relationship can be said to have its seat in a given state, Judge Burke developed the idea more fully than I attempted to carry it. I do not think Judge Fuld correct in attributing to the majority the rule that "controlling effect must be given to the law of the jurisdiction in which the relationship originated." Understandably, Judge Burke's initial effort to articulate the concept has left areas of uncertainty, but I should

[21] I assume that the minority would deny the benefit of the New York law to a plaintiff from a state with a guest statute but grant it to a plaintiff from a state following the common-law negligence standard. See note 14, *supra*.

[22] See p. 166, *supra*.

suppose that he would not apply *Babcock* to an Ontario driver who, having picked up an Ontario hitch-hiker in Buffalo, negligently injured him in Toronto. Nor do I think he would apply *Dym* to a New York student who, at the close of his summer school session in Boulder, offered a ride back to New York to a fellow New Yorker and then negligently injured him before they had crossed the Colorado line.

In thus employing the seat of the relationship as the key to the choice of law in the principal case, Judge Burke takes pains to limit its applicability. He points to its use in other situations (interspousal immunity, workmen's compensation, and carrier's liability)[23] but refuses either to prescribe it as prerequisite to the application of a law other than that of the state of injury or to assert the paramountcy of the seat of a relationship in all cases. This seems to me wise. The court is using the principle as a guide to decision in a field where the variables are many. The bar's natural liking for certain rules is sure to create pressures to convert a guideline for judgment into a straight and narrow path. A refusal by the court to allow itself thus to be fenced in cannot be made too soon.

Chief Judge Desmond's "Public Policy"

Although no doubt Judge Fuld is disappointed by his inability to persuade enough of his brethren to accept his conception of the policies and interests at stake in the *Dym* case, he has reason for satisfaction in the court's acceptance of the methodology of which he has been a pioneer. Many commentators will, I am sure, prefer his clear-cut allocation of the policies of the states involved and will note his progress in giving

[23] The New York cases cited were Mertz v. Mertz, 271 N.Y. 466, 3 N.E. 2d 597 (1936) (New York law applied to deny wife recovery for injury caused by husband in Connecticut, which had abolished interspousal immunity); Matter of Nashko v. Standard Water Proofing Co., 4 N.Y.2d 199, 201, 149 N.E.2d 859 (1958) (New York employment relationship sustained application of New York workmen's compensation law to injury in New Jersey); Kilberg v. Northeast Airlines, Inc., *supra* note 18 (New York law applied to deny Massachusetts ceiling on recovery for wrongful death of New Yorker who flew on New York ticket from New York to Massachusetts where plane crashed).

sharper definition to the choice-of-law process he has been employing. However, though he seems to have won over the dissenters in *Babcock* to his approach to choice of law, he has made no convert of Chief Judge Desmond. In concurring with Judge Fuld in dissent, Chief Judge Desmond has reiterated in his separate opinion the theme of his majority opinion in *Kilberg*[24]: his choice of law comes in response to the imperative of New York public policy.

Chief Judge Desmond repeats with gusto the characterization by Judge Van Voorhis in the latter's *Babcock* dissent of "contacts," "center of gravity," and state "interests" as "catchwords," useful only as "considerations to be employed in setting up the new rules of law required by changing times." Yet, while declaring the impossibility of comparing the "interests" of Colorado and New York, the Chief Judge proceeds unhesitatingly to deny that Colorado had any interest in *Dym*, Massachusetts, in *Kilberg*, or Ontario, in *Babcock*. In each of these cases, he finds New York to have had a "public policy" calling for the employment of its law, a public policy which in application looks suspiciously like what the other judges have called a state "interest." Could it be that Chief Judge Desmond is speaking the language of interest analysis as M. Molière's bourgeois gentleman spoke prose?

I am not prepared to cede him to Professor Currie, however. It seems plain that the Chief Judge is seeking broader categories as the bases of decisions in choice of law, even, as he admits, at the risk of seeming "mechanical." I see in his desire to develop "new decisional formulae" a search for legal principles not unlike the principles of preference I have been advocating. Perhaps he would give them a larger role than I have seen for them, rejecting the reservations I have made for the cases that present false or clearly avoidable conflicts or are susceptible of solution by statutory interpretation. He might wish to convert principles into rules more rapidly than I would think prudent, and it is plain that the content of his principles would not be identical to those that I have proffered. Thus, he might accept the first two principles I have proposed for the law of torts

24 *Supra* note 18.

but subject them both to the qualification that, when both parties are from a state having a different standard of conduct or financial protection, that state's standard should be chosen instead of the standard of the place of injury.

He leaves no clue to his disposition of the case where the defendant resides in the state of injury which has a less exacting standard than the plaintiff's home state, New York. Though the plaintiff were to invoke New York's public policy ever so vigorously, I should be surprised if the Chief Judge's sense of fair play did not restrain his inclination to apply New York law. I doubt that he would shelter the wayfaring New York resident "from foreign State deprivations of reasonable protection and indemnity" when this would have to be at the expense of a resident of "the foreign State" for whom those deprivations serve as "reasonable protection."[25]

Some Points in Passing

Jurisdiction-Selecting Rules? In a comment on *Babcock v. Jackson,* I expressed concern lest Judge Fuld's opinion in that case be treated as establishing a rule selecting as the source of law the jurisdiction in which the driver lived and his car was garaged, regardless of whether the law of that jurisdiction imposed liability on the driver.[26]

My concern seems justified. Only a month before *Dym,* the Supreme Court of Delaware chose the common-law liability rule of New Jersey as against the guest statute of Delaware.[27]

[25] *Kilberg* is not inconsistent with this hope. Though Northeast Airlines is a Massachusetts corporation with a Boston office, many of its activities are in New York, including the initiation of the flight ending in Kilberg's death.

[26] For a brief comment on "jurisdiction-selecting rules," see note 24 on p. 9, *supra.* I discussed whether *Babcock* laid down such a rule in Cavers, "Comment on *Babcock v. Jackson,* A Recent Development in Conflict of Laws," 63 COL. L. REV. 1212, 1222-6 (1963).

[27] Friday v. Smoot, 33 U.S.L. WK. 2637 (Del. 1965). The court refused to apply *Babcock* to the New Jersey injury chiefly because a canvass of a number of variations on the facts in *Babcock*—varying the place of picking up the passenger, varying his residence, adding to the number of passengers, and so forth—excited the court's fears of confusion, uncertainty, and forum-shopping. The court fell back upon the *lex loci delicti* with

The case arose out of an accident in New Jersey in which a Delaware passenger was injured by a negligent Delaware driver in the course of a short motor trip that began in Delaware. The court explicitly rejected *Babcock*, but showed no awareness that, because the law-fact pattern was the reverse of *Babcock*'s the problem raised by its case was any different from that confronting the New York Court of Appeals in *Babcock*.

When one turns to the opinions in *Dym* with the question whether they have produced jurisdiction-selecting rules, distinctions must be taken. Since the majority has found the seat of the guest-host relationship in the state of injury, judgment would not differ if the law-fact pattern were reversed. The state from which the parties hailed would have no greater claim to the application of its law. If such a case were to come after *Dym*, the product would be a synthetic jurisdiction-selecting rule, made by combining the two decisions based on opposite law-fact patterns. However, would the majority's rationale lead it to apply New York law if the seat of the relationship had been found to be there and if the laws of New York and Colorado were reversed? The analysis pursued by the majority argues that they would recognize that the new case was different from *Dym*, but the opinion suggests at points that the law of the seat of the relationship would apply even when it had the guest statute and the place of injury, the common-law rule.[28]

---

evident comfort, finding that the adoption of a "flexible approach" fell "within the peculiar province of the General Assembly." *Id.* at 2638. Had it considered *Babcock* as restricted to its own law-fact pattern, the court might have reached its result without having to retreat to a rule which it concedes "in some instances may appear arbitrary and unfair." *Ibid.*

28 The chief indication that a jurisdiction-selecting rule is intended is the fact that nowhere is the opposite conclusion indicated. Quoting *Kilberg*, the court states that its conclusion "does not subject 'the traveling citizens of this state to the varying laws of other states through and over which they move.'" This statement could be confined to the law-fact pattern before the court. However, extended to a case where it was the state of injury that had the common-law standard, the statement would be true only if the majority considered that in *Dym* it had adopted a rule selecting the law of the seat of the relationship as controlling, regardless of its content.

A court faced by such a case might prefer the law of the state of the

In the case of Judge Fuld's dissent, which views *Babcock* as the controlling precedent, there is less room than in his earlier opinion for intimations that the law of the place of injury should always be subordinated to the law of the parties' home. The choice-of-law problem for the court is seen as that posed by the law-fact pattern the case presents. Reverse that pattern, and a new case would have to be decided. This I also find in Chief Judge Desmond's opinion. If New York had a guest statute and Colorado did not, would he feel constrained to protect the New York driver defendant "from foreign State deprivations of reasonable protection"? One can only guess.

The Place of Registration and Insurance. Since the majority opinion finds the seat of the guest-host relationship to have been in Colorado, it thereby rejects any view that the place where the car was registered and insured should have a dominant role in identifying the seat. Indeed, Judge Burke is explicit in denigrating these "alleged contacts," characterizing them as merely "a long-handed method of reciting that the parties were domiciled in New York." They lack "independent significance" and are but the "natural incidents of domicile."

Judge Fuld's dissent alludes to these phenomena at three places, twice in drawing parallels between *Dym* and *Babcock* and once in quoting from the latter decision, a quotation Chief Judge Desmond also employs. At no point does Judge Fuld develop the significance of either circumstance.[29] In the normal situation, where the driver's domicil is in the same state where his car was registered, "based," and insured, it seems reasonable to consider these factors as simply enhancing the significance of domicil.

---

relationship to the law of the state of the injury, a position consonant with the fifth principle I presented (but did not propose) in Chapter VI. See p. 177, *supra*. Surely the choice is not an easy one. It should be reached on its own merits, not as an undiscussed consequence of deciding the question posed by the quite different law pattern in *Dym*.

29 Any temptation to make much of these contacts may have been subdued by Professor Currie's crushing criticism of the proposal, based on "economic realities," by Professor Ehrenzweig to make the place of permanent garaging decisive. See Currie, Book Review, "Ehrenzweig, *Conflict of Laws*," 1964 DUKE L. J. 424, 432.

Suppose, however, the case of a New York domiciliary, a junior in the University of Washington who has acquired a car and a liability insurance policy in Seattle. When he injures his fellow-student from New York in a car accident en route to the golf course and is sued upon his return to vacation in New York, would Judge Fuld consider the case an apt one to apply the domiciliary law as against the Washington guest statute?[30]

If Judge Fuld were to apply New York law, what would be left of the significance of the New York based and insured car as a contact? If he were to apply Washington law, would he be moved to do so by solicitude for the Washington insurers? Washington's law may have held down insurance premiums in the state, but one can be sure their level would not respond perceptibly to the occasional cases in which the common-law rules of other states were applied.

Yet the fact that the car is insured in New York does have an impact in these cases, an impact to which, I submit, only an insurance lawyer or an insurance executive can be immune. In greater or less degree, the rest of us resent the idea that a New Yorker's liability insurance company can get out of paying a claim to another New Yorker simply because the state where the accident happened has a law that is softer on defendants and their insurers than the New York law. Yet I am sure Judge Fuld does not think of his opinion as implementing that deeply-felt lay sentiment, nor would I urge it. Even if a court could so limit its rule as to permit only judgments *quasi-in-rem*, the *res* being the amount for which insurance had been written, I still should be disturbed by this candid shaping of liability to fit protection.

"The Ordinary Processes of Construction and Interpretation." As I noted in Chapter IV,[31] these are the processes by which Professor Currie would have the courts reach choice-of-law decisions. Did the opinion-writers in *Dym* conform to his counsel? Both Judge Burke and Judge Fuld endeavor to identify the policies that underlie the statutory and common-law rules they are examining, a step that surely represents construction and

[30] WASH. REV. CODE ANN. § 46.08.080 (1963).

[31] See p. 88, *supra*.

interpretation. By finding a policy in the Colorado law limiting its purposes to the protection of Colorado insureds and insurers, Judge Fuld felt free to fill the resulting vacuum by New York law. He did not pause to consider whether the latter law was designed for the protection of New Yorkers (not to mention citizens of other states and countries with like laws) against careless New York drivers everywhere on earth, an inquiry in which the ordinary processes of construction and interpretation would have afforded little help. Judge Burke's view of the Colorado law left him with a potentially true conflict. Did those ordinary processes enable him to avoid it?

Professor Currie might say that Judge Burke gave to the New York common law "a moderate and restrained interpretation,"[32] even though he might question the aptness of the occasion for doing so. I see instead a search for a principle of preference to enable the court to arrive at a just accommodation between two laws, the purposes of which rendered each of them relevant to the problem before it. The result of the search, which we have already canvassed, has, to be sure, the effect of curtailing the reach of the New York standard of care and of achieving recognition for the Colorado act in the New York forum. This may be an example of construction, but is it "ordinary"? Perhaps "constructive construction" would be a better term.

As for Chief Judge Desmond, he finds New York's public policy in New York's tort law and applies it forthrightly to protect New Yorkers against "foreign State deprivations." His process seems closer to the "ordinary processes of construction and interpretation" than those of his colleagues, yet even he is seeking "new decisional formulae."

Picking and Choosing Laws. Since *Pearson v. Northeast Airlines, Inc.*,[33] the constitutional sequel to *Kilberg*, writers on choice of law have been apprehensive lest courts, in approaching choice-of-law questions on an issue-by-issue basis, should feel free to pick and choose among the legal systems involved

[32] This alternative has been recognized by Professor Currie, especially in his recent writing, as open to a court which appears to be confronted by a true conflict. See p. 73, *supra*, especially note 25.

[33] 309 F.2d 553 (2d Cir. 1962), *rev'g*, on rehearing *en banc*, 307 F.2d 131 (2d Cir. 1962).

and, by joining a law drawn from one state to a law drawn from another, should now and then produce a teratoid hybrid that each system would disown. This hazard was the subject of an interchange between Judge Currie and Judge Cavers in Case 3 in the series of Knickerbocker Nature Study Society cases stated in Chapter II.[34] I shall not return to the problem here, but I think it interesting to note that neither in *Babcock* nor in the dissenters' position in *Dym* has this problem occasioned concern. *Babcock*, I should suppose, can be explained only on a "local law" theory[35] since Ontario gives a guest no cause of action whatsoever. In *Dym*, however, a court could view the guest's cause of action as of Colorado origin,[36] in which the New York standard of ordinary care would replace Colorado's "willfull and wanton" standard. Either theory seems to me suitable for solving a problem that in these cases is only theoretical.

Fortuity and Its Consequences. I have sometimes remarked to a class in the conflict of laws that, if the teachers of that subject were deprived of the adjective "fortuitous," instruction in its mysteries would soon slow to a halt. As one reads opinions in current choice-of-law cases, one wonders how their authors would have fared if they had been deprived of the epithet. Judge Fuld put it to work in *Babcock*, and Judge Burke has made much use of it in *Dym*. He observes that in *Babcock*, where the guest-host relationship had its seat in New York, the place of the accident in Ontario was "entirely fortuitous," whereas in *Dym* the accident's occurrence at the seat of the relationship in Colorado "could in no sense be termed fortuitous."

Fortuity has become a conclusion of law. If a court considers that the significant contact in a case is, say, the place of the injury, then the fact that one or both of the persons involved were from another state becomes fortuitous. If, on the

[34] See pp. 38 and 41, *supra*.

[35] But only if the local law theory is taken as formulated by Professor Walter Wheeler Cook. See p. 7, note 20, *supra;* Cavers, "The Two 'Local Law' Theories," 63 HARV. L. REV. 822 (1950).

[36] Guest statutes are viewed not as creating a new cause of action but as imposing a limitation on the pre-existing common-law action for negligent injury. Goodwin v. Goodwin, 5 Cal. App. 2d 644, 43 P.2d 332 (1935); Massa v. Nastri, 125 Conn. 144, 3 A.2d 839 (1939).

other hand, the significant contact is deemed to be domicil, then it is the place of the injury that becomes fortuitous. Despite this, I believe there still is a condition which I can call factual fortuity.

This has led me to wonder whether Judge Burke's opinion leaves us with a compulsion to find the seat of a guest-host relationship somewhere, however factually fortuitous the circumstances may be. Or do we start with a principle that the lower standard of the place of injury is to be applied unless we can locate the seat of a relationship in another, higher-standard state on the basis of facts that are not merely adventitious and transitory?

An application of the principles of preference in Chapter VI would lead to the latter conclusion. However, those principles are not designed for literal application; they are guides proffered as aids to judicious judges. I can readily imagine cases in which the place of injury was so factually fortuitous that no court possessed of good common sense would employ its law. Plainly, in choosing among the laws of the fifty states in this mobile nation of ours, our courts must become inured to fortuity and not be bullied by it.

TABLE OF STATUTES

TABLE OF TREATIES AND CONVENTIONS

TABLE OF CASES

INDEX

Printed and bound by CPI Group (UK) Ltd, Croydon, CR0 4YY

16/09/2026

14963492-0002